Made in the USA
Coppell, TX
01 December 2019

CHAPTER 1

THE BOOKSTORE HAD ONCE BUSTLED WITH THE DEAD. As a child, Samantha Hamilton had spent hours with Mr. Abernathy's ghost in the mysteries. He loved to make her guess the plots to his favorite books. Susan Pratt had always lamented about not finding love, her spirit pacing up and down the romance aisles, while Sam did everything she could to make her laugh, to forget her sorrow even for a moment. But Sam had been frightened of Peter Kneller, holed up in the conspiracy section, shouting warnings about black ops military groups capturing people with special abilities.

All were residents of the realm of Entwine. A realm Sam used to see. But years ago she'd ended her curse.

Now when she gazed across the narrow stretch of worn carpet and past the chipped shelves, all she saw were the living, here for her book signing. Were the ghosts still there, still hoping someone would listen?

She ducked back behind the large cardboard cutout announcing her new book and tamped down a sudden swell of longing. It couldn't be longing for Entwine. That would be ridiculous. It was just nostalgia. Being back in her hometown bookstore stirred up memories.

Cynthia Lerner, the bookstore owner and her old next-door neighbor, hurried over with a steaming mug of coffee. "Stampeding elephants in your tummy, hon?" She handed her the mug and held up Sam's latest book, *Ghostly Paramour*. "Want some distraction?" A carefree Sam smiled at her from the back cover, happiness in her green eyes, an extra bounce in her blonde hair.

"I hate that picture." Sam took a sip of the coffee, the burnt taste so familiar. "I look plastic. Author Barbie."

Cynthia frowned and turned the book around to the cover. "Oh stop it. I meant this side. Guaranteed to keep your mind off the signing."

A smoldering Englishman fairly leapt off the cover, ready to ravish her. Dark hair lying in waves against strong cheekbones, deep brown eyes with just the hint of amber glinting at the promise in his heart. Even with a hint of ghostly transparency, she had to admit, it was definite historical eye candy.

She still couldn't believe she'd written about a ghost in her latest book. And made him the love interest. She'd wanted to trash it, but her editor had seen the first few pages and pestered her to finish writing it.

But writing about ghosts didn't mean she welcomed back that part of her. At thirteen, with scalpel-precision, she'd cut away the dead. She'd been accused of severing her ties to the living in the process. But sometimes when a tumor was sandwiched up against healthy tissue, everything had to be removed. It was the only way to heal.

A touch on her shoulder startled Sam. She jerked, spilling coffee on the already-stained carpet.

"Sorry," Michael said. He held up her favorite writing pen. "You forgot this at my office."

Sam took the pen from him. "But you were on shifts today."

He smiled, and it warmed his blue eyes, bringing out a hint of hazel. "I rearranged my schedule. Your first signing at home. I knew . . . I thought you might need the support."

Dr. Michael Forbes could have been one of her book covers. He was tall, had broad shoulders and a slim waist honed from hours of swimming. With his tailored suit and short blonde hair, he always reminded Sam of a civilized Viking.

Cynthia leaned over and whispered in her ear. "You were crazy for breaking up with him."

Sam didn't bother responding. She'd known Michael for two years, ever since he'd saved her butler, Bronson, from a heart attack. Several months back, they'd tried the dating thing and made it through about three and a half dates. For Sam, that was a record.

She handed the coffee back to Cynthia and gave Michael a quick hug. Some of the tightness around her chest eased. He always had that effect on her.

"Thank you." She pulled back and rolled the Montblanc pen in her hands, staring at the reflective silver surface. "I've never done a signing without it. My dad gave it to me when I was twelve."

Michael's face softened. "Your parents would both be so proud of you."

"It's fine. I'm fine," Sam said briskly. *And I don't really want to talk about them. Not in the bookstore they loved so much.* "I'm ready, Cynthia."

Cynthia gave her an assessing eye behind her glasses, but finally walked around the cutout to stand near the desk they'd set up for Sam. "Thank you so much for coming, everyone. The world knows her as the best-selling author of the *River Chronicles*, the *Lost Fireflies* trilogy, and her latest, *Ghostly Paramour*, but here in Kingston, we know her as our hometown girl. Samantha Hamilton."

The applause was immediate and thunderous. Sam would never get used to that reaction. She'd come a long way from the crazy girl who used to see ghosts.

Michael gave her a thumbs up. Sam took a deep breath and walked out to greet her readers.

Aᴛᴏ᷉ᴇʀ ᴛʜᴇ ꜰɪʀsᴛ ʜᴏᴜʀ, ᴛʜᴇ ᴛᴇɴsɪᴏɴ ɪɴ Sᴀᴍ's sʜᴏᴜʟᴅᴇʀs eased. Having a signing in Kingston was risky. People here knew her past, but Cynthia's store really needed the boost. The old school taunts still rang in her ears. Schitzo Sammy. Haunted Hamilton. Her parents had tried to hide what she could do, but sometimes concealing her abilities was impossible.

Sam shot a quick glance over at Cynthia. Her old friend hummed to herself, watching the register ringing up sale after sale. She gave Sam a wink, her salt and pepper curls bouncing against her rounded cheeks. *You're killing it*, Cynthia mouthed.

Sam took selfies with members of the *River Chronicles'* fan club, accepted homemade cookies from a grandmother who'd dissected every moment of *Ghostly Paramour*, and signed a full set of the *Lost Fireflies* trilogy for a pug named Theodore. And his owner, Rachel.

Michael and Cynthia kept her stocked with water and energy bars. Finally, the line ebbed, and Sam walked over to the picture window at the side of the store. She looked out at the Kingston streets. Cobblestones erupted here and there from within the cracked concrete. Though the sun had set, an orange glow hovered above the deep purple sky. The warmth of the June day still remained, heating her skin through the window the longer she gazed.

Beth and Kate used to race her down the sidewalk outside while trying not to tip over their ice cream cones. Sam had always won. It seemed like a lifetime ago.

She looked back over her shoulder. Michael and Cynthia stood near the table, munching some of her chocolate-chip cookies.

Michael's suit jacket was long gone, along with his tie. "I never get presents from my patients. Maybe I should become a writer."

Sam walked over and snagged a cookie. "I've read your writing. Stick to surgery."

He grabbed a rubber band from the table, priming it to shoot. Sam laughed and ducked behind the book cut-out.

She'd been very lucky to keep Michael as a friend. He'd quickly become like a brother.

"Are you fondling your book cover again?" Michael said from the other side of the cut-out. "You do realize no man can live up to Ghostly Paramour."

"That's why it's called fiction," Sam replied. "And I'm not fondling the cover." Though when she looked, her hand *was* on Robert's chest, the ghostly love interest. She removed it quickly, feeling suddenly guilty, and peeked around the cutout to find Michael had dropped the rubber band. Her cookies were almost gone.

Cynthia smiled at both of them. "Tell me again why it didn't work between you two? You get along better than most couples I know."

Michael shook his head. "It was my fault. My job always sabotages any relationship. No time."

"Gallant as always to take the blame," Cynthia said. "Yet you made time in your busy schedule to be here for Sam today." Cynthia fixed Sam with a stern stare. "And what's your reason, missy? Michael's right about your cover. Men like that don't exist. Maybe you should focus on what's right in front of you. Hmmmm?"

"Maybe you should focus on your store and less on relationships," Sam said sweetly. "Like how Bonnie has been close to sending up smoke signals to get your attention?"

Cynthia glanced at the front desk where a frantic Bonnie waved her hands like she was trying to land a plane. "It's obvious you two aren't going to fess up with the whole truth. I best go be useful where I'm wanted." She walked to the front desk muttering about people being blind.

Michael watched her for a moment and then turned back to Sam. "Cynthia's not the only one who wondered about us. Everyone at the hospital thought we were perfect. But I knew something was missing. That spark that would finally get me to put my job second." He touched her hand. "I know you've been searching for that connection too."

"I have." She wasn't sure how she'd ever find it with someone who didn't know the real Sam. "That's why I knew we were better as friends."

Michael laughed softly. "I'm happy with our friendship, thankful for it actually. I don't have many women friends." His gaze met hers and held. "But I can't shake this feeling something else is going on. We've known each other a while now, Sam. I hope you know you can tell me anything."

Sam's mind scrambled. She didn't want to lie to him outright. And she had a sinking feeling he'd know somehow if she did. "You want to get into this now?"

Michael nodded. "Yes, *now*. You're done with the signing, away from your laptop, and away from Bronson, who hovers over you like a protective hummingbird with very sharp teeth."

Sam laughed. "Bronson wouldn't appreciate the hummingbird reference. But I don't mind that he's protective. He's really the only family I have left. And I'm not counting some distant cousins in Scotland."

"Well, from what you've shared, your parents sound like they were pretty incredible."

"Yours sound wonderful too," Sam said. Michael didn't talk much about his family, but always had good things to say about his parents. Though she didn't know any concrete details except they lived in Scotland. Another reason they couldn't be together. She'd never go back there.

"I love my parents." Michael frowned. "It's my siblings I can't stand. Well, most of them anyway." He shook his head like he could get rid of whatever thoughts had tightened his face into sharp angles. "You're dodging my question. Was something else going on beyond our lack of chemistry?"

Sam grabbed a water bottle and untwisted the cap slowly, giving herself time to think. She couldn't share the real reasons.

Because I can't tell you about my curse, because I can't tell you about my past, and because I can't tell you who I really am.

The familiar chasm of loneliness yawned wide inside her. Only a handful of people knew her, *really* knew her. And she wasn't sure she'd ever find someone who'd accept her completely. Who she could be honest with. Every book she finished reminded her that the best-selling romance author might never find love herself. Maybe the Universe had gotten the last laugh after all.

Tears rushed to her eyes. She turned away from Michael, hoping he hadn't seen it. "There was something else. I've got trust issues. It's hard for me to open up with anyone." *Please don't ask why.*

Michael let out a long breath. "Are you afraid to let anyone past your walls because they might leave you?" He lowered his voice into a gentle whisper. "Your parents died, Sam. They didn't abandon you willingly."

Sam blinked and tears fell in a hot trail down her cheeks. "I don't want to talk about this right now." She wiped her face with her knuckles. "You don't know the whole story."

Michael came around the table and faced her. He handed her a handkerchief. "I hope you'll tell me the whole story one day. I'm usually pretty good with getting past trust issues." His gaze was curious and a bit wistful. "But not with you."

"Well, they recalled the mold after they made me." Sam managed a small laugh. It helped push the tears back. "I'm not the only one. Beth and Kate would give you a run for your money too." She traced the scar on her thumb with her nail. "We all went through a lot when we were kids. Having barriers kept us sane." *And alone.*

"Beth." Michael frowned like he'd swallowed vinegar. "I know Beth Marshall is your friend but—"

"Ex-friend."

"That fraud will get what she deserves." His tone was intense. "Using people's pain for her own profit is deplorable. No one has special powers, except in stories."

She didn't bother to assure Michael what he saw on Beth's reality show was real. Even if her ghost-seeing days were gone, he wouldn't believe her. Or worse. He'd think she was nuts.

"Excuse me," a voice said. Sam looked over to see a man who looked familiar, but she couldn't place him. His thick beard hid a weak jaw. Nothing rang any recognition bells.

He had one of her books in his hands, but didn't hold it

out for her to take. "Did you need me to sign that for you?" she asked.

"You don't remember me?"

Michael seemed to suddenly grow taller. He moved to stand slightly in front of Sam, shielding her. Now *who* was being protective?

"Did we go to school together?" Sam said.

The man nodded and gave her a small smile. "Fourth and fifth grades before I moved. Jeremy Reynolds."

Finally, Sam saw the boy underneath the man. He'd been shy back then, too. "I remember. It's great to see you. Do you live here now?"

Jeremy shoved his hands in his jeans' pockets. "I do. At my mom's place. She passed away last month."

Michael finally relaxed his stance. "I'm sorry for your loss."

Sadness tugged on the lines around Jeremy's mouth. "Thank you. It was a blessing actually. She was in a lot of pain." Jeremy took a step closer. "That's actually why I wanted to talk to you. I need to communicate with her ghost."

"Ghost?" Michael let out a soft chuckle. "Sam's new book has ghosts in it, but that doesn't mean she can talk to them."

Sam wiped her suddenly damp palms on her jacket. She'd been worried all day someone would mention this and now it was in front of Michael. *Great, just great.*

"Jeremy's talking about a rumor at school," Sam said. "Back when we were kids." Her voice was calm. She'd learned at a very young age how to lie. Her life had once depended on it.

"I know you must see them still," Jeremy said. "You can't

stop a power like that." His words were rushed, rising in volume.

Michael touched his arm. "Take a breath, Jeremy. You're not thinking straight."

"I *am* thinking straight."

"Your mother just died." Michael's voice was soothing. "I know what it's like to lose someone." Sam wondered who Michael was talking about.

Jeremy looked like he was going to protest more, but then let out a long breath. "My mom. I miss her so much."

"I'm sorry," Sam said. "The ghost thing was just something the bullies made up at school to hurt me. To humiliate me."

Jeremy looked at Sam, disappointment heavy in his eyes. "I know you're lying." His words dropped into a tortured whisper. "You used to help people. What *happened* to you?" Without another word, he turned and left the store.

Sam felt the sucker punch to her gut just as surely as if he'd struck her. *What happened to you?* That's what Kate had said when Sam had buried her curse.

She'd gotten her life back, that's what happened. And she'd refused to be the Universe's slave any longer. But Sam's conviction didn't erase the open pain she'd seen on Jeremy's face. For a split second, she wished she could help him.

Michael grabbed his jacket. "I'm going to give him the card for one of our counselors. I'll be right back." He followed Jeremey out the door.

Cynthia marched over. "Just about everyone has cleared out. Was that the Reynolds' kid?"

Sam nodded. "Jeremy. He wanted to talk to his mother's ghost."

Cynthia pulled on the hem of her tunic, fixing the embroidered stars until they all lined up again perfectly. "I'm not surprised. He's been in a bad way since her passing. Didn't get to say goodbye."

"I can't do anything anymore." It hadn't been like a faucet she could turn on or off. She'd had to bury it so deeply it would never emerge. That had been the only way.

"You were a lifesaver to a lot of folks," Cynthia said. "Whether you want to remember that or not."

"It's always the awful things that stick with me." Sam shook her head slowly. "The energy drain, the ghosts showing up out of nowhere, bleeding and screaming. Never leaving me alone." Her hands twisted together.

"If you hadn't let me speak to my son, I don't know what would have happened." Cynthia paused and then cleared her throat. "Well, I do. I don't think I'd be here. You'd have been talking to my ghost next."

Sam remembered Zach. How it had felt so natural to talk to the ghost of a child her own age. She gazed at Cynthia's careworn face, noting the fine lines etched around her eyes, her mouth. What would her own mom have looked like if she hadn't died so young?

Her phone buzzed in her jacket. She looked at the number. "It's Kate." In the echo of Jeremy's words, she didn't want to answer the call.

Cynthia grinned, all sadness dismissed. "Tell her she needs

to give me a discount at her Scottish B&B and I'll be there in a shake of a snowflake."

"I will," Sam said. She walked back into the stacks and finally answered. "Hey Kate, how are you?" Her voice sounded weak. She tried again. "How's business?"

"Crappy."

Sam knew it had been rough on Kate having to run the B&B all by herself after her husband had died two years ago. Moral support and loans—*that* she could easily give. "What can I do to help?"

"I need you to do your ghost shit."

Sam's grip on her phone tightened. "I don't see ghosts anymore. We've been over this."

"Well, you need to figure out how to do it again because my B&B is haunted." Kate's voice hardened. "And they're not the friendly Casper kind. They're scaring away the guests."

Sam's knees suddenly felt ancient. She leaned back against one of the bookshelves. The hardcovers dug into her shoulder blades. "Sorry to hear that."

"Sorry to . . . are you friggin' kidding me?"

"I can give you some names of reputable mediums." Sam kept her tone friendly, but couldn't help the frost creeping around the edges. She couldn't believe Kate was even bringing this to her. She knew better.

"I *have* tried other mediums, but they couldn't fix things. I need someone who can really see ghosts. And my best friend." Kate's voice was firm, but Sam heard the tremor underneath.

"Ghosts are in my past. I can't help you." Sam enunciated each word carefully.

"I'm desperate." Kate's long exhale filled the connection. "If the B&B goes under, we'll have nothing. I can't do that to my girls. Patty and Emily are counting on me now that Paul's gone."

Sam stared at the books in front of her. They blurred into the greens and blues she remembered of Scotland's hills. The last time she'd seen them was while she watched her parents' car burn.

"I can't go back there, Kate." Panic scrabbled at her chest.

Kate's voice came through so razor sharp Sam was surprised her ear didn't bleed. "I know you're scared, but I need you. The girls need you. Are you really going to turn your back on us again?"

She wanted to drop the phone, but the vines of Kate's friendship wound about her tight, welcoming yet inescapable. Sam had almost lost her once before. If she didn't go to Scotland, their friendship wouldn't survive. And she didn't have many friends to lose.

Sam pushed herself up straight and stepped away from the bookshelf. "I'll come, but I can't help with the ghosts."

"I'll email you the details." Sam thought she'd hung up on her, but then Kate said, "You'll see ghosts again, Sam. It's *who* you are."

Sam hung up and slid the phone back into her pocket. Kate was wrong. Her curse wasn't coming back. It wasn't who she is. She'd never allow it to ruin her life.

Not ever again.

CHAPTER 2

SAM TURNED AWAY FROM THE HALF-PACKED SUITCASE IN HER room and made her way downstairs. She'd left her itinerary on the armchair by the fireplace. The heat reached her even before she'd made it to the chair. She welcomed the warmth. Every time she thought about the promise she'd made yesterday to Kate, it chilled her bones.

Had she really agreed to go back to Scotland?

Sam spotted the itinerary and grabbed it. Bronson cleared his throat behind her and she spun around, the paper slid from her grip.

Bronson picked it up and paused for a moment to scan it. Short, gray hair framed his square face, as tidy as always, but his dark blue eyes were wide with shock.

"Scotland?" The one word held the straining weight of concern.

They stared at each other, and she knew he was thinking about when he'd rescued her from the police station. She'd barely been coherent after the car crash. Since then he'd been mother, father, and confidant all rolled up in one. He'd helped her survive that aching loss.

"Kate needs me." Sam crossed her arms, burrowing into the warmth of her sweater. She wasn't going to make any excuses. There had been only truth between her and Bronson since that awful day.

Bronson smoothed the lapels of his black jacket. "Why did Kate ask you to come?"

"Her B&B hasn't been doing well since Paul died." Sam took a deep breath. "She says it's haunted. I told her I don't see ghosts anymore, but she wants me there. I couldn't say no."

Bronson nodded. "So, *it's* not back, then?"

"No. The curse isn't back."

Bronson placed his hands gently on her shoulders. "Stop calling it a curse. No one has ever believed that except for you."

Sam didn't speak, just pulled him into a hug, burying her face against his shoulder and shutting out the world. Just like she'd done when he'd taken her home from Scotland. Like always, his arms wrapped around her and the scent of pipe tobacco washed over her.

"I'm scared," she mumbled against his arm. "I've always managed not to dwell on the memory, thinking of something else when I get too close, but I can't any longer. I keep seeing their faces." She shuddered. "It's been almost seventeen years. I should be past this by now."

"You were in the car with them right before they died. That's not something you get past. It's something you have to accept. But your parents wouldn't want you to be afraid." His words vibrated through her forehead, ruffling her hair. "Perhaps, it's a blessing in disguise? To heal old wounds?"

She hadn't thought of it like that. Maybe this was a way to move on. To accept that she survived somehow when her parents hadn't.

Sam pulled back. "Michael's annual trip to see his parents is coming up in a few weeks. Maybe I can spend extra time with Kate and the girls, then join Michael and meet his family? Another good reason for the trip." It didn't ease the fluttering in her chest, but having something else to focus on besides ghosts and her parents' deaths was a very good thing.

Bronson smoothed her hair back from her cheek. "There's my Sam. Already focusing on the plan ahead." He gave her a long stare. "Why haven't you told Michael what you can do? Used to do," he amended.

"You know he despises anything supernatural. Including Beth and her reality show."

Bronson stiffened. "What she's doing is ridiculous. Flaunting her gifts to make money. I'm happy she's no longer in your life."

"Hmmm," Sam replied as she always did when Bronson began the usual rant about what had happened when they were kids. He blamed Beth. Sam did too. The old anger began to ignite, but she tamped it down. Now was not the time.

She squeezed his shoulder. "Let's not talk about Beth. I'm going to Scotland to be there for Kate."

Sam tried to shake the cold which still clung to her skin, but it burrowed through her pores, freezing her bones. Bones which suddenly felt brittle and weak under the weight of the past.

She let out a long breath, pushing the cold out with it. "I can do this."

"I'm proud of you."

Just those four words brought tears welling into Sam's eyes. "Took me long enough to face going back, huh?"

"Nonsense. Everyone heals at their own rate. Take a nice long bath, and I'll be by in a while with some sandwiches and tea."

Sam didn't protest when he pushed her toward the stairs. She walked slowly up to her room, her mind already going through what else she'd need to pack and the book signings she'd need to reschedule. She turned on the hot water in the tub and stared into the white porcelain as if it somehow had the answers. What if this was a huge mistake?

But if not now, when? Kate needed her. She had to do this. It was time.

CHAPTER 3

ROBERT GRENNING TURNED RIGHT AT THE EDGE OF THE wall and delved once more into the shadows. The Rinth was a never-ending maze of stone wall, muddied path, and lost souls locked in this journey.

Ever since he had died, this was the only place he had known. At first, he had supposed it was torture, for it was. The mind playing tricks on you, making you believe that this time, *this time,* you would come to the end and be free. But he had discovered the Rinth was a place of waiting. Waiting for the mythical release others hinted at. Likely a lie told to soften the truth. No one escaped.

Another turn to the left, and he walked back the way he had come. In the beginning, he had attempted to leave a trail by marking the stone, tearing bits of his clothing to leave behind, anything to show he had passed this way before. But nothing lasted. Clothes were mysteriously mended. Stone reshaped. Nothing he did mattered.

His steps slowed, anticipating the next turn, but Robert

found himself at the edge of a large open grassy field stretching toward the Chasm of Deighilt. The tall grass came to his knees. Though he felt no breeze, the grass bowed under the weight of wind. On the other side of the Chasm was the realm of Entwine.

The field was a place he had not glimpsed since his arrival. The entrance to the Rinth. He remembered running across the grass, believing he had somehow escaped his hanging. Until someone had stopped him. A figure in a cloak the color of autumn leaves. The stranger's hand had touched his shoulder, robbing his body of warmth.

Even now, Robert felt the cold imprint of fingers against his skin. He shivered. It had been like ice burrowing deep inside him.

Why was he here now, back at the entrance?

"Are you ready, Robert?" a voice said from behind him.

Was it the mysterious stranger again? Robert whirled around, sweat coating his skin. But there was no cloak, no concealment. The man before him wore a long black vest over a gray shirt and black pants. He looked a bit older than Robert, perhaps approaching his fortieth year, but he appeared in fine form.

He was not alone. Another stood with him—a boy, though he was tall enough to be a man. His hair was the color of sunset, but it was his eyes that startled Robert. One was blue and the other brown.

"Who are you?" Robert said. His voice was rough. He had not spoken to another soul for weeks.

"Darrin. I'm a Runner for the Wardens." The man smiled, his face softening. "And this is my apprentice, Connor."

Runners. Robert had heard of them. They ferried the ghosts from Entwine to their final resting place, wherever that might be. They worked for the Wardens who ruled the Rinth and Entwine. No one he had met had ever seen a Warden. He had almost believed they did not exist.

Robert gave them a small bow. "I am pleased to make your acquaintance. I did not realize Runners were allowed in the Rinth."

"We are when the Wardens deem it necessary." Darrin gestured back over his shoulder toward the Chasm. "It's time for you to leave here, to go to Entwine. Don't you see the light?"

The gloom of the Rinth was absolute as always. He only made out Darrin's features and Connor's because they stood close. "There is no light. I think you must be mistaken, I do not—" Wait, there was something in the distance.

A glow, like when a fire is first catching hold to kindling. Brilliant flashes warring with the dark until the flames took control.

"What is that?" Robert stretched his hand toward the brightness. It grew in strength like a small sun rising over the shadows of the Rinth.

The light fell upon him, bathing his chest in blazing heat, stretching down his arms, his legs, until every part of him was captured in its glow. For a moment, he remembered what it had felt like to be alive.

"You've been called," Connor said. His voice was lower than

Robert had expected. It held confidence. Darrin had trained his apprentice well.

"Called? I had heard only rumors." Robert met Darrin's gaze.

Darrin lifted his hand and the silver cuff at his wrist caught the light. The symbols etched in the metal seemed to glow. "They're true. The one who can help you is finally ready."

The other ghosts only whispered of those who allowed them to leave the Rinth forever. Robert did not dare utter their title, afraid speaking it would somehow shatter his chances of escape. "Let us depart."

"We're not taking you," Darrin said.

"Then why are you here?" Robert drew himself up, standing straight. It seemed ages since he had felt the burn of frustration.

Darrin took a step closer. "We needed to draw you from the maze. To get you *here*." He spread his arms wide to encompass the entrance. "The rest is up to you."

"I am not one for games," Robert said. The frustration galloped into anger. "*You* are to take me from here."

Understanding glimmered in Darrin's eyes. "I can't even if I wanted to. There's only one way out. You need to jump across the Chasm."

"But no one survives the leap."

Connor crossed his arms. "Who told you that?"

Robert gazed at the Chasm. It looked wider than before. "When I first arrived, a ghost made it halfway before his essence dissolved like dirt in a rainstorm." A chill doused his skin, erasing the earlier warmth. "His screams echoed afterward." It was on the edge of his tongue to tell them both of the cloaked figure who had stood beside him while they watched the ghost's demise, but something kept his silence.

He looked back at Darrin and Connor. "You send me to my death."

"You're already dead." Connor's words were neutral, but the symbols on his cuff blazed bright blue. Robert squinted against the sudden glare.

Darrin gave his apprentice a sharp look before gazing at Robert. "That ghost wasn't called. It wasn't his time. Do you want this chance or not?"

Robert did not answer, could not. His thoughts scattered with the promise of helping his family and the uncertainty of nothingness should he leap.

Darrin shook his head. "Don't you understand? This is a way for you to find peace."

"I do not deserve peace, nor do I seek it." Robert turned and looked back at the maze. "Not after the horror I visited upon my family."

"It's true, the Grenning name didn't fare well after your death," Darrin said. "But you didn't kill Sarah. You're entitled to absolution."

"Forgiveness? No. Never." Though he had been wrongfully convicted, he had contributed to his demise by his own arrogance. Robert's memories flashed back to the feel of the noose squeezing his throat shut. The rough pieces of rope cutting into his flesh. Sparks danced in front of his eyes. Robert staggered forward. Only a hiss escaped through his lips.

Connor grabbed his arm, steadying him. The boy was stronger than he looked. Robert's lungs released, and he sucked in a long breath.

"There are reasons we do what we do," Connor said. "Our *intent* matters, regardless of the actions we take."

Robert shook his head slowly, the phantom hold of his past loosening. "Lillian warned me to stay away from Sarah, but I thought I knew best. I was foolish. Stupid."

Darrin looked disappointed. "Add selfish to that list too if you're going to wallow in your own pain when you've got the chance to make things right. You say you want to clear your family name?" He pointed toward the fading light in the distance, urgency gleaming in his eyes. "Then *go* do it."

"Surely there must be more to it than just leaping."

Darrin touched Robert's chest, where his heart was. "Hope. Faith. The belief you can make it across."

"After two centuries in the Rinth, I have scarce supplies of any of those."

"I have it on good authority that you're not the type of man to let fear rule your actions." Darrin gestured to Connor, and they both began to walk away. "I hope I'm not wrong."

His last words wafted through the air. The Runners disappeared into the Rinth's gloom. As if sensing Robert's uncertainty, the light flickered, growing even fainter. There was not much time left.

Darrin was right about one thing. Robert had never given in to fear, and he was not about to now. Staying was not an option, not when this chance would never come again. The light weakened further, just a bare slit of promise breaking through the darkness.

He sent a prayer to whomever was listening, and then ran with everything his tired legs had. His muscles screamed at the sudden effort, but he pushed on, the Chasm approaching in his sight. The edge was suddenly under his boots. With no more doubts or hesitation, he leapt.

He kept his eyes on the dimming glow, willing it to pull him forward. The Chasm yawned below him like a creature eager to devour his being. And then he was in a bedroom.

A bedroom?

The furnishings were sparse, but it was difficult to tell much more than that against the powerful light blazing from the woman in front of him. Steam rose about her, mingling with the luminous glow emanating from her pores, through every strand of hair.

He knew what she was, but not that she would shimmer with such inner light. It called to him like a lantern placed in a window to guide him home. A home he would never see again. But if she helped him to right the wrongs of his past, it would ease the burning regret in his soul.

"What in hell?" She stumbled back a step, but her glow beckoned him forward. She was dressed very strangely in what looked like a green plush tablecloth wrapped tightly around her body.

"No, I was not in Hell," he replied and then amended his stern tone. "What is your name, lass?"

She gripped the tablecloth, pulling it up higher, almost to

her neck. "You're obviously a stress dream about Scotland and I'm asleep in the tub." She glanced at her fingertips. "I'm going to prune up good."

"Your name?"

"Samantha, but you can call me Sam for short." She picked up a brush and drew it through her long blonde hair. With each stroke, her glow lessened, finally dimming to the point he need not squint any longer.

Now that he could see her more clearly, words fled. He had enjoyed arrangements with many beautiful women in his time, but none with such fire sparkling in the depths of her eyes.

She stared at him so fixedly, he felt laid bare. "My subconscious certainly whipped up a drool-worthy leading man. Too bad you aren't real."

This was the second time she claimed he was not real. "I am not a dream," Robert said, finally registering her extreme state of undress. Peeking out from under the fabric wrapped around her, shapely legs glistened with a fine layer of dew.

"Oh boy. You're ogling me." Samantha sighed. "It's going to be one of *those* dreams. Usually, I'd play along, but I'm really not in the mood." She ran her hands through her wet hair. He saw them tremble. "No ravishing tonight, okay? Just go back from whence you came."

"I do not wish to go back. And I would never take liberties with a woman I just met." Robert began to pace. This was not what he expected. Samantha should know why he was here.

Samantha grabbed her brush again and brandished it at him. "Look, we're not playing the hard-to-get scenario. Now shoo." She smacked his shoulder with the back of the brush.

A flash of pain lanced through his arm. He reacted without thinking, knocking the brush from her hand and gripping her shoulders, drawing her close.

"I am here on business not a dalliance." His words were tight. "You are supposed to help me." The tablecloth had slipped, revealing the tantalizing swell of her breasts.

Samantha shook her head. "You smell incredible. Like lavender and moss. I wish I could wake up and write this down for my next book."

He pulled her closer, quelling the urge to shake some sense into her. "I am real."

The sweet scent of her breath bathed his skin. Heat flooded his body, awakening him in ways he had thought gone forever.

A glimmer of a smile quirked her lips. "You certainly feel real." She touched his jaw with her fingertips. "And maybe this *is* what I need. A break from the anxiety over tomorrow. Over Scotland."

Robert had no idea what she was talking about. Right now, every fiber of his being was struggling against the urge to rip the tablecloth from her. "So you will help me?"

Samantha's skin flushed. "Sexy dream, you win. No more arguments. I'll help you." Her hand slid down his chest, past his waist, and further.

Robert's eyes flashed open. He stumbled back, putting much-needed distance between them. His trousers were uncomfortably tight. "I believe there is a misunderstanding, Samantha." He stalked over to the chair by her dresser, standing behind it. "Only someone who can help ease a ghost's burden can call them from the Rinth. *That* is the help I seek."

Samantha frowned. "A ghost? Of course, let's turn this dream into a nightmare." She grabbed a blue robe from the edge of her bed and put it on, the tablecloth now a puddle of fabric at her feet. She gestured with her hand. "Pray tell, fine sir, what am I supposed to help you with?"

He ignored the sarcasm in her tone. "You will clear my name. I am Lord Robert Grenning. I was wrongfully convicted of killing Sarah Covington and executed in 1790."

She tucked a long lock of her blonde hair behind her ear. "Robert. Of course. Just like Robert from my book. But the backstory is different." She squinted at him. "You do resemble the cover a bit too. It appears my subconscious is as tired as I am. Nothing new, just recycling."

"Are you tetched?" Robert reached her in a few long strides. "Or trying to shirk your duty?"

"Said the reinterpretation of my romance novel character."

"Stop prevaricating and start acting like who I know you to be."

"And who exactly do you know me to be?" Her words were clipped, hard. Though she did not move, her energy rose through the air, pushing at him like a hot wind.

He held his ground. "You are who every ghost knows you to be, once they have laid their eyes upon you."

This time it was Samantha who turned away. "Enough. This is my dream, and I don't want to hear my fears spoken by a delusion. Even with an adorable Scottish lilt."

The fragility of her voice almost stopped him, but she was his only chance. Whispering in her ear, he said the name he knew instinctively in the core of his ghostly essence. The name the others had spoken in the Rinth.

"Necromancer."

CHAPTER 4

Sam turned around slowly. A laugh bubbled up from someplace dark inside her. "Necromancer? I've never been called that before. My subconscious finally came up with something from the movies. How unoriginal."

"It is a noble title." He gave her a deep bow as if she were someone important.

Dark, dashing, dangerous and obviously a dream. But she certainly enjoyed the view. His broad shoulders were barely contained in a cream linen shirt. He might be a Lord, but he had muscle on him.

She pinched her arm, hard. "Ow. Okay, not waking up." Her mind must want her to work through something. "All right handsome, what's the Rinth?"

Robert's eyes narrowed, but he complied. "It is a Purgatory of sorts. Where ghosts wait until the one person who can assist them with their unfinished business calls them from the darkness."

"Like on a phone?" She knew she was being facetious, but

she wanted this over and him gone so she could wake up.

He gave her a long disapproving look. "It was your glow which beckoned me here."

She raised an eyebrow. "Am I glowing now?"

He nodded. "But dimmer than before. Perhaps because I have found you now."

Maybe this really was an idea for a new book about ghosts. If so, she'd better mine it for all the details before the bath cooled and woke her up. "Is the Rinth on the same plane as my world?"

"I know not how things work. But the Rinth is next to the realm of Entwine."

It didn't surprise her that he mentioned Entwine. He was her own hallucination, so it made sense. She looked at him more closely. "My mind may have used my book cover as inspiration, but there are differences. You're taller, and your brown hair has hints of red." Sam took a few steps closer. "Is that a scar near your left eye?"

Robert nodded. "I was marked so while climbing a tree. Well, falling from it actually. Beatrice was quite cross with me."

He suddenly looked younger. Around thirty. Her age. "I hate when story ideas come from dreams. I'll probably forget all this when I wake up.

A concerned look molded Robert's features into something more regal. She could picture him commanding an estate. "I sincerely hope your questionable mental state will not impede your steps to clear my name."

Sam rubbed her temples against the headache beginning

to pound. "Of course I would have a fantasy man who is rude."

"I am not," Robert stopped and ran a hand along his brow. "I am not rude. I seek your help and you must give it. That is the role of a Necromancer."

Rule #2: The ghost must ask for help.

Sam froze, her gaze dropping to the floor. Where had that come from? She hadn't thought about the Rules since her parents died. This wasn't happening. He was just a dream. Albeit the best dream she'd had in a while, but he wasn't a ghost.

"Samantha." She looked up at his voice and realized he was holding her hand. It felt natural. "Perhaps you need sustenance? You look pale."

She squeezed his hand, feeling a little more steady. Squeezed his hand? "Wait a second, you can't be a ghost. I can touch you. I can't touch ghosts."

He lifted her hand to his lips and kissed her knuckles gently. Heat rushed down her fingers. "For the last time. I. Am. A. Ghost."

Sam pulled her hand out of his grip. "Fine, Mr. Ghost. I got rid of my affliction years ago. Why can I see ghosts now?"

"Why do you feel it is an affliction?"

"Answer my question."

He shook his head, sending a dark lock of his hair falling over one eye. He pushed it back with practiced ease. "Your ability is not something you can give up. It is bestowed upon you by the Universe. Why do you despise what you can do?"

Sam walked past him and sat on the side of the bed, tucking

her legs up under her. "You're my subconscious, me, so I'm just rehashing what I already know. This is a waste of time."

"Please seek a priest after you have cleared my name. I fear for your sanity."

She shot him what she hoped was a deadly stink-eye, but he just stared at her, like he had all the time in the world. "Are you sure you weren't killed for being extremely frustrating?"

"Well, apparently, I am you." He pointed at her. "A figment of your mind, so you are truly the one who is frustrating. Not I."

Sam wanted to protest, but instead couldn't help smiling. This was absurd. Robert smiled back, like they were friends, sharing a moment of amusement. "What am I doing?"

Robert's gaze sobered. "You were about to tell me why you hate being the Necromancer."

"I was going to do no such thing." Yet the urge to share it with him rose through her. Maybe it was the understanding in his eyes?

"I must disagree. If I am truly your mind, you *do* want to tell someone."

She couldn't fault his reasoning. Perhaps she just needed to be honest with herself.

Sam took a deep breath. "I buried my ability after my parents died in a car accident." Robert looked at her in confusion. "A car is . . . a metal horse and carriage we use for transportation." He nodded. "They died in Scotland."

Robert sat down on the bed, a few feet separating them. "I am sorry you suffered such a loss."

Just remembering that day squeezed her chest tight. She

clutched at the comforter, struggling for control. Robert's hand found hers again, their fingers threading together like they'd done it a thousand times.

"I should have been able to see their ghosts, to say good-bye," Sam said. "But they never came. *That's* when I knew it was a curse. A joke on me by the Universe or whatever I'd been helping all those years." She gripped his hand so tightly, she was sure it was painful, but he never flinched. "The *one time* I needed my ability, it failed me. What's the point of suffering like I did if I couldn't see the ones I loved?"

"How did you rid yourself of your gift?" His voice matched hers, soft, secretive. Like they didn't want anyone to hear.

"I wished it away. Wished what I could do to disappear."

He tilted his head toward her, his face open. "I lost my mother when I was seven."

"That's horrible. How'd it happen?"

"Influenza." He gazed down at their hands, not looking at her. "She took care of the sick at the local church and ended up one of the victims herself. My father called in every doctor money could buy, but she had weak lungs from pneumonia. Once the illness settled there, we could do nothing but wait for her to die."

Seeing his bowed head, his shoulders sagging, Sam wished she could help him somehow. Let her power back in and then banish it again. If he were truly a ghost, that is. But he wasn't. And even if he were, she couldn't waiver on her resolve. Her powers were dead.

A knock sounded on her bedroom door and Robert disappeared almost before she could blink. Her hand clenched the comforter instead of Robert's hand.

"Are you all right, Sam?" Bronson asked, coming in carrying a heavily laden tray of tea, scones, fruit, and sandwiches and placed it on her dresser.

"This dream was getting weirder." Sam stood slowly, feeling chilled. She looked around her room, expecting to see Robert hiding somewhere.

Bronson raised his eyebrow. "You're not dreaming."

She peeped into the bathroom. Nothing. She walked over to the closet and opened it. Just clothes. "I don't see him any-where, but this could still be a dream."

Bronson grabbed a teacup from the tray and went into her bathroom. She heard water running. He came out, the cup filled with water. "You're not dreaming." He threw a cupful of cold water at her chest.

Sam gasped, instantly getting goosebumps. She took the towel he offered. "Fine. I'm not dreaming *now*. But I was."

Bronson favored her with a raised eyebrow. "And why do you think that?"

"I met a man, a Lord, he was in my bedroom. He looked like my book cover. Said he was a ghost which is absurd."

"I think you need to sit down." Bronson helped her into the chair by the dresser.

Wait, there was a way she could absolutely prove he was a dream. She grabbed her phone. "I am Lord Robert Grenning," she said under her breath, typing his name into the search engine.

An entry popped up. No, several entries about the notorious Lord Robert and his murderous past. He'd been convicted of killing Sarah Covington.

"No." Sam dropped her phone, spots dancing in front of her eyes.

Bronson crouched in front of her. "It's going to be okay. Focus on me, Sam. There's nothing you can't handle. That we can't handle. Two for two . . ."

"Is what we do," Sam replied, feeling stronger already. It was the saying Bronson had come up with after her parents died.

"What's going on?" He took her hands. "Is this about returning to Scotland? You don't have to go. Kate will eventually forgive you."

"I think I just saw a ghost."

Bronson's grip tightened and then released. "Why do you think that?"

"He came to me." She showed him her phone. "How could I dream of a Lord Robert whom I didn't even know existed, right down to whom he was convicted of murdering? And I touched him. How is that possible?"

Bronson's face grew still. "You banished your powers right when you were reaching puberty. I wouldn't be surprised if they've shifted." He stood and widened his stance as if preparing for battle. "You might be able to touch all ghosts now."

Sam got to her feet and gazed at the picture of her parents by her bed. The picture was from a family skiing trip, their arms wrapped around each other. She'd been ten. She remembered that cocoon of warmth. And how they'd tried to help her get over her fear of her curse. Talking about destiny, how they would sacrifice anything for her. Thinking she might be part of something larger still scared her, but Robert needed her help. And maybe it meant she could help Kate with her ghost problems too.

Obviously, the Universe wasn't done with her yet.

But it didn't mean she had to go quietly. She'd gotten rid of her burden before. She'd do it again. Resolve, like a rod of metal slid through her back, tightening her shoulders. If it was possible, she felt taller than her five-foot-ten frame. Not invincible, but more than able to help out at Kate's B&B to kick some ghostly ass.

Bronson's face filled with pride, though she still sensed his worry. "You know what you need then."

Sam nodded. "I can't take any chances." She went over to her bed and kneeled. The heavy box underneath protested a moment before allowing her to pull it free. It was dusty, but when she opened it, the two iron daggers inside were pristine.

They'd been forged with the express purpose of battling ghosts. At least that's what her father had told her when he brought them back from Scotland.

Sam grasped one of the daggers. It was like picking up a shard of ice. "I'll be checking an extra bag."

CHAPTER 5

SAM WAS PREPARED FOR SCOTLAND TO BRING BACK PAINFUL memories, but she'd forgotten just how much she used to love this country. The heady scent of grass and rich dark earth rushed into her lungs on the wind. Gazing out the cab's window, she watched shadows race across the fields from the game of hide and seek the sun played with the clouds. Puffs of white dotted the green hills with sheep.

She tugged at the edges of the blue and red scarf wrapped around her neck. It was the tartan of Clan Hamilton. The last gift she had ever received from her father. She'd almost left it in her dresser at home. Now, it felt like a bright talisman against the impending horrors.

"Do you know Kate Banberry?" the driver asked, his eyes meeting hers in the rearview mirror.

"We're old friends."

"She was very insistent I be the one to pick you up, not one of my lads."

"Lads? How many sons do you have?"

He smiled at her. It was warm and comforting. More than she would have expected from a stranger. "By lads, I mean my employees. But I hope to have children someday. With the right woman." There was a faint tinge of sadness in his tone, though his smile never wavered.

"I hope to be a mom someday, too. I lost my own mother when I was young." She hadn't meant to talk about the accident, but being back in Scotland seemed to have loosened her tongue. "Sorry. Oversharing."

He glanced back over his shoulder at her, and then turned away, but not before Sam saw understanding in his gaze. "Don't fret about it. We've all had sorrows in our lives. It nearly killed Katie when she lost Paul. There were many times all I could do was be a shoulder for her to cry on. It tore me up inside."

Sam studied the driver more closely in the mirror. Tousled short hair, kind brown eyes, slightly long face, wide shoulders. And interested in 'Katie'. That much was obvious by the way he said her name and the anguish she heard in his voice when he talked about comforting her. A fine Scotsman indeed.

"How long have you and Kate known each other?"

"Since she moved here four years ago." He shot her an apologetic glance in the rearview mirror. "Where are my manners? I'm Graham Dunning. My brother, Logan, is the Detective Chief Constable of this town. We've both been looking after Katie." They headed up a steep hill, and Graham shifted gears before speaking again. "It's been tough on her, taking care of the B&B and her two wee ones on her own."

"Paul was an amazing man," Sam said. "But he's been gone

over two years now. I'd hoped she'd find someone else to share her life with."

Graham nodded. "That's my hope too. Life is too fleeting to be alone." His cell phone trilled. "Pardon me while I take this. I've got two lads out sick, so I've been troubleshooting all day." He tapped the bluetooth receiver in his ear, and his voice dropped to a low tone. Too low for Sam to follow.

Leaning back in her seat, she let her eyes drift shut. The flight had been long, and she hadn't been able to sleep at all on the plane. Graham's voice dimmed to a dull drone of noise. The tires crunched over some gravel, and the sound morphed into the crackling of flames. Drowned out by her dad's screams.

Images swam joining the sounds and smells. Blood. There'd been so much blood.

"Are you all right, Ms. Hamilton?" Graham's voice jarred her out of the past and shoved her painfully into the present.

Sweat coated Sam's skin. She willed her fingers to unclench from the handles of her purse. "I'm fine," she lied. "Just tired." No matter how many deep breaths she took, she couldn't seem to clear the phantom scents of smoke and death.

She'd been worried about facing old memories here, but the raised hair on the back of her neck told her something else was going on. Sam might not have Kate's gift of seeing the future, but she had an awful feeling there was more danger in Scotland than she'd realized. Just what was she heading into?

D ouglas Manor, Kate's B&B, loomed in the distance, rising up tall amongst grassy fields and thick woods. The brick was a weathered peach with stains of charcoal gray smudged across the surface.

This was Lord Robert Grenning's old home. Sam had found it during her research on his life. If what he said was true, her decision to come back to Scotland must have been what pulled him from the Rinth. Which meant there *was* something here that could help him. Some clue.

So after paying her fare, she took her time looking over the outside of the manor. To her left, a tower rose several stories above the ground, casting a long shadow up to the doorway. The main house directly in front of her had a sloping, uneven roof. Here and there, windows gaped at her like small, dark graves.

This place was different than she expected. Robert seemed so warm and full of life. Strange for someone who was a ghost, but that's the impression he'd made on her. But the manor was nothing like him. It felt forgotten. Lonely.

A shiver worked its way up her legs and through her shoulders, leaving her wool cardigan and scarf feeling like tissue paper against the cold. Her gaze swept over the front door. Impatiens spilled from the hanging orange pots in shades of purple and pink, finally, one happy touch that told her this was Kate's home.

"Hullo," called a voice from her right, quickly followed by another voice, this one chiding. "Show some manners, Stu."

An older couple approached across a gravel parking area.

They looked to be somewhere in their sixties, but their strides hummed with energy. The man was tall with short red hair shot through with gray. The woman was almost his height, thin and gangly. Long gray hair flowed out behind her like a cape.

"You must be Ms. Hamilton." The heavy creases on the man's face softened into a smile. "I'm Stuart Kelly, the caretaker."

"And I'm Agatha, his wife. But everyone calls me Aggie." She grabbed Sam into an unexpected hug.

Sam pulled back and smiled. "Pleased to meet you both." The B&B couldn't have been doing too badly if Kate still had staff around.

Stu gestured toward her scarf. "I see you're wearing your clan's colors. Very becoming a Scottish lass such as yourself."

"Welcome to our fine estate." Aggie lifted her hands. "My husband manages the grounds. I do all the rest."

"Ach, now woman, don't be giving off airs to our guest." He grabbed Sam's luggage. "Let's get her settled in per Ms. Banberry's request." The stern look he gave his wife lasted about a second.

"Airs?" Aggie looped her arm through Sam's. "She'll know what's what soon enough. She's a smart cookie, I can tell." She leaned in close to Sam and whispered. "I read all your books. Stu thinks they're too steamy." She giggled just like a young girl.

With muttered complaints about women always thinking they know best, Stu led them into the house.

Inside, dark red woods offset the beautiful light yellow

wallpaper. A staircase curved up, disappearing into a second floor. To her right, a massive oak desk stood covered in brochures, with a guest book almost falling off the edge. The calendar draped over the side was from last year. Kate hadn't been exaggerating after all. The business was hurting.

The sparkling sound of children's voices came from down the hallway. Stu set her bags at the bottom of the stairs, but Sam moved past him, eager to see Kate's daughters.

Sam peeped her head inside the room off the main hallway. It was a large study dominated by a fireplace, massive enough to fit several people inside its impressive girth. Heavy logs burned bright, and the scent of cedar clung to the air.

Two girls sat in front of the flames, their heads bent together as if they were one. The last time she'd been with them was at their father's grave. Had it really been two years now?

The familiar guilt sank heavier on her shoulders, rooting her by the door. She rubbed her face, loosening her jaw. The girls would want to see happy Auntie Sam, not wracked-with-regret Auntie Sam.

Plastering a smile on her face, she said in a loud voice. "I've been here for five whole seconds. Where's my welcome hug?"

The girls spun around and stared at her in unison.

"Auntie Sam!" Emily, the older one, squealed and scrambled to her feet. She raced across the floor toward Sam, her red braids flying out behind her. With her solid nine-year-old frame, she almost knocked Sam off her feet with a running hug.

Emily fired questions at her quickly, but with excellent diction. She still had her American accent. "How was your trip?

Where's Bronson? Do you want to play dolls with us? Would you like some tea?"

Sam smoothed Emily's bangs back from her forehead and kissed her nose. "Great. At home. Later. Yes." It was a game they always played, and Emily's face split into a huge smile, revealing a charming gap between her two front teeth. Kate had wanted to fix it with braces, but Emily had refused. She told her she liked being different.

Patty hadn't moved from her spot in front of the fireplace.

"Auntie Sam, please go sit with Patty. I'll get the tea," Emily declared.

"I best help her with that," Aggie said, joining them. "If you're fine here rather than scooting up to your room right away?"

Sam nodded. "Patty will keep me company." Emily's younger sister seemed to be ignoring them. Just barely seven-years-old, she looked tiny against the huge fireplace, as a mouse against the yellow fur of a great lion.

Aggie took Emily's hand. "Come on, I'll help you get the tea ready while they play."

"Excellent idea, Mrs. Aggie." Emily brightened at the suggestion, and they headed back out to the hallway.

She heard Emily's excited chatter even over the crackling of flames from the fireplace. Sound apparently carried in this old house.

Crouching next to Patty, Sam picked up one of the rag dolls the girls had been playing with. It felt limp in her hands, as if the stuffing had been crushed down by years of use. Red yarn sprang unevenly from its scalp, and the doll's smile seemed to have been stitched on many times. If only it were so easy with people. To sew on a smile when yours had long worn away.

"That's Mommy," Patty said in a voice suited to a library. She shot a quick glance at Sam, and then turned back to the doll in her hands.

Dark circles bruised the pale skin underneath the girl's eyes, and her light brown hair looked dull, tied back into a low ponytail. Sam knew Patty had taken Paul's death harder than Emily, but she hadn't known it was this bad.

Looking down at the array of dolls on the floor, Sam had a good idea what Patty might be using them for. When the doctors had treated Sam after her parents had died, they'd worked with pictures and role-playing to help her process her grief.

Sam angled the Mommy doll toward Patty. "And how's my baby girl?" She tried to mimic Kate's voice, but heard right away she'd failed. "Will there be cookies with our tea?"

Patty didn't reply immediately, but the girl scooted a bit closer to Sam. "You're doing it all wrong," Patty said. "The dolls don't talk to us, they talk to each other."

"They do?" Sam frowned and hunched her shoulders. "Sorry I messed up. Will you help me get it right?"

Nodding slowly, Patty picked up another doll. This one had pieces of black yarn clinging to the scalp. A mustache had been scribbled onto its face with a black marker.

"Don't cry, Katie," Patty said, using her doll to talk to the one in Sam's hands. "I'm still here. Watching over my girls."

Patty lowered her chin, the movement so reminiscent of Paul that for a moment, Sam couldn't breathe.

Grabbing the Mommy doll from Sam's sagging grip, Patty turned it toward the first one. "Why did you have to die, Paul? Why?" The dolls fell to the floor, and Patty's hands flew to her face. Big heavy tears rushed down her cheeks. "Why did Daddy have to die?"

Sam scooped the girl up. "If I could take the hurt away, I would."

Patty curled into Sam's arms. Her tears felt hot against Sam's skin. "Why did he leave us?" Each word became more labored, and Sam felt the heavy sobs shaking through her.

"He would have stayed if he could have, monkey. That's the absolute truth."

She grasped Sam's hands, squeezing them so hard it became painful, but Sam didn't pull away.

Patty forced words out of her mouth in hard breaths. "Did I tease Emily too much? I was never quiet when he needed to work. And I didn't mean to dig up the garden and ruin the flowers, but I was looking for buried treasure. Was it my fault he died?"

Hearing the same kinds of questions she'd asked herself all those years ago, felt like someone reached into Sam's chest and pinched. Hard. Dizziness blurred her vision. "It was nothing you did. You couldn't have done anything to prevent it."

"But I could have. Before he died, I *knew* it would happen."

The serious look on her face frightened Sam almost more than her words. Sam's throat was tight. Kate had never mentioned

Patty had inherited her ability. "Do you always know what's going to happen before it does?"

Patty leaned in close. Close enough, Sam saw every freckle on her nose clearly. "Not always, but I'm getting bad feelings again. Like when Daddy got sick."

"What are these feelings telling you, monkey?" Sam asked, not really wanting to know the answer, but knowing she had to.

Patty's words were just a breath on Sam's face. "Mommy's going to die."

CHAPTER 6

ROBERT WATCHED SAMANTHA DISAPPEAR INTO THE MANOR. He had known of her destination, but once she had arrived, he found himself in front of his old home in the merest blink of an eye. Not wanting to intrude while she fought her own personal demons, he had kept his distance. He had his own battle to suffer through. Seeing his old home once again, but not as one of the living.

He scanned the manor buildings, noting time's bootprints upon their surface and structure. The tower continued to command the landscape. His home.

Robert crouched, his hand frozen above the ground before it clenched into a fist. He would never be able to touch the earth, feel the damp soil slipping through his fingers again. He was merely a spectator.

But lamenting his death would not accomplish his goal. He must save his energies for the struggles he could affect, could change, such as clearing his name.

He straightened and stared at the front door. Instead of the heavy iron lanterns which used to guard his family home, baskets hung on either side of the entryway, spewing forth fragile flowers.

How changed would the inside of the manor be? Had everything been blackened and tarnished, like he had done so with his family's legacy?

The Grennings had been one of the most respected families in Scotland. From what he had read of Samantha's research over her shoulder, they were only mentioned briefly in history. For the murder of Sarah Covington.

He could not change the past, but Samantha could help him rewrite the ending for his family and remove the stain.

He stared again at the manor entrance. Delaying outside would only fuel his fear of what he might find. He needed to see for himself. Eyeing the sturdy front door, Robert knew it would take extreme concentration to pass through it effectively.

He approached the door and laid a hand above its surface. *I will pass through, I will pass through.* His palm sank through the surface, and then his whole hand followed. The particles of wood vibrated through his form. When his entire body dissolved into the door, he became one with the wood, without human shape. It would be so easy to let go.

I am Lord Robert Grenning. The pronouncement blared loud within his mind, clearing away any hesitation. He was through the door, almost falling to his knees. His body trembled from the effort, but he had made it inside.

There were changes upon the surface, but the bones of his home had remained strong. The staircase still wound its way to the second floor, the mahogany bannister gleaming in the light of the small chandelier above, but the wallpaper was a pale yellow rather than the beautiful cornflower blue his sister, Lillian, had chosen. The overstuffed chaises and grandfather clock were gone. His old desk had been shoved into the right corner. Why wasn't it in the study?

It felt like only a few months since he had been here, rather than over two hundred years. His gaze flicked to the stairs again, where Allistair, the Justiciar's lackey, had dragged him to his death.

A shadow of anger reared its head, but he pushed it back. It would serve no purpose here. He could no more go back in time than he could wish himself alive.

His gaze swept across his desk once more. The papers and book scattered upon its surface beckoned him. When he got closer, he realized the papers were pamphlets of a sort. Blazed across the top of the incredibly shiny paper were the words "Explore Scotland" in a garish print. Underneath were paintings of strangely dressed commoners with enormous smiles on their faces. Were they drunk? Or tetched?

He moved his attention to the book. Where it lay open, he found names and dates of stay. It could not. The proud Grenning home had been turned into a boarding house? Had his conviction fueled the ghoulish interest of the public? Did they wish to stay in the same place where the murderous Lord Robert had laid his head?

Rage exploded through him. He swept his arm across the desk, unable to bear the sight any longer of the Grennings' demise. For a brief moment, he thought he felt the weight of the book against his hand. But like a breeze buffeting against stone, he moved nothing, affected nothing, changed nothing.

His shoulders drooped, despair dousing the flames of anger. He had not murdered Sarah Covington, but he had killed his family's name. Samantha had to help him right this wrong.

As if summoned by his thoughts, her voice reached his ears. It rode the air like an irresistible scent.

Drawn toward the sound, he saw the iron lanterns from his youth, now framing the open archway into the study. About the length of his forearm, they were just as imposing as he remembered.

Taking a few steps into the room, Robert watched Samantha playing dolls with a young girl. The gentle way in which she spoke to the child reminded him of his mother. Samantha pushed a lock of the girl's hair back from her face, and Robert could almost feel the touch of his mother's fingers against his skin. How deeply he missed her.

Samantha turned slightly, and the firelight caught the curve of her cheek and the deep pink of her lips. Strands of her hair tumbled over her shoulders like rivers of honey against her sweater.

He already stood transfixed at the sight. And then she smiled.

Again that feeling of home spread through him, like she was the sun and he craved her light. He wondered if all ghosts who were freed from the Rinth felt this way about their saviors? It would do no good to feed the flames of a fleeting attraction.

This was a business arrangement and nothing must get in the way of their goal.

He turned away slowly and then walked back to the iron lanterns in the hallway. He remembered his father's strong arms lifting him up so he could touch the intricate pattern along the bottom of the lantern, the proud "G" for the Grenning name.

Robert reached for a lantern, but stopped just an inch away, knowing he would not be able to feel the hardness of the metal underneath his palm or the raised scrollwork. Just like the desk, objects from the living world were forever beyond his dead grasp.

An itching sensation burrowed into his nails and marched up his hand. He pulled back, and the sensation bled away. He must know the meaning of this.

Without another thought, he gripped the lantern. Rather than his hand passing through, it felt like he had plunged it beneath the depths of an icy lake.

Alarmed, Robert yanked his hand back, but it remained pinned to the iron as if they had been forged from the same mold. He tried to brace himself against the wall, but kept sliding through. Without leverage, he could not break free, shackled to the metal.

His hand shimmered in front of him as if the fibers of his ghostly form could not hold together. The chandelier flickered above, almost extinguishing.

He heard movement behind him. Arms encircled his waist in a tight grip and with a high screeching sound of metal upon metal, he found himself flung down the hallway.

Robert scrambled for balance, his body still reeling from the iron's sharp bite.

He was free. But how?

"My lord, now why would you ever do something so foolish?"

It was a chiding voice Robert had never dared hope to hear again. He turned quickly.

Beatrice, his family's housekeeper, stood with her hands on her ample hips. The disapproving look on her face almost had him stammering with an excuse like the boy he used to be, but his first inclination overwhelmed the rest.

He dragged her into a tight hug, his chin against her temple. "How is this possible?"

Beatrice's hands trembled for a moment against his back, and then she pulled away to look up into his face. With red hair escaping from her bun and skirts dusted in flour, she looked just as alive as he remembered. He touched her cheek lightly, then her shoulder until finally, he squeezed her hand. She was indeed before him. This was real.

"I'm dead, my lord. Just like you. That's how it's possible." Her gaze roved over his face as if memorizing it. "Why aren't you in Heaven with your sister?"

"I was in the Rinth."

Beatrice shuddered and then steadied. "I guess I shouldn't be surprised. You had a whopping heap of unfinished business."

"Speaking of unfinished business, did Lillian find Sarah's journal?" Robert was eager to know her answer. "I left it for her in our childhood hiding spot, the crawlspace between our rooms. It contains clues to the identity of Sarah's killer."

"I don't know if Lillian ever found it. I fled Scotland, as you'd urged me to." Beatrice's lips tightened. "Though I almost came back just to wring that bastard's neck. Allistair knew you were innocent. He wanted you out of the way."

Robert nodded. "It was my fault I ended up in the web of lies surrounding Sarah's death, but he gloried in robbing me of my life and everything I could have had. Children. A family." The words choked off, his throat growing tight. Heat built from his feet up through his body. How he had longed to kill Allistair. That thought had been a constant companion for many months when he had first entered the Rinth. His hands clenched, nails digging into his palms.

The guestbook slid off the desk and smashed into the back wall, crushing the spine and spilling pages onto the floor. Beatrice flinched.

Shock stole the heat from his body, replacing it with a chill. Robert glanced from the ruined book to Beatrice and back again. "Did you do that?"

"I think you did, my lord." Beatrice's eyes were wide. "You must calm yourself, lest you turn into a geist."

His anger shrank to a mere ember. "You used to tell me geists would eat me if I was not a good boy."

Beatrice grinned. "Well, it worked, didn't it? Geists do exist, but they don't dine on bad little boys. They're troubled spirits who rain destruction and mayhem through our realm and the world of the living." She gave him a short quick nod so violent that several more strands of graying hair slipped free of her bun to mix with the red. "I'll be damned if I let you turn into one."

"I will endeavor to control myself accordingly." Robert gave her a bow. Deference usually calmed her.

Beatrice let out a long sigh. "See that you do. And stop touching iron. Did they teach you nothing in the Rinth?"

"Nothing of merit." The darkness of that place returned to him, robbing his words of any emotion. "Just that pain and regret would walk beside us always."

"I'm sorry, my lord." Beatrice cupped his cheek. "That can't have been easy." She dropped her hand and gave him a stern look. "You must be careful around iron. It's a plague to spirits. Rips apart the energy holding them together. Holding them in Entwine."

"How is it that *you* are still here? After practically raising me alone, if anyone deserves Heaven, it is you."

Beatrice tucked some of her hair back into her bun. "Those that keep the lists can be persuaded to move you to the bottom. For a price."

Robert's eyebrow raised at her words. "So, one can buy extra time in Entwine. But why would you stay?"

Beatrice's fingers fumbled with the strings of her apron, worrying the bow tied in front. "I've got to watch over my family. I was shocked when Kate and her husband purchased the manor, like they'd been drawn here." She dropped her hands and smoothed her apron. "Kate's husband died two years back. It's been rough on her lasses. If only I could hug them, comfort them."

"Why are you unable to hug them?" Samantha had

commented that their touching was unusual. He had not given it much thought until now.

"Ghosts can't touch the living." She favored him with an indulgent smile.

"I can. I can touch Samantha."

"The Necromancer? Stop jesting."

"I do not jest."

"Only a geist can touch someone living." She looked at him in a sideways glance, as if worried he might be becoming one of these dreaded creatures.

"I am not a geist, and I am telling you I can touch the Necromancer."

"It would be very dangerous if you can do as you say." Beatrice glanced around the hallway. He did not know who she was looking for. "You must have imagined it."

He strove to control his tone. "I did not imagine it."

They stared at each other for several long moments. She needed proof. He took her arm. "Come with me into the study, so we can learn the truth. Together."

"You won't let this rest?" At the shake of his head, she finally nodded. "Let us be quick about it before any others show up."

"Others?"

Beatrice led him into the study. "Other ghosts. Information is a useful currency in Entwine. Now don't let her see you. Don't materialize."

"Why?"

"If I'm to prove you wrong, we need to make sure she'd only be reacting to your touch, not the sight of you." She squared her shoulders. "You've always been too stubborn for your own good."

"As are you." Robert placed a quick kiss on her cheek. She could rail at him all she wanted. He was just so thankful not to be alone any longer.

Samantha held the little girl he had seen her with earlier. They still sat by the fire, but now both looked exhausted and worried. What had happened while he tarried with Beatrice?

Without any warning, Beatrice reached toward Samantha. Her hand slid through the sweater, the flesh, the bone.

"Hurry now," Beatrice urged, her gaze darting around the room.

Robert tapped Samantha on the shoulder. She rubbed the place he had touched and looked around.

Beatrice's gasp cut off almost before it escaped her lips.

Robert smiled. "There. I have proved it."

Beatrice whispered. "Can you touch all the living?"

"I have not tried."

"Try." Her words were a command, not to be trifled with.

Robert did as she ordered and tugged on the girl's ponytail, feeling every fine strand.

"Hey," the girl said, whirling around. "What was that?"

Beatrice's eyes darkened to a heavy gray. She pulled him back, away from the fire. "This is bad. This is very bad." She gripped his arm, nails digging into his skin. Her whisper was almost a hiss. "If they find out, they will use you for their own means."

Robert nodded. "The Wardens."

"They are part of both worlds—the living and Entwine."

Her gaze held his. "I've never heard of any ghost doing what you can do, and I wouldn't put it past them to use you for their own purposes. Maybe even as an assassin. Death by ghost. No clues, no evidence, nothing."

Robert drew himself up to his full height. "I would refuse. I would rather go to Hell without clearing my name than kill an innocent."

She leaned in close, her voice barely a breath against his cheek. "If you refused, they'd threaten to harm anyone you care about."

He knew they'd use Beatrice against him if they could. Would he really be able to refuse to do the Wardens' bidding if her existence hung in the balance?

Beatrice's eyes shifted to Samantha. "We'll have to be very careful. And whatever you do, don't touch anyone until your name is cleared. You never know who's watching. Information like that would ensure decades in Entwine."

"I will do as you ask, Beatrice," he replied. There should be no need for him to touch Samantha ever again.

He tried to ignore the hollow feeling in his stomach. It was much like the iron had felt, leaching his very soul.

"SOMEONE TOUCHED ME," PATTY SAID. SHE DIDN'T SOUND afraid, just interested.

Sam sensed two ghosts. She hoped one of them was Robert, and that he'd been the one who tapped her shoulder. If not, then her worry had become a reality. All ghosts could touch her.

She leaned closer to the fire and put her arm around Patty's shoulders.

"You believe me about Mommy, right? Something bad is going to happen, Auntie Sam."

Patty's proclamation of Kate's death rushed back through Sam's mind. She trusted Patty just like she'd trusted Kate and Beth, all those years ago. Which meant Kate really *was* in danger.

She couldn't lose Kate. And what would happen to the girls? Was the threat to Kate even something Sam could stop? "I believe you, Patty. You were very brave to tell me about not only your mom, but also your gift." Sam took the girl's cold hands in hers and rubbed them until they warmed. She remembered what it felt like to tell someone for the first time. To acknowledge you were a freak.

Patty squeezed her hand. "You're trembling, Auntie Sam. Are you frightened?"

Sam nodded. "I am, Patty. I don't want anything to happen to your mom."

"I should have said something about Daddy. I messed up."

Sam pulled gently on her hand until she looked back at her. "You told me about your mom while we still have time to do something. That's what counts."

The lines around Patty's mouth eased, and her shoulders dropped. The cloud of despair lifted from her face, some color returning. "You really think we can save Mommy?"

Sam nodded quickly, though she couldn't be entirely sure how they were going to manage it until she knew more about the threat they faced. "Do you have any details that might help?"

Patty shook her head. "No. Just an awful feeling in my tummy. That's when I know something bad is going to happen to that person." She looked down, picking at a piece of loose wool in the rug. "Emily thinks I'm making things up."

She smoothed back the hair from the girl's sweaty brow, and then leaned in close. "Don't be too upset with Emily. It's tough for people to understand at first, even family. She'll come around. She's your sister."

"Why did you believe me?"

"I'm like you. I can do something special, too." She'd never described it as anything positive before, but Patty needed reassurance.

"You can?" Excitement lit her eyes.

"I can see ghosts, and talk to them."

"Really?" Patty exclaimed in a loud whisper. She touched her hair. "I think a ghost pulled it earlier." Her face held a mixture of fear and excitement. She whipped her head around, gaze attacking every corner as if she could pull ghosts into existence by will alone.

"You could be right."

"Riley can help you find out," Patty said with a wisp of a smile. It was the first sign of happiness Sam had seen since she arrived. "He's a little younger than Em, but much smarter. He hunts ghosts."

The last sentence was delivered with such authority, Sam almost expected the boy to burst through the entryway, armed to the teeth with EMF detectors and infrared scanners.

The floorboards creaked in the hallway, and that, along with Stu's humming, announced his entry into the study. The B&B caretaker had a bemused smile on his face. "I see my grandson has somehow made his way into the conversation. Again. He and Patty are like this." He held up his hand and crossed his first two fingers with a slow deliberate motion.

A blush flooded Patty's cheeks, and this time a full smile stretched across her face reminding Sam of the girl she used to know before Paul had died. "He's my best friend, Auntie Sam. You'll love him."

"I'm sure I will." Sam rose to her feet.

"Why don't you go help your sister in the kitchen, eh lass?" Stu said. "Aggie just pulled some shortbread cookies from the oven, and she needs help icing them right quick, with the spoils going to the helpers." He bent down so he was closer to Patty's level and cupped his hand to his mouth as if imparting a big secret, though his whisper was as loud as Patty's had been. "But, don't be telling your mother I said that."

Patty shook her head so fast, Sam was surprised she didn't make herself dizzy. "I promise I won't tell." She thrust the rag doll that looked like Kate into Sam's hands. "We'll protect Mommy together, right?"

"Absolutely." Sam hoped Patty wouldn't detect the tremor of worry in her voice. "I'll join you and Emily in the kitchen in a bit. Mr. Stuart is going to show me to my room."

Patty gave her a quick kiss on the cheek, and then walked from the study. As soon as she was out of their sight, Sam heard the slap of her shoes against the floor in a run.

"They're good lasses, those girls. You should see them with my grandson. The three musketeers, they are."

Though Stu's comment was innocent, Sam experienced a moment of deja vu. That's what they used to call themselves. Her, Kate and Beth. The three musketeers.

The scar on her thumb itched. It was hard to believe they were once so close, they had performed a ritual. Shared blood.

She felt Stu's heavy stare. "Sorry, lost in thought. Just thinking of Kate and me when we were around Patty's age. How old is your grandson?"

"Eight going on twenty. Fancies he knows everything about everything." His words held a rumbling of mirth, and the skin around his eyes crinkled.

"Well, Patty thinks the world of him. That much is obvious."

Stu nodded and grasped his chest like he swooned. "Riley worships the pebbles she kicks with her shoe. Young love is the most beautiful. Now, if you'll just follow me, I'll get you settled in finally."

Sam trailed behind Stu up the stairs and down the hall. A long wool runner covered the entire length of the hallway, just as plush as the rug downstairs. The hard pounding of Stu's boots hushed.

The further they walked, the more the walls of the narrow hallway loomed in closer. The flowers and vines on the rug swarmed against a green background as if fighting for air. The wallpaper echoed the same design of the rug. Yet, here and there Sam saw splotches of red, almost like spatters of blood on the paper. When she stopped to peer more closely at the design, she couldn't find the crimson spots anywhere.

"Gives you the willies too, I see," Stu said, with a shiver. "I've suggested Ms. Banberry replace it, but as you know, we're low on guests. And money."

Sam leaned closer to the wall, and the hairs on her arms rose in response to a current of energy vibrating just above the surface of the paper. It felt as if tiny pins jutted forward to touch her and then scurried back before they sank too deep into her skin, tasting her blood.

Adrenaline rushed through her system, pushing out a clammy sweat onto her skin.

Only one kind of ghost caused this type of volatile reaction. A poltergeist.

When Kate said the B&B was haunted, Sam hadn't expected to fight this level of ghost again. Normal ghosts could move things at times and scare people. But a poltergeist could kill.

Her power was untested after all these years. She only hoped she remembered enough. Rule #15 floated into her mind. *Invading a poltergeist's space issues a challenge. You must counter immediately.*

If she didn't face the ghost now, it would keep attacking her until she left. Untested or not, she had to do this. For all of them. Once the poltergeist was done with Sam, it would continue on to the others.

She took a deep breath and then another. Her shoulders slid back. She widened her stance for balance and then reached into her purse for the iron daggers. She unwrapped them carefully, her hands steady.

"Those are awfully large letter openers," Stu exclaimed, though she knew by the concern in his eyes he realized they were no such thing.

"Kate might not have told you this, but I see ghosts." After telling Patty, this admission was strangely easier. "You've got a poltergeist who wants a fight. It's already measured my aura, assessed my strength." Those pinpricks hadn't been random.

The daggers' cold metal stole the warmth from her hands. She welcomed the chill, urging it to course through her. Joining with the iron would give her the strength she needed, would help her target her intent against this malevolence.

"I knew it." Stu jabbed his finger in the air. "I told my niece, Yasmin, this particular hallway was filled with something dark. Something foul."

"You were right."

The earlier tiny pinpricks flew into a swarm of invisible stinging bees. Sam flinched, and then steadied herself. This was a strong poltergeist. More powerful than the last one she faced.

"What are you going to do?" Stu's whisper was breathy.

Sam kept her focus on the wallpaper. Poltergeists always had a favorite point of entry into the living world. For Kate's poltergeist, it looked like the wallpaper was its door. "I'm going to show this thing I'm not to be trifled with. That the people here are under my protection."

"You've done this before?"

"Once."

"How'd it go?"

Sam swallowed before answering. She struggled with telling

a lie to make Stu feel better and finally decided on the truth. "This time will be better. And I've got these." She rolled the iron daggers in her hands, her palms already numb. "You might want to back up a bit."

The wallpaper pattern swam before her eyes. The vines contorted into the outlines of a man's face. The buds of the flowers reddened and slanted into eyes. The paper bulged forward, and Stu stumbled back against the opposite wall. Heavy emotions rushed through Sam. Anger, despair, regret. She felt like she'd swallowed tar.

But the iron protected her, shielded her from taking on the ghost's emotions. Otherwise, she would have been lost, unable to separate her own thoughts from its horrors.

With a loud screech, the paper split down the center. Shadows oozed out like oil, dousing the hallway into darkness, devouring any light. Though she couldn't see it, she felt the core of his essence, moving toward her. The swarm of bees grew into a tornado of razor blades.

Slashing into her, they nicked her skin over and over again until blood slicked down her cheeks, her neck, and into her mouth.

Images of her mother's body from the car crash flashed into her mind, but she pushed them back. It was what the poltergeist wanted. If her focus wavered, it was over.

"Samantha!" Stu yelled, but she couldn't go to him. She had to wait for the right moment. The poltergeist was still in Entwine. She needed him here, with her. So she could strike.

"You've had your run of scaring these people. Now you've

got someone who can hit back," Sam said. "Coward. Afraid to face me?"

Okay powers. I know I'm stuck with you for now, so help me wound this thing. Guide me with the iron.

A trickle of energy slid down her arms, then grew to a stream, and then a flood. Light burst from the iron blades, bathing the hallway in a gray gleam. A dark maelstrom of energy churned in front of her. Glass crashed, and something heavy hit the walls. She didn't see Stu, but she buried her concern and took a step toward the poltergeist.

"You shouldn't have come here," the poltergeist said, though it was more a scream of wind rather than a voice.

The dark energy stuttered for a brief instant, and Sam saw his face in the center. Hands reaching for her.

Now.

She stabbed the daggers toward it. They rammed hard into something solid. The chill of the iron reversed, blazing hot. Sam held on even when the smell of her burning flesh gagged her.

The poltergeist shrieked. Pictures fell from the wall. Under her feet, the hallway floor bucked as if an earthquake rumbled through the manor. Sam held on with everything she had.

The razor blade storm ebbed, and finally died. The unnatural darkness seeped away, retreating back into the ceiling, the walls, the floor. Sam blinked against the sudden brightness, and then dropped the smoldering daggers. Stu rushed forward, throwing his jacket over the flames eating their way through the rug.

Sam slid down against the wall She felt completely drained.

Empty. But the poltergeist would think twice before it came after them again.

And this time, no one had died.

CHAPTER 7

S AM OPENED HER EYES, SURPRISED TO FIND HERSELF IN A bed and not on the smoldering hallway rug with two iron daggers beside her.

Kate sat on the side of the bed. Her deep red hair had escaped its haphazard braid as usual, tendrils curling around her heart-shaped face. Though she still looked as beautiful as the last time Sam had seen her, there was a layer of exhaustion coating her porcelain skin with an ashy tone.

"You look tired." Sam hadn't meant to say that out loud. "I mean, considering everything you've been shouldering, it's expected."

"Oh, the art of tap-dance. You never really mastered that." Kate winked. "But don't give me any crap over how I look when you look like someone microwaved you. On high."

Her friend sat back, pulling on the bottom of her mustard brown sweater that looked two sizes too big. Obviously an old sweater of Paul's. An oval gold locket hung from her neck. It held pictures of Paul and her kids in it. Sam had given it to Kate at Paul's funeral.

Sam rubbed her face and came away with blood on her bandaged hands. The razor blade storm from the poltergeist had left its mark.

"Not sure how you got the cuts on your face." Kate gave her a long look. "They're shallow, but I cleaned them anyway. You also had some nasty blisters on your hands," Kate said. "Yesterday, Stu's niece gave me some miracle salve for burns. She's handy that way. Anticipating unknown needs."

"Thanks." The blisters itched. Sam rubbed her right palm against her hip.

"Don't." Kate's mom voice was set on stun, and Sam froze instantly. "No scratching."

Sam pushed herself up with her elbows and leaned against the headboard. "Is Stu okay?"

Kate handed her a glass of water. "Shaken up, but fine."

Sam took a long drink and finally gazed around the room. "Wow," she whispered.

A long oval mirror stretched above a gorgeous dressing table as if holding court over the room. An ornate brush and hand mirror glistened on the table. Resplendent in plum velvet, a fainting couch cuddled with a pair of matching easy chairs along the wall. A large portrait window bathed the room in sunlight.

Kate took the glass from her hands and put it on the bedside table. "You can admire the room later. Stu said it was a poltergeist. I told him he was crazy."

"It's a poltergeist."

Kate just blinked at her for a few seconds. "No friggin way."

"You had no idea?"

Kate stood, her arms flailing out to the side. "How was I supposed to know? I'm not the ghost expert here."

Sam rubbed her temples with the tips of her fingers. Her head felt like nails were being driven into her brain stem. "Sorry. There's no way you could have been sure. Even normal ghosts can move minor things when they're upset."

Kate sighed and sat down on the bed. "I didn't mean to saddle you with the biggest bad of all ghosts. But on the bright side, your powers are definitely back." The last was said with true happiness.

"I've faced a poltergeist before."

"When?"

"Remember the bruised ribs and a broken arm from my bike accident?" Sam made air quotes around *bike accident*. "A parting gift from the poltergeist on Oak Lane."

And it could have been worse. If she hadn't tucked herself in a ball when it threw her down the stairs, she would have died. Just like the owner of the house.

Kate's mouth dropped open, and she shook her head. "Oak Lane. That's where Mr. Montgomery died. Holy crap." She waved a hand at Sam. "I won't put you in that kind of danger. You'll have to leave. I'll call in a priest or something. Do an exorcism."

"That's not going to work. Poltergeists aren't evil spirits or demons. They're just warped by their pain." Sam touched Kate's shoulder. "I can't leave you and the girls to fend for yourselves."

She dropped her hand and let it fall to the comforter. The blisters throbbed under her bandages, and she fought not to rub them. "Though I'm not sure how to get rid of it."

Kate held up one of Sam's iron daggers wrapped in a sock. "So, 'ghost poker' didn't do the trick? I didn't think you still had these. Cleaning this was no fun, by the way."

Sam didn't take the dagger from her. "I kept them just in case. Besides, they came from some distant muckity-muck relative in Scotland. A family heirloom."

Kate put the dagger back down on the bed. "So, the iron didn't get rid of the poltergeist?"

"Nope, only wounded it. It was a warning."

"What, that you're a badass?"

"Yup. If I hadn't held my ground, he would have attacked me until I had to leave. It would have been non-stop torment."

"The torment thing, is that Rule #717 or something? I still don't understand how you've always known the ghost stuff instinctively, but I think that just confirms you can't get rid of it. It's part of you."

Sam just frowned at her, refusing again to rise to the bait.

Kate looked down finally, playing with the frayed bottom of her sweater. "Sorry that my poltergeist was the first ghost you've seen in years. Talk about starting with the big Kahuna."

"He wasn't the first."

Kate clasped her legs close to her, chin on her knees. "Excuse me? You gave me the whole 'I don't see ghosts anymore, Kate' party line when I asked you to come."

The image of Lord Robert Grenning flowed into her mind.

So handsome, she'd thought he had to be a fantasy.

"You're blushing," Kate declared like it was a guilty verdict. "This is going to be juicy. He was hot, wasn't he?"

"It's not juicy. It's embarrassing really. I thought he was a dream, and he thought I was crazy for not realizing what he was." She flung back the comforter, finding it too warm.

Kate pointed at her. "Your cheeks never lie—you only blush about one thing. You know I'll just keep asking until you finally give in."

Kate's smile fought against Sam's reluctance, wearing it away. She missed this. Though they'd stayed in touch, things hadn't been the same since they were kids. The destruction of Sam's friendship with Beth had wounded the one with Kate.

"I forgot how much of a pain you are," Sam said.

"You say that with love." Kate's voice was singsong.

Sam laughed, and it felt really good. "Fine. He's gorgeous."

"Are we talking sex-on-a-stick beauty or refined unreachable hotness?"

"Both."

"Oh man." Kate grinned. "This is the one time I'm bummed I can't see ghosts too. I can't wait to tell Beth that the first ghost you saw again is Mr. Delish."

Sam shook her head. "This is none of her business. You keep this to yourself."

"Well, it's going to be a little hard to do that since she'll be here tomorrow." Kate delivered this with such a casual air, Sam almost didn't process what she'd said.

"What?" The word ended on such a high note, Sam was

surprised she didn't break the mirror over the dressing table. "Why is Beth coming?"

Kate touched Sam's shin, her fingers so light, they barely registered. "She found something that belongs to someone here. She's bringing it tomorrow."

Flight mode quickly engaged, sending adrenaline troops throughout her body. "Did you know she was coming when you called me?" The last time Sam had seen Beth was at Paul's funeral. This would be different. She'd have to talk to her, spend time with her.

Kate slid to the edge of the bed and got to her feet. "Your feud is ridiculous. Whatever happened all those years ago shouldn't erase the bond we all had. I'd like to think we could all be close again. Like we used to."

"Is that your plan?" Sam pushed the last of the covers aside and swung her legs around. "Invite both of us here so we can hash it out."

Kate crossed her arms. "No, I didn't ask her to come. She called."

"How much is she charging for her services?" Sam said. "She doesn't find things for free. She only thinks of herself, always has."

"That is not true, and you know it. Beth was our best friend."

Sam rushed to her feet. "Not after she . . ."

Kate put her hands on her hips. "Not after she what? Why won't you tell me?"

Anger swallowed the adrenaline inside Sam. "Let's just say you don't know her as well as you think."

"Jesus, Sam. No one's perfect. Everything has to be just

so with you." Kate made orderly little boxes with her hands. "Otherwise it's shit. Beth did the best she could to stay afloat. She was just a kid. Alone. You and I were fortunate to have other people in our lives to help us."

A harsh laugh burst through Sam's lips. This time sadness wove together with her anger. Fortunate? She'd lost both her parents. "Beth had an awful past, but she's come through it just fine. Mansions, cars, a private jet. Better than fine."

"Don't you think she'd trade it all to have had a normal loving family? Not parents who abused her and abused her gift?"

Sam used to feel that way too, but not after what Beth had done to her. She grabbed her boots and slid them on her feet. "I'll check into the nearest hotel. I won't stay under the same roof with her."

"You little coward."

Sam's head whipped around toward Kate. Her heartbeat boomed loud in her ears, pounding. "What did you call me?"

"You heard me." Kate drew her petite frame up to its full height, hands still on her hips. "One mention of Beth, and you're scurrying away like a bug escaping the light. If that's not cowardly, I don't know what is."

The disdain and disrespect in Kate's eyes wrapped around Sam, crushing her. No one would ever make her feel less than she was. Not ever again.

Sam wavered on her feet. Wait a second. No one had made her feel that way in years. Not since grade school. What was going on?

Her question was swept away in a surge of rage so

overwhelming, Sam could barely breathe. She stomped over to Kate until she loomed over her.

"How dare you judge me? You who have both your parents. You who have two beautiful daughters." Her words lowered into a barely contained growl. "You who had the love of your life."

The hard lines of Kate's face broke apart. "I just want you back, Sam. The way you used to be. When you turned away from the dead, you shut out the living too."

The brush and hand mirror twitched, banging against each other from the dressing table. Both Sam and Kate jerked at the sound. The rage receded from Sam just enough she could think again.

"Poltergeist?" Kate said.

"No." It all made sense. The onslaught of emotion. One of the heavier tolls of dealing with ghosts.

The iron wasn't going to help now.

"Sam?" Kate reached for her, but Sam stumbled back.

"Don't touch me. Don't ever touch me again." The last was almost a scream. Sam heard someone else's voice over hers. Another woman's. Fear stampeded through her, dragging her along. She was losing control again.

Kate's eyes widened. "Calm down. I'm just trying to help, that's all. I didn't mean to push you so hard."

"Ghosts," Sam said through gritted teeth. "Feelings." She leaned over, hands on her knees, breathing so fast she knew she was close to hyperventilating.

"Oh God, I forgot about that. Here's the ghost poker." Kate

tried to hand her the sock-sheathed dagger.

Sam shook her head. "Need it before." Each word was hard won. "Too late."

She struggled to remember how to block the ghosts' emotions. A wall. She'd construct a wall in her mind, but she couldn't concentrate. Pain had always helped in the past. Sam slammed her right palm against the corner of the bedside table and shooting agony throbbed from her hand up through her arm. She'd just popped the blisters and sliced raw skin.

But she could think again.

The brick wall inside her mind came together quickly. First layer done. Second layer of brick locked in with the first. But when the third layer hit, everything crumbled under a sledgehammer of despair.

Sam fell back onto the bed. She managed to lean over the edge before she threw up what little she'd eaten in the wastebasket Kate had somehow gotten under her in time. Then the dry heaves began, her stomach clenching as if it could thrust the foreign emotions from her. Kate stroked her back and held her hair out the way.

"It will be all right, Samantha." Robert's voice reached her ears. "I am here. And I have help." Sam craned her head up and saw Robert and an older woman dressed like a maid standing at the foot of the bed.

"No, do it this way, my lord," the woman said gently, yet firmly, reminding Sam of her first grade school teacher. "We use our energy to form a shield of sorts. Picture something soothing. Stretch it around the lass." Her mouth widened into a proud smile. "There, that's it."

The pressure in Sam's chest released, like someone had finally stopped sitting on her lungs. "It's working. Whatever you're doing, keep doing it." The emotions she'd felt before were still there, but muffled. She didn't know ghosts could do something like this. Shield her.

Robert's puckered brow smoothed. The smile he turned toward the older woman beamed with a sense of accomplishment and love. Who was she to him?

Kate handed her a tissue and continued to rub her back. "I'm glad it's working. Rubbing their back always calms the girls down."

Sam wiped her mouth. "It's great, but I was talking to Robert. He's the ghost I mentioned and . . ."

"Beatrice," the older ghost said with a curtsy. "I took care of my lord since he was a wee bairn." She gave Sam a firm look. "And with your help, I mean to see him on his rightful path."

"Now is not the time to talk about paths," Robert said to Beatrice. "Samantha just recovered from her skirmish with the poltergeist, and now she must hold audience with more ghosts who need her help."

"Hold on a second," Kate said. "Your first ghost in seventeen years is named Robert just like the love interest in *Ghostly Paramour*?" She laughed. "Oh man, Beth is going to have a field day with that one."

Sam got to her feet slowly. The room didn't spin. Progress.

"Drop it, Kate. Robert isn't alone." She hoped that piece of information might head off any further embarrassing outbursts.

"Who's hunky Robert with?"

"Hunky Robert?" Robert repeated slowly.

If the floor would have opened and swallowed Sam up, she would have welcomed it at that moment.

Beatrice patted his arm, drawing his attention away from Sam. "Hunky is a term women use today for handsome men with . . ." Her words faltered, and then she brightened. "With broad shoulders," she finished with a sharp nod of her head.

A surprised grin lit up Robert's face. "You have told your friend of me. I am honored."

Kate jabbed Sam in the ribs, her elbow feeling like a knife. "You're blazing so hot I could light a candle from your skin. What are they saying?"

Sam frowned at her. "Robert is with Beatrice, who took care of him as a child." She paused. "She had to explain to him what hunky meant. He's from the eighteenth century."

Kate laughed but covered her mouth with her hands. "Good thing they weren't listening earlier."

Beatrice cleared her throat sharply. "The ones who pushed their emotions upon you are still waiting to talk to you."

"And so it begins," Sam said under her breath.

"Come, my lord." Beatrice grasped Robert's hand. "We must go and let them have their time with the Necromancer." Before Sam could blink, they'd disappeared.

Necromancer again. The title didn't sit well with her. Like she was more important than she really was.

"Some other ghosts want to talk to me," she told Kate.

She knew the moment the ghosts had materialized behind them. Lethargy gripped her limbs, and she braced herself against the bed frame to stay upright. Ghosts always pulled from her energy in order to materialize. Yet Robert and Beatrice had hardly affected her. Why?

"Are they here?" Kate whispered, but it was as loud as Patty had been downstairs.

"They're here," Sam replied. Taking a deep breath, she turned to face them.

CHAPTER 8

SAM BUILT ANOTHER WALL INSIDE HER MIND. UNFORTUNATELY, no barrier she constructed would stop the energy pull. One ghost was bad enough usually, but having three latch onto her to remain visible felt like it sucked the cartilage from her knees.

She wobbled, and then caught herself. "Kate, have there been any recent deaths?"

"A few." Kate's voice sounded wary.

The three ghosts in front of her were young women, dressed in modern clothes. They appeared to be in their early twenties to early thirties. They all looked like they could have been Kate's sisters.

"They look an awful lot like you." Sam didn't try to keep the accusatory tone from her voice. Something was going on here. Something she wasn't going to like.

"There are a lot of women around here who look like me." Kate gazed around the room, avoiding Sam.

Sam crossed her arms. "You know they're just going to tell me anyway, so spit it out."

"Fine. The cops think it's a serial killer." Kate's words were defiant, but Sam saw the tick in her jaw.

A serial killer who's targeting short women with fair skin, blue eyes and red hair? What the hell are you still doing here?"

"I've been careful."

Patty's warning screamed through Sam's ears. *Mommy's going to die.*

"Careful might not be good enough." Sam softened her tone, trying to sound reasonable. "Close the B&B for a while. It's hurting for business anyway. I've got more than enough room for you and the girls." She uncrossed her arms and took a step toward Kate. "Think of it as an extended holiday. At least until they catch the killer."

"I don't run from my problems."

"This wouldn't be running," Sam said. "It's being smart."

"Don't you have ghosts to deal with?" Kate pointed to the air around Sam.

"You can be so damn stubborn at times." Sam grabbed her arm.

The muscle in Kate's jaw tightened. "I could say the exact same thing about you."

Sam dropped her grip on Kate's arm. Nothing she said was going to get through to her. Maybe Beth could convince her to leave. If it saved Kate's life, she'd tolerate Beth's involvement.

Sam turned back to the three ghosts who'd been waiting patiently. Well, two of them had been patient. The one in the bootcut jeans and a plunging burgundy top looked like she might fidget herself through the wall.

Rule #1: When seeking a Bargain, ghosts cannot speak unless you address them first.

"I'm Samantha Hamilton, but you can call me Sam. What are your names?" She kept her voice soothing and welcoming. If the emotions she'd felt earlier were any indication, they were still dealing with the horror of what had happened to them.

"I'm Ellie Croft," the ghost in the burgundy top said. She gestured toward the woman in the yellow sundress and scuffed cowboy boots. "This is Wendy Drummond." Wendy gave Sam a shy smile.

"I'm Inspector Monica Blair." The last ghost stepped forward, holding out her hand a moment before it trembled and dropped back to her side. Though she wasn't in uniform, with her hair back in a severe ponytail and an outfit which consisted of a dark blue blazer, matching slacks, and serviceable white blouse, Sam could easily see she had been a cop.

Kate nudged her shoulder, and Sam knew she'd have to repeat what was going on. Otherwise, Kate would be unbearable with questions.

"Ellie Croft, Monica Blair and Wendy . . ."

"Drummond," Wendy supplied.

"Sorry," Sam said. "Wendy Drummond. They're all here."

"Monica, Wendy, nice to meet you. Ellie . . ." Kate's voice faltered. "Ellie, I'm so sorry about what happened."

"You knew her?" Sam hadn't thought about that possibility, but this was a small town.

"She used to help out when we had more guests." Kate clasped her hands together. "They found her in the forest.

On our grounds. I was home at the time."

"And still you don't want to leave," Sam said under her breath, but loud enough so Kate could hear. She didn't hide her frustration. Kate didn't come back with an immediate retort. A small step.

"We have to stop this psycho before he kills again," Ellie said. "Ms. Banberry could be next."

Monica touched Ellie's shoulder, coming closer. "She's right. Your friend fits the killer's profile."

Wendy stepped forward to join them, and Sam's knees finally buckled. She almost spilled face first onto the floor, but Kate grabbed her in time.

"Are you okay?" Kate's voice rose.

"Just being unraveled like a sweater with a loose thread." Sam's words were slow. She was so tired. The hardwoods looked incredibly inviting for a nap. "Ellie, you can stay, but the others have to go. It's too much of a drain."

Ellie nodded quickly. Wendy and Monica faded away, and Sam was finally able to stand without hunching. The weight on her shoulders had lessened to that of a large dog. She felt more steady.

Kate's worried gaze skimmed over her face.

"I'm fine," Sam said. "Remember, this is what happens when ghosts pull on my energy to become visible. Once the Bargain is reached, I'll be okay."

She turned away from Kate. Protocol had to be followed. She spoke the words that hadn't passed through her lips in seventeen years. "What is your need?"

Rule #3: The need must be clearly defined by the ghost.

This meant no broad statements. It had to be specific.

Which lead to *Rule #4: You must not volunteer to help.*

Anything she said could be construed as the Bargain. There was an order to this. Even now, she felt calm. The Rules had guided her for years.

Ellie pointed at the angry marks on her throat, the outline of fingers. "We need you to find our killer. He stole our lives, our future." Ellie's round face twisted, looking like something yanked from a nightmare.

A burst of rage battered Sam's wall, unable to touch her. Still, it took energy to continuously reinforce her shield and allow Ellie to stay visible. Doing both would eventually make her comatose.

"Control your emotions, Ellie. Or I won't be able to help you."

The harsh edges of Ellie's face fell and softened into a torn look of despair. The claws of anger retracted, scraping off Sam's wall. She took a deep breath, and then another.

"I'm sorry." Ellie shoved her hands in her jeans' pockets. "It's just hard to stop what I'm feeling. To hold it back."

Sam nodded. "You need to be careful. You don't want to become a poltergeist."

Kate whistled. "Shit. Is that how they start? When you're murdered?"

"No, it's more complicated than that. But hiding pain behind strong emotions is a ghost's first step toward becoming one." Sam focused back on Ellie. "Who killed you?"

"Paul."

A sharp stab of fear lanced through Sam. "Paul what?"

"He never gave any of us his last name."

"His name is Paul?" Kate's words sounded curdled.

"I'm sure it's fake," Sam said. If the serial killer was using Kate's dead husband's name, things might be worse than she thought.

"Has she mentioned what he looks like?" Kate pulled over the chair from the dressing table and sat down.

Ellie shook her head. "We've got nothing. Wendy, Monica, and I compared our memories, and they don't match up except that he had a tattoo, but we can't remember what it looked like." She waved her hands in the air. "It doesn't help that he drugged us. Bastard." A waver of heat rose in her last word, but she tamped her lips together and looked contrite.

Sam glanced at Kate. "Sounds like he wore disguises. He has a tattoo, but they can't remember it. He drugged them."

"Disguises? Maybe it was more than one killer?" Kate said.

"No, when multiple people die at an accident together or are killed by the same person, their ghosts cluster. There is only one killer."

It was all coming back to her. The way she knew things instinctively. The Rules. The consequences.

Kate shook her head slowly. "I'll be damned. Logan was right. It is a serial killer."

"I'm not sure what I can do." Sam lifted her bandaged hands toward Ellie, fresh blood soaked through the white. "I'm not a private investigator, and the police aren't going to share their casework with me."

Ellie's eyes glowed, light circling her irises until they blazed.

"You're the only one who can hear us, who can help us." The mirror above the dresser cracked in a corner, a shivering line screaming its way through the glass.

"Dammit, I just got that replaced," Kate muttered, and then raised her voice to the best stern-mom-level Sam had heard in a long time. "Ellie Croft, you stop that right now. Behave yourself."

The crack threading its way through the glass halted with a high-pitched whine.

Some of the fire dimmed in Ellie's eyes, but her lips still remained firm. "Will you kill him for what he's done? Give us justice?"

"I'm not killing anyone."

"Do you have to kill someone if they ask you to?" Kate said.

"Nope. It's Rule #11."

Ellie stared at her a moment longer, and then her shoulders eased. The anger tumbled from her face as if it were too heavy to hold any longer. She just looked sad and frightened and alone.

Sam took a deep breath and let it out slowly. These poor women. Kate couldn't join them. She wouldn't let that happen. There was one thing that might get the information she needed to find the killer, but it carried a heavy price.

Already a wash of energy tingled across her skin, as if an army of electric ants marched over her body. Even though she hadn't said the words yet, the Universe knew her intent. She was going to agree to the Bargain.

Sam held out her hands towards Ellie, palms up. She had

listened to what Ellie had said, but had also felt what burned in Ellie's heart. In all three ghosts. This would be a Bargain with all three of the murdered women. They needed their killer found.

She took a deep breath. "I agree to do everything I can to find the identity of your killer. Is this acceptable to your need?" The ghost had to agree to seal the Bargain. That was Rule #5.

Tears glistened in Ellie's eyes. She nodded and then whispered. "Yes."

Sparks of light like embers appeared in the air, wafting toward Sam, reminding her of feathers drifting down on the breeze. She'd almost forgotten about them. The one part she didn't mind.

Sam lifted her right hand. The first spark touched her skin and then sank through her, almost with a sigh.

"Are they here? The fireflies?" Kate's voice was hushed.

Sam nodded. That's how she described them to Beth and Kate when they were kids. Would it still work the same?

A welcoming warmth seeped through Sam, sinking deep into her muscles, around her tendons, and a burning began in her throat. When she spoke next, her voice would be deeper. Powerful enough to bind the weight of purpose to each word. There would be no going back. No escape.

Opening her mouth, Sam felt the heat rush up her throat, past her tongue, through her lips, riding on the edge of her words. "The Bargain is struck."

The floorboards creaked, and the shutters banged against the window panes. Then, for a moment, everything was silent.

Not even the wind dared ruffle a leaf outside.

Sam stumbled forward, drawn by the newly formed bond between her and Ellie. It stuttered, shifting in strength when it connected with Wendy and Monica. Sam felt their energy join the flow, and then seek balance. They were bound.

"I don't remember your voice being that powerful," Kate said. "Or that deep. But it's still freaking cool."

The earlier drag on Sam's body had disappeared with the Bargain. At least that remained the same.

"Thank you for agreeing to help," Ellie said in a cautious tone like she tiptoed around a slumbering bull. "But how are you going to find our killer if we can't give you more clues?"

"I'm going to go into your memories from the day you died. See through your eyes." Sam felt Kate's gaze boring a hole into the side of her face. She'd never told her about this before. It was something only she and Beth had done together.

"Wicked," Ellie said with a huge smile. "Is there anything we can do to help?"

Sam nodded. "I'll need something of yours that you either wore the day of the murder or had with you. Not clothes. Something with meaning. Ask Wendy and Monica, and then let me know what those items are. I'll have to get them from your families."

"I'll chat with them and give you a list."

"Good." Sam paused, feeling the need to warn Ellie. Ghosts in pain tended to seek out others who shared their anguish. She didn't want Ellie to make that mistake. "Stay away from the poltergeist in the hallway. He's dangerous."

Ellie's face paled. "We've heard Ray can kill ghosts."

A large crash sounded from the bedroom across the hall.

Sam jumped, but Kate just rolled her eyes. "He knocks that bookcase over at least once a day. Then lifts it up and knocks it over again. I keep that room locked so no one can get hurt."

"Poltergeists can harm ghosts," Sam said. "Be careful." Sam tried to touch Ellie's shoulder, but her hand just slid through. As usual. So why could she touch Robert?

Ellie smiled, and Sam could see just how beautiful she'd been when she was alive. "Beatrice knew you'd help." She reached out her hands toward Sam, and a rush of gratitude washed over her like a mist of refreshing raindrops. "Once we saw you, we knew it too."

"You did?"

Ellie nodded. "To us in Entwine, you glow." Her words echoed through the room, and then she was gone.

Robert had said the same thing. Sam studied her hands, though with the bandages, she couldn't see much. Her blisters weren't itching any longer. She tried to peek through the edge of gauze.

"Stop that," Kate said. "They need to heal."

"I know it doesn't make sense, but they feel like they already are."

Kate gave her a what-have-you-been-drinking look, but gently unwound one of the bandages. No sign of blisters, just perfectly smooth skin. She looked up at Sam's face, eyes widening. "The cuts on your cheeks are gone too. Was it the fireflies?"

"Could be." Sam touched her face. No sign of her injuries.

"But I felt something right before Ellie left."

"I thought you said ghosts only take. Now, you've had three ghosts who've helped you."

Sam shook her head. She didn't want to deal with a shift in her ghost world-view right now. "I found out the poltergeist's name is Ray."

"My poltergeist is named Ray?" Kate tilted her head. "He seems less scary now that he has a name."

"Don't underestimate him. We'll need to know more about Ray if we have any hope of getting rid of him. Robert might be able to help."

Kate didn't say anything, but mouthed, *hunky hunky Robert.* Accompanied by a wiggly dance that was sexy and silly all at the same time.

Sam giggled, and the tension in her back released. "Stop it. You're worse than I remember."

"I was always this bad. You just loved it more back then." Her face grew serious. "So how are you going to get what you need for the ghost memory thing? And don't think I don't have twelve million questions about how that's going to work. Or why it's the first I've heard of it. I'm not letting that one go."

"Duly noted. As for getting the personal items, it looks like we'll be visiting the families."

"We?" The question was almost a squeak. "I don't think I'm cut out for field work."

"You got me into this, and now I'm stuck with three murdered ghosts, Ray the poltergeist, and who knows who else will come out of the woodwork. So, yes. *We.*"

CHAPTER 9

KATE CUT UP THE REMAINING BEEF AND SLID IT OFF THE cutting board into the stew. Their quick lunch was almost boiling. She glanced over her shoulder at Sam.

Her friend hadn't moved a muscle since they'd come down to the kitchen. She just sat staring off into space. Maybe seeing the three ghosts on top of the poltergeist and hunky hunky Robert had been too much for her?

The rich aroma of red wine and onions filled the air above the pot in a steamy plume. If she closed her eyes, she could almost hear the sound of her husband's footsteps, the sound of his laugh, the sound of his deep voice calling her name. If only she could forget the sound of his last breath.

"You okay?" Sam said.

"Nope. I'm not okay."

The scrape of the kitchen stool sounded loud. Sam joined her at the stove. "I can go and visit the families myself. I didn't stop to think how hard it might be for you. I know you still miss Paul."

Kate added some vegetables to the stew. "It's not the family visits. The kitchen was our favorite place. Paul loved to cook." Her voice broke, and the wooden spoon fell from her hand, clattering onto the counter.

Sam pulled her into her arms. "I'm sorry, Kate."

Kate leaned her cheek against Sam's shoulder, the tears flowing free like they'd just been waiting under the surface. It felt so good to let it all go. There was no one here she could really cry to, and she didn't want the girls to see her fall apart.

"This was his dream, his love, the B&B," Kate said in breathy sobs. "And I'm letting it go down the tubes. The one thing he wanted to leave the girls. A legacy."

Sam rubbed her back much like Kate had done upstairs. "You're not screwing things up. The B&B is gorgeous, and we'll get things back on track. I'll figure out a way to give Ray the heave-ho. It's under control."

"It is *so* not under control. And when did you become Olivia Optimistic?"

Sam squeezed her more tightly and kissed her temple. "You're benched at the moment. Someone's gotta step in and be the sparkly cheerleader for positivity."

Kate pulled back. "Well, with that new attitude, will you shake your pom-poms for Beth when she gets here?"

Sam stiffened, and Kate wondered again just what had happened between the two of them. They'd never told her. In that one matter, they were united.

"I'm not going to run, if that's what you're worried about." Sam leaned against the counter, crossed her arms and then uncrossed them, letting them fall to her sides. "Those things you said up there, about me being a coward—"

"I might have been a tad out of line." Though everything she'd said was true, Sam was in a vulnerable place and she'd pushed too hard. Kate grabbed a tissue and blew her nose loudly, feeling her ears pop.

"As much as I hated to hear it," Sam said, "you were right. I *was* a coward. I let you down when you really needed me."

Kate touched Sam's shoulder. "It killed me to lose you twice. Once when you checked out of our friendship, and then again when Paul was dying."

"I know. I blew it."

"I miss what we had, you know that. But . . ." All the planned speeches she'd practiced in her head fell away. Their friendship had always been messy even when they were kids, but it had been honest. "I've got to think of my girls, Sam. You can't be a part-time aunt. I need to know you'll be there. For all of us."

Sam wasn't smiling. She looked dead serious, and Kate was glad she understood how big this was. If she let Sam back in fully and her family was hurt again, it was done.

Sam gripped the edge of the marble island, her knuckles white. "When I got rid of my curse, everything was jumbled together inside me. What I could do, what we all were to each other, you, me, and Beth. I had to distance myself from it all."

"Because it was easier."

Sam met her gaze, her eyes brimming with regret. "Because it was easier. I have no excuse. But as frightened as I was, I came back to Scotland. For you. For the girls. If you want me to stay away after this, I will."

Kate pried Sam's hand from the countertop and held it in hers. "What do *you* want to do?"

A tear spilled over Sam's lashes. "I want you, Emily, and Patty back in my life. I can't promise to be the perfect aunt or best friend, but you're stuck with me. If you'll have me."

Kate smiled at Sam's determination. Once Sam made her mind up about something, it was done.

"The Bargain has been struck," Kate said in her best try of Sam's creepy voice. "Let's eat. I'm starving." She filled up the bowls.

"That's it?" Sam grabbed the bowls and brought them over to the table in the corner of the kitchen. "Just like that, we're good?"

Kate put napkins and spoons down. "You know I'm all about giving second chances. And for the first time in years, you were honest with me. Even on the ugly parts." She grabbed the loaf of bread she'd cut up. "Besides, you don't have many friends to lose. So taking you back is an act of charity really."

Sam laughed, a few tears still glistening in her eyes. "I really don't deserve you, do I?"

Kate broke off a piece of bread and dipped it in the stew. "Nope, but then we've known that for years."

Sam took a long sip of water. "Now that we're buddies again, I heard something today I wanted to ask you about."

The amusement was gone from Sam's face again. Kate's heart fluttered, skipping a beat. She didn't need to have a vision to know that whatever Sam was going to ask, it wasn't good.

Sam stirred her stew. "Aggie said you couldn't drive anymore. They have to take you everywhere."

"You try driving when you could black out at any moment."

"You're blacking out?"

"The visions, Sam. They've gotten worse." Kate pushed back her bowl, realizing she was almost yelling. She was thankful the girls were out playing with Riley. She managed a quick breath. "I've tried to keep things as normal as I could for the girls, but . . ."

"Tell me what's happening."

Kate shook her head. "We've got more important craziness on our plates than dealing with my failure as mother of the year."

"You're not failing the kids. Never think that." Sam stared at Kate until she finally met her gaze.

Kate's voice was a whisper. "I tried to hide it, but they've seen it happen. Mommy having a seizure. Mommy collapsing in a store." She rubbed her hands together. They were slicked with sweat.

Sam's voice was low. "What do you tell them?"

Kate laughed, but it sounded shrill. "At first I made up every excuse—Mommy had low blood sugar or that Mommy had a bad reaction to something she ate. But they didn't believe me. I finally had to tell them the truth after Paul died."

"And how did they take it?"

Kate sighed. "I don't think they really understood. And as if my visions of the future weren't enough to deal with, when

I lost Paul, I suddenly started having glimpses of the past. Actually being in someone else's memory."

"It sounds like the memory journey I'll do to help Ellie and the others. But I can only see right before the moment of their death." Sam grabbed a slice of bread and buttered it. "What are your visions of the past like?"

"It's never their death. It's usually something from the past that relates to an event happening now." She tilted her head toward Sam. "Tell me more about this memory journey. I wondered how you were going to help the ghosts."

"Later." Sam's gaze narrowed. "The blacking out piece is bad, but something else is going on with your past visions. Isn't it?"

Kate thought seriously about lying. But Sam's ghost lie detector skills always seemed to extend to the living too. At least they used to.

"You don't give up, do you?"

Sam shook her head. "Not when my best friend is obviously in trouble."

After giving her the "you need to be more involved" edict, Kate couldn't very well tell her to stuff it. Though she wanted to. Just talking about all this made her worry it might bring on a vision. Past or future.

Kate looked out the kitchen window, the sky still overcast with clouds. "On the visions of the past, I don't just see what happened, I live it. It sticks with me even when it's done and I wake up."

"Sticks with you how?"

"Like talking with my daughters in French or trying to run

off to England to get word to Parliament about spies." She shivered, remembering all too well the feeling of not being herself. "It's absolutely terrifying. I need to figure out a way to control what I can do, but so far, nothing's worked."

Sam grew serious. "As much as I hate that Beth is coming, maybe she can help you. She's got connections."

"Or maybe all three of us can figure something out. We were always stronger when we were together."

Sam didn't say anything further, just looked into her bowl of stew as if it were a crystal ball and rubbed the tip of her thumb against her finger. Kate looked down at her thumb with the matching scar. She wondered if Sam ever thought of the ritual.

Kate had thought of nothing else for the past month. She'd had a vision. Something bad was coming. Something that would change all three of them forever.

Robert's eyes swept the clearing. He stood with Beatrice deep within the forests that surrounded the manor. All around them, massive beech trees loomed pale against the blue sky. Their exposed roots covered the grassy area like pale gray serpents in search of new prey.

"You believe this Caleb will help us?" Robert said to Beatrice. Though he did not see anyone, they were being watched.

"For a price he will." Beatrice did not appear to be nervous, but he had seen her stare down the ire of his father with barely a quiver. It was difficult to know if she was hiding her fear, or if Caleb was someone they could trust.

"She speaks the truth," a booming voice announced, and the trees shivered in a rustling of leaves.

Bursting free from the branches, several dark shapes took flight. Crows. Their calls echoed back through the air in sharp squawks of sound.

A long dark shadow stretched out across the clearing toward him, and then disappeared when a cloud smothered the sun's face.

Robert stepped in front of Beatrice. "Show yourself," he demanded of the voice. "If you seek to cause us harm, you shall answer to me."

A rough laugh ruffled through the forest. It seemed to echo from everywhere and nowhere. "No lack of confidence there. The bravery of the naive. So tragic."

Beatrice moved around Robert before he could react. She jammed her fists onto her hips and stared at the largest tree in front of them. "That'll be quite enough theatrics, Caleb. This is Lord Robert Grenning, and he deserves much more than your shenanigans."

"I know who the hell that boy is," came the voice again. "I watched him take his first steps." The voice slid into a sly whisper. "I saw him run for his life before he was dragged back to prison. For justice."

"It was no justice," Robert said loudly. He focused on the tree in front of him as Beatrice had done. "I did not kill Sarah Covington. I was wrongly convicted."

The tree they had addressed jerked and twitched like it had an itch it was unable to reach. Then it leaned forward, its trunk swelling and bulging.

Robert glanced quickly at Beatrice. "We should leave. It is not safe."

"Don't worry," she whispered out of the side of her mouth. "Caleb likes to show off."

With a loud snap of noise, a ghost emerged from the pale bark, like he had been birthed from the wood. He stumbled a bit before he regained his footing with the use of large walking stick.

Robert studied him closely. Long and gnarled limbs, like the beeches around them, poked out from under a dark spun tunic and trousers. A thick white thatch of hair seemed frozen in a whirlwind, with leaves and twigs hiding amongst the pale strands. Caleb observed them with keen sharp eyes, reminding Robert of a bird, gaze darting here and there.

Caleb leaned heavily on the walking stick. A shaft of afternoon sun, freed from the clouds, cut across the clearing. It struck the stick, making the dark wood gleam as if it had been recently polished and oiled. Thick deep lines cut through the wood in patterns Robert did not recognize, but the nearer the ghost approached, the more his skin felt like it wanted to pull away from his bones. Whatever Caleb was, he was powerful.

"Ah, Bea, it's been too long since you've visited me." Caleb pursed his thin lips. His next words were dry. "What do you want?"

Beatrice's face remained serious. "Your assistance."

"That much is obvious." Caleb frowned. "No one visits me of their own free will. Though I don't know why. I'm pleasant company."

Beatrice snorted, but then sneezed at the end. Robert saw the smile she hid behind her hand.

Waving his staff toward several tree stumps nearby, Caleb said, "Sit." Though the one word was soft, it had a hard edge to it, and Robert found himself obeying immediately.

Beatrice sat, smoothing out her skirt and apron. Robert settled on the large stump beside her. Why could he pass through certain objects, while others held weight and substance, like the ground, the floor of the manor, the tree stump?

He realized Beatrice had been speaking while he had mused. ". . . the journal," she said. "We couldn't find it where my Lord left it, concealed underneath a false piece of flooring. What do you know about it?"

Caleb rubbed his pointy jaw. "Well, there have been a total of twenty-two journals left behind in that manor by its former residents. Not all have been found."

Robert leaned forward. "Are you saying the one we seek is still on the manor grounds?"

"No, it's gone," Caleb said.

"Where?" Beatrice's question was calm, but her hands clenched the fabric of her skirt, bunching it.

Caleb eased himself slowly down to sit on the largest stump across from them, all the while rubbing his lower back. "The Wardens say we only feel pain if we believe we will. Well, unless we get struck by iron." His laugh had a deep wheezing sound to it like wind crushing dry leaves. "I heard about your mistake with the lanterns, boy."

It would appear Caleb had eyes everywhere. Robert hoped no one had seen him touch Samantha. Suddenly Beatrice's warnings became all the more prudent to obey.

"I am still learning the rules of Entwine," Robert said. "I am sure that will not be my only mistake."

Caleb opened his mouth. Beatrice held up her hand. "We didn't come here for chit-chat. It's obvious you know nothing and simply seek to keep us here for company." She stood.

"Prickly, that one," Caleb said to Robert. "Always has been." Though his face looked forbidding, Robert heard appreciation in his tone. "I know of the journal you're seeking."

Beatrice sat slowly and crossed her arms. "I'm listening."

Caleb picked at his teeth with a fingernail and then squinted at the results of his plunder. "What are you planning on trading?"

Robert remembered what Beatrice had said earlier about information being used as currency in Entwine. The only piece of value he had was the very thing Beatrice swore him to keep secret.

"I still have one last favor you owe me," she said to Caleb. "Consider it called in."

Caleb shook his head. "That one was called in when I covered for the little one, Patty. Making sure the Wardens didn't hear of her gift."

Beatrice reached a shaking hand to her chest, her breath quickening. "But she's just a child."

"You know the young are the easiest to manipulate." Caleb's

words held an old sadness to them. "The Wardens don't discriminate when it comes to their power."

Robert had never seen her this frightened before. He grasped her free hand in his. "Beatrice, what is he talking about?"

"Patty's got the sight. Just like her mother." Beatrice's gaze flicked up to meet Caleb's. "I never asked you to intervene or protect my family." Her tone trembled with gratitude.

"You didn't have to. I know what they mean to you." This time Caleb looked everywhere but at Beatrice.

"Thank you." Robert stood and offered his hand.

Caleb stared at it for a long moment before he finally took it. His bones felt like sticks in Robert's grasp, but his grip was strong, almost painfully so.

"Yes, thank you," Beatrice said. Her gaze shifted to Robert. "My Lord, this means we need something else to offer."

Robert's mind raced to think of an alternative. "Would the name of the killer plaguing this area be an appropriate trade?"

Caleb shook his head. "I already have that deal with the victims. They'll tell me when the Necromancer discovers his identity."

"What could those lasses possibly need from you?" Robert asked. It was not as if Caleb could breathe life back into them.

Caleb barked out a sharp laugh. "I don't reveal the nature of my deals. It's why folks come to me." He winked. "Discretion."

Robert had dealt with those of Caleb's ilk when he was alive. This forest ghost already knew what he wanted, so there was no point prevaricating. "What will it take to get the information we need?"

Running his gnarled hands against the carved symbols on his wooden staff, Caleb appeared to ponder this question deeply. "There is something."

Beatrice sighed. "Out with it already."

Caleb's eyes gleamed. "Get rid of the geist."

Beatrice shot to her feet. "That would be payment for much more than the journal."

Caleb shrugged. "You asked me what it would take."

Robert shook his head. "Given the geist's activities, I can understand the desire for this boon. However, I sense the immense power and darkness surrounding this entity. It would not be a fair trade."

"And Ray's been pestering you here in the woods," Beatrice added. "This task is of great value to you personally."

Robert clasped his hands behind his back. "What are you prepared to pay for the added danger in our quest?"

Caleb's eyes narrowed, becoming thin lines with just the barest glint of white and brown visible. "Mayhap, I was wrong about you, boy. You're not as dull as I thought."

"Caleb," Beatrice said, her tone sharp. "You will not insult Lord Robert."

Robert was not bothered by Caleb's words. He had heard them from others many a time when he was alive. Being underestimated had assisted him in the past. "Beatrice, in your estimation, what would be sufficient motivation to take on the geist?"

"Caleb shall owe us a favor," Beatrice declared. The sun dipped lower on the horizon, cloaking her face in shadow.

"I'm done with owing favors." Caleb stood slowly. "No more."

The trees shook in the still air. Crows stalked into the clearing. Their eyes, like shiny black stones, remained fixed upon Beatrice and Robert. Their talons tore up the dry grass, sending tufts of dirt into the air. The message was clear.

However, the scare tactic had no merit. Robert had witnessed the concealed affection Caleb had for Beatrice. Neither of them would come to any serious harm by his hand.

Robert took a few steps toward Caleb, but stopped when the crows began to hop along the ground, almost in a gallop, coming closer. "You want the geist gone. We seek the journal. Agree to our terms and we both get what want."

Caleb's eyebrow arched, dislodging what looked like a piece of bark from his forehead. "I can see neither of us will back down. Even if I agree, a future favor is very dear. In addition to ridding this realm of the geist, I'll require visits from Beatrice."

"That can be arranged," Beatrice said briskly.

"Are you sure?" Robert said.

"He protected Patty without me asking. Besides, it will give me someone to rattle."

"You know I can hear everything you're saying," Caleb said with a loud smack of his lips.

Beatrice smiled, and she looked like a little girl who had gotten her way. "I know, you old coot."

"Who're you calling old? You're not exactly the picture of dewy Spring."

She did not seemed bothered by his words in the least. "I'll come to the forest to see you."

"Be specific." Caleb pointed his stick at her. "I make deals for a living and know the value of what you say."

"Fine. I'll visit you once a month."

"Twice a week."

"Twice a month." Beatrice crossed her arms.

"Once a week."

"Three times a month."

Caleb smiled broadly. "Done."

Robert looked between the two of them, both seeming satisfied and happy with their deal. But how were they going to get rid of the geist?

CHAPTER 10

SAM STARED AT THE POLICE STATION SIGN ON THE SMALL BRICK building in the center of town. Kate said Logan, Graham's brother, could help them with the introductions to the families.

Her phone buzzed. Another missed call from Michael. She knew he must be worried about how she was doing being back in Scotland, but with everything going on, she didn't know what to tell him since she couldn't tell him the truth.

The morning sun flitted in and out of the passing clouds overhead, casting the worn stone in shadow and then light. The longer Sam gazed at the rusted sign, the more her stomach tightened, into a ball. The last time she'd been in a police station had been after the accident. The night her parents died.

"Have they ever handled a murder?" Sam said.

Kate pulled the edge of her knit cap down lower. The pale blue wool deepened the red in her hair. "I'm happy to say not until recently."

Sam realized her hands were clenched into fists. She released them slowly.

Understanding washed over Kate's face, smoothing out the tension. "This can't be easy for you. Why don't you wait in the car?"

"No. If you're going in there, I'm going in there." *And hoping that I don't barf all over their furniture.*

Kate tilted her chin toward Sam, approval glowing in her gaze. "Come on. We'll be in and out before you know it."

They made their way up the steps and through the station's heavy wooden doors. An official-looking desk sat in the front with orderly cubicles beyond it. Nothing like the last police station she'd been in. That place had been as chaotic and out of control as she'd felt. Officers, or rather constables, running this way and that. Three other cars had been involved in the accident, but only her parents had died.

Sweat pushed out through her pores. Her turtleneck felt like it strangled her. She walked over to the tiny waiting room and sank into one of the chairs. Portraits cluttered the cream walls, making the room feel even smaller. Sam drew quick breaths in and out.

The bergamot odor wafting in the air transformed into the metallic smell of blood. The way it smelled that night in the car. Her hands gripped the armrest until the wood dug into her skin.

Kate approached, looking over her shoulder at the desk. "Sheila's going to tell Logan we're here." She turned toward Sam and froze. "Holy shit. Are you okay?" Her voice was pitched low though they were alone in the waiting room. She crouched in front of Sam. "Deep breaths in, honey. That's it. You've got it. Long one out. That's right. One more time. That's good."

Kate's breathing instructions actually helped. "I'll be okay," Sam murmured.

"I should never have brought you here." Kate shook her head slowly. "I'll walk you out to the car. I can chat with Logan myself."

Sam straightened from her hunch, realizing she'd been on the way to curling into a ball. She took the tissue Kate gave her and patted her forehead. It came back wet. Another deep breath in and out. "No, I'm staying. It's one of the reasons I came back here. To face my past."

Kate squeezed her knee. "I'm proud of you. Though I'm still worried about what's going to happen when Beth shows up."

"I'll deal with it."

"That's what I'm worried about." Kate's tone was dry. She pointed at the portrait on the wall. The man's forbidding gaze pierced Sam even from across the room. "Hey, at least Beth isn't like that guy."

"Ick, who's that?"

"Logan's great, great, great or something along those lines, uncle, Oscar." Kate shivered. "He always gives me the creeps. You don't see his ghost do you?"

"Nope. He's haunted-house scary though, like he'll leap out of the picture and attack us." Sam felt steadier. Concentrating on something else really helped. As Kate had intended, no doubt.

"There are rumors about that." Kate waved her hand. "Not the leaping-out-of-the-picture piece, but that he was a very dangerous man. It must be strange for Logan and Graham to have that kind of family history."

"Graham seems like a really nice guy. Or is Logan your favorite Dunning?"

Kate's eyebrow lifted. "Who said either was my favorite?" Her cheeks grew pink. She cast a quick look back over her shoulder. "There's Logan. He's here."

Sam followed her gaze to the man by the front desk. Logan was definitely easy on the eyes. Nice face and strong shoulders. His brown hair was the same color as Graham's, but it was shorter, cut very close to the scalp. He wore a long-sleeved black dress shirt and matching slacks.

He walked toward them, and Sam found herself sitting up straighter in her chair. He oozed law enforcement in every tightly controlled step.

Kate stood and Sam followed suit. "Not another word about favorites. Got it?" Kate hissed.

"Got what?" Logan smiled. The expression softened his face, and his posture relaxed, like being near Kate soothed him.

"Just chatting about Patty and Emily. They're pretty excited to have their Auntie Sam in town." Kate danced back and forth on her feet as if she weren't sure whether to shake his hand or hug him. She finally settled for clasping his shoulder quickly and then releasing it. "Thanks so much for seeing us. This is my friend, Sam, who I told you about."

"Very pleased to meet you," Logan said with a quick nod. "I've heard you two were inseparable as children."

"We were," Sam said. His smile was so engaging, she found herself smiling back. "Many adventures with this one." She hooked her thumb toward Kate. "Don't let the unassuming facade fool you."

Kate began to sputter, but Logan ignored her. "I've always thought so," he said, and then his voice lost the Scottish accent. "Our Kate is very tight-lipped about her past. Any embarrassing details you could share?" He sounded like an American talk show host. The only things missing were a microphone and camera.

Sam laughed, seeing why Kate liked him. Easy-going, cute and funny. Just what she needed to get through the loss of Paul. In fact, both brothers were good choices. "Excellent work on an American accent. My Scottish one is awful."

Logan looked pleased with himself. "I've been practicing. It helps sometimes when I have to call the States. So how about those Kate stories?"

"No one is sharing any of my stories," Kate said firmly.

Sam tilted her head toward Logan. "There are quite a few bits I can share with you, but they'll require copious amounts of chocolate."

"I love chocolate." Logan's took out his phone. "How about tomorrow evening?"

Kate cleared her throat. "Are you two done vying for ways to embarrass me?"

Logan let out a dramatic sigh. "For a while. Since I see that familiar fire flaring in your eyes, why don't we get down to business? What can I help you fine ladies with today?"

Kate leaned in close to Logan. "We need to talk to the families of the victims."

The humor drained from Logan's face. "No. I want you nowhere near this case, for obvious reasons."

"I wouldn't ask if it wasn't necessary." Kate tipped her head in Sheila's direction and kept her voice at a whisper. "Too many ears here. Can I treat you to some pastries and an explanation at Shandy's?"

Sam took Kate's lead. "I'd love to check out some local food," she said loudly. "Where do you suggest?"

Logan frowned. "I'm not going to like this, am I?" He turned to Sheila, a cardboard smile hastily taped in place. "I'm taking a break to show Kate's guest our finest bakery."

Sheila's perusal of Sam ended with a sniff, but she gave Logan a quick nod. "Bring me back a chocolate croissant?"

"Sure thing." He took Kate's arm and almost hustled them outside.

Sam followed them for about a block until they reached the bakery. It sat in the bottom floor of an old house. The building leaned to the right like it was trying to rest against the newspaper offices next door.

The doors opened, and the warm air carried the promise of freshly baked bread, cinnamon, and something savory.

The tables were packed, but there were a few open toward the front where they'd come in. The large picture windows let in a light dusting of sunlight. Sam snagged a spot in line.

"Any requests?" Logan asked. "They make amazing apple turnovers here and, of course, Sheila's favorite, chocolate croissants."

"Kate's turnovers are much better," a deep voice from behind Logan chimed in.

Sam turned around. The stranger was a little taller than Logan. His tanned complexion spoke of days outside, and his strong arms looked like there wasn't much he couldn't handle, though all he held now was a to-go bag. Dark wavy hair fell over one eye until he brushed it back. He almost gave Robert a run for his money. Almost.

Sam realized her mouth hung open. She closed it quickly. "Damn," she whispered to Kate.

"Hi Max," Kate said smoothly and brightly.

Logan looked like he wanted to grab Kate and flee. "Afternoon Mr. Grady. All done with the work at the Canfields'?"

Max smiled, and if it was possible, became even more gorgeous. *They sure do grow them right in Scotland.*

"Just finished this morning," Max replied, barely giving Logan a glance. "Your baking truly is the best, Kate. I'm lucky I get to sample it for free."

Sam didn't miss the heat he put in the last few words. Was Kate getting busy with Max?

Kate's hat dropped from her hands and hit the floor. Logan grabbed it before Max could and handed it back to Kate. He laughed, but it sounded a bit strangled. "Oh, she brings by treats to the station all the time. A very kind soul, she is."

Kate waved her hands at Logan. "Treats are the least I can do. Your extra patrols stopped my vandal problems." She turned to Max, her smile not changing an iota in wattage. "Since you won't take any money for all the work you do in the garden, baked goods are just a small token of my gratitude."

"That's my Kate. Always thinking of others." Logan gave her a one-armed hug.

Max smiled and put his arm around her shoulders. "She's certainly one of a kind."

As intriguing as *Days of Our Scottish Men* was, Sam needed to break this up before they ended up arm-wrestling for Kate.

"I'm Sam by the way." She held out her hand to Max. "I hate to steal Kate away, but Logan's on the clock, and we need to chat with him about a story idea I have. I'm an author."

Logan glanced at his watch. "Yes, you're absolutely right. Busy day."

Kate nodded. "Sorry, Max. We'll catch up on Thursday. Emily can't wait to try out her new gardening gloves."

Max leaned down and gave Kate a quick peck on the cheek. "No worries, Kate. I was on my way out anyway." He shook his to-go bag. "See you on Thursday."

Sam watched him leave. She thought she'd have to worry about Kate not making a move with Logan or Graham, but Max was primed and ready to pounce.

"I'll get us some pastries and tea," Logan said. Sam took out her wallet, but Logan waved her away. "Go and find us a seat."

Sam and Kate made their way to a small table near a large oil painting of flowers. She sat next to Kate, leaving a chair open across from them for Logan. "Since Logan and Graham are off limits as topics of discussion, how about Max?"

"Graham has a girlfriend, just so you know."

Sam was surprised given Graham's obvious affection for

Kate, but maybe they were just close friends. "Okay, so we can talk about Max?"

"No."

"You didn't tell me you had a drool-worthy handyman who's obviously pining for you."

Kate took the toothpicks from their holder and arranged them on the table in different geometric patterns. "He's too young."

"Not buying it. He looks your age."

"He's too handsome."

"You're adorable and you know it."

Kate looked up from her toothpicks. "So, what about you and Michael? Are you going to give it another try?"

"Deflect much?" Sam sighed. "You and Bronson are broken records about Michael. We're much better as friends, and we like it that way."

Kate stared at her a moment longer and then blew out a long breath. "Fine. I think about Max. Believe me, I do. God, he's built." She shook her head like she fought for composure. "But whenever I think of Max or Logan in a relationship-way, I feel guilty."

Logan walked up on the last word, a tray in his hands piled high with croissants, turnovers and blueberry muffins, still steaming. "Guilty? Guess I'm going to have to arrest you, Kate." Logan gave her a stern look, but it was ruined by the twitching of his lips. "I have my handcuffs with me."

Sam grabbed a warm blueberry muffin and dropped it onto a plate. "Oh, Kate loves handcuffs."

Kate kicked her hard underneath the table. "Sam loves to cause trouble." Her voice was almost as sweet as the pastries looked.

Logan took Kate's hand and kissed the top of her knuckles. "I can see why you two are friends. Now, why do you need to see the families? Is it the story idea Sam mentioned?"

She wondered exactly what excuse Kate was going to use. They'd brainstormed, but hadn't been able to come up with anything remotely believable. She'd just thrown out the story excuse to get rid of Max, but Kate said she'd work out a Plan B and to trust her. It was either something completely ridiculous or the truth. God, she hoped it wasn't the truth.

"Sam sees ghosts," Kate blurted.

Conversations around them had already been staggering, but they now stumbled to a halt. Someone moved their chair back, and it scraped loudly against the wooden floor.

"Gee Kate, I don't think the pastry chef heard you, but everyone else did." Sam's words almost didn't make it out past the tightness in her throat. She kept her eyes glued on the table. She didn't want to see the looks.

Kate stood and addressed the other patrons in a fierce imitation of Beth. All smoothness and fakery, but it sold well. "For those of you interested, keep your eyes open for my friend, Samantha Hamilton's book." She gave them a it's-between-us look like they were all sharing a big secret. "It's about ghosts and murder. Our fine Detective Chief Constable is helping us with the plot, so please don't share anything you hear. It'll spoil the ending."

There were several chuckles and smiles, but more importantly, the rolling murmur of conversation picked back up again.

Logan shook his head, the smile gone from his face. "What are you playing at, Kate?"

"I'm telling the truth about Sam." Kate reached for his hand on the table, but he pulled it away. "What I said to the crowd was to hopefully cover my blunder. Being interested about her book is one thing, but if they find out what she can really do, they'll become obnoxious."

Sam pinched the bridge of her nose, wishing for something stronger than tea even though it was only two o'clock. "She's right. Even with the act, I'll probably get folks coming by the manor asking me to talk with their dead aunts."

Logan's gaze moved back and forth between them. "So, I'm supposed to believe that a romance novelist who can commune with the dead conveniently came to Scotland in time to solve the murders?"

The next moment was crucial. Either he was willing to listen or he would walk out. "I don't like what I do, but I do talk to ghosts. And right now, they want me to find their killer, which gives all of us the same goal."

Logan took a long swig of coffee. "It's not like I haven't run into someone with gifts before, but I knew them. You're a stranger."

Sam gave Kate a quick look, but her friend appeared surprised by the news too. "I didn't realize you'd met others with abilities."

Logan looked down at a scar on the back of his hand. "My best friend could touch you without moving." When he gazed up again, determination blazed from his eyes. "But I've never met someone who can talk with the dead. Tell me something about the victims that an outsider wouldn't know. I won't have you toying with these poor families unless you can truly do what you say."

Sam tapped the table with her nail. "Ellie's very confident, has a temper and loves Tunnock's Tea cakes." Tap two. "Wendy's timid, doesn't make eye contact for more than a few seconds, and slept with a stuffed penguin named Herbert until she was twenty." Tap three. "Monica is poised and collected, but she has a nervous gesture of smoothing her blazer even when it's perfectly even. Her dad's talked about moving back to the States for the last few months, and you told Monica you didn't want to lose your best constable." Leaning back in her chair, she took a hefty forkful of blueberry muffin, pausing before stuffing it in her mouth. "Satisfied?"

Logan rubbed his face. "Can they tell you who killed them?"

And just like that, he believed her.

Sam had never had it happen that quickly. She liked him even more. "No, they can't. That's the problem." Sam explained what the ghosts had told her. How none of the descriptions really matched.

"Are we looking for multiple killers?" Logan said.

"No, it's just one," Sam said. "Otherwise, all three ghosts wouldn't be joined together, and I wouldn't be able to make one Bargain with all three."

"Bargain?"

Kate piped in, sounding official. "It's a deal between her and the ghosts to find the killer."

Logan took Kate's hand in both of his. "I'm sorry for my earlier reaction. Do you really believe she can find the killer?"

"I do." Kate squeezed his hand back. "I trust Sam one-thousand percent. If she says she can do it, she'll do it. If nothing else, then at least we've exhausted another avenue to help these women."

"And to help you too." Logan stared at Kate. "All the victims look like you. We've talked about this before. You should leave town for a while until this gets resolved."

Sam waited to see if Logan's argument would have more weight than Sam's had, but Kate gave him the same stony shake of her head. Logan let go of her hand slowly, as if he were reluctant to lose her touch.

He got out his phone. "Let me make some calls. See if I can convince the families to meet with you."

"What are you going to tell them?" Kate said.

"I don't know yet. Probably the truth."

Logan began to speak on the phone, and Kate turned to Sam. "See, I told you we'd get this done. You'll find the murderer. I know it."

Sam nodded, but inside a worm of worry worked its way through her chest. She'd taken a chance on accepting the Bargain. She still didn't know if her powers had changed. If they had, the consequences of not fulfilling her promise might be deadly.

S AM TURNED INTO THE MANOR DRIVEWAY AND PARKED NEAR the front door. She shut off the car and glanced over at Kate in the passenger seat. "You've said barely two words since we left the bakery. What's wrong?"

"I'm sorry I told Logan what you can do."

Sighing, Sam leaned back in the car seat. "It got the job done." Though for a moment, she'd been back in school. Free on display.

Kate's face looked pinched in the fading afternoon light. "I haven't told Logan about my gift, so it wasn't fair to spill your secret. I just panicked."

"You should tell him about your visions." Sam kept her words gentle. "He's crazy about you. And he believed about *me*. He'll accept you. I know he will."

"Isn't that the same argument you shot down about Michael?" Kate lifted an eyebrow.

"Logan didn't freak out like Michael would." Sam felt the frown digging into her face. "Michael hates anything supernatural. Beth's show is his top rant ever since he found out I knew her when we were kids."

Kate gripped her locket, running her thumb over the engraving on the back. "If I did tell Logan, eventually everyone would know. Nothing stays quiet in a small town. I'd either be avoided like Joe Stine's stinky socks or be pestered for readings. The B&B is having enough trouble without throwing either outcome into the mix."

"Wow, Joe's socks must be worse than your Uncle Harold's."

A sharp giggle erupted from Kate. "They are."

"Maybe everyone knowing about your gift could work to your advantage? Market your place as a haunted B&B. You definitely have a bunch of ghosts, and seeing the future would be a great draw."

"I actually thought about that," Kate said. "For a nanosecond. But since I can't control my visions, it wouldn't be something regular enough for guests. Stu and Abbie's niece, Yasmin, said she could come out and help. She does readings at her shop."

Sam cast a sideways look at her. "Well, now you have extra notoriety by having a writer friend, a *best-selling* writer friend, I should add. Once Beth gets here, you can parade her around town too and create a trifecta of interest. They probably love her TV schtick."

"Beth would be fine with the attention. But if anyone found out that we weren't just talking about your book . . ." Kate gave her a searching look. "You haven't changed your mind about revealing your gifts, have you?"

"No." Sam played with the keys on her lap. "It's always so difficult explaining to people why I can't call up specific spirits." The last few words brimmed with a bitterness Sam tasted in her mouth.

Kate took her hand. "It's not fair."

"Yeah, well, I guess that's the Universe's big joke on me. I'm its janitor with no pay."

"Stop being so dramatic."

The whole deal with the Universe wasn't being dramatic. It was real, and Kate knew it. Sam saw the glint of mischief in her eyes and calmed. "Fine. I'll stop being so dramatic if you will."

Kate gave her a sharp look. "I'm the least dramatic person I know."

"You've claimed you only find true love once. That's pretty dramatic."

"It's the truth."

Sam shook her head. "No, it's not. It's fear. I should know. I've got a whole helping of that when it comes to relationships too."

Kate's eyebrows lifted so high, they disappeared under her side-swept bangs. "And how exactly did we segue into this topic?"

"I've been thinking about it the whole way home after meeting Logan and Max. You deserve to be happy again, Kate." There, she'd said it.

Kate pulled her hand back. "Paul was it." She got out of the car and stalked toward the front door. Her boots crunching through the gravel.

Sam got out and ran after her. "You don't really believe that, do you?"

Kate stopped and took off her wool cap. She looked down, the strands of red falling over her cheeks, shielding her. "I loved Paul with everything I had. You don't get that twice." Her voice shook slightly. "I just wish I wasn't so damn lonely."

"You *can* get something like that twice, Kate. Or three times or more. If anyone deserves another round with love, it's you."

Kate looked up at her, a maelstrom of emotions flitting across her face so fast Sam couldn't read them. "You sound uber sure of yourself. I'm the one with the ability to see the future, remember?"

"You've never been able to see your own future. Which means anything is possible." Sam smiled and after a few moments, she saw the shadow of an answering smile on Kate's face. "You'll find love again, I promise."

"Sammy's promise and few bucks wouldn't even buy you a latte," said a familiar voice which scraped across Sam's skin like a saw blade. "We know how she is with promises."

Stomach acid surged up Sam's throat. She hadn't been called Sammy in years. There was only one person who used that name for her. The person who'd once meant everything. The person who'd ripped open her already bleeding heart the day of her parents' funeral.

CHAPTER 11

"Beth." Sam turned around slowly. "I'd hoped you'd changed your mind about coming."

Beth's smile shrank for a moment, then blazed again, revealing white teeth against her sun-kissed skin. "I thought you'd have left by now. Still running?"

Was she calling her a coward, like Kate had? Sam stiffened. "If you're implying—"

"That running has kept you looking amazing?" Beth said smoothly. "That's exactly what I'm doing."

Sam's mouth dropped open. Beth didn't compliment, but she'd hid the dig expertly.

Kate rushed over and hugged Beth. "Why didn't you let me know you'd arrived?"

Skinny jeans showed off Beth's lean muscled legs, and an oversized black sweater hung artfully in an asymmetric cut. A chin-length bob and straight bangs made her look like a starlet from the twenties. Mysterious.

Beth tucked a strand of Kate's hair behind her ear. "No

worries. I was playing with the girls before they left for Stu's." The smile she gave Kate was softer, sweeter. Real.

Sam remembered that smile and how it felt to have that warmth directed toward her. They used to be so close, it was almost as if they were one person, one mind. That seemed eons ago. But they couldn't go back. Whatever they had shared as friends was gone. Dead.

Beth sauntered down the steps and past Sam, the movement causing her dark hair to dance against her cheekbones. High heeled leather boots almost brought her to Sam's height, but not quite. She stopped by the ivy trellis leading into the garden. "Aggie showed me around. This is quite a spread you have here, Kate."

"Guess it doesn't compare with your mansion in Beverly Hills." Sam's tone was as chilled as the early evening air. "How much does one make pandering to the masses?"

"Oh, not nearly as much dough as you made when your parents died." Beth's perfectly lacquered lips almost curled. "Has your silver spoon tarnished so soon?"

"You bitch." Every muscle in Sam's body trembled with restraint.

"Just returning old favors, Sammy." Beth's voice caught at the very end. She turned and looked back into the garden.

Kate held up her hands in defeat. "Will one of you please tell me what happened at Sam's parents' funeral? We were blood sisters once. Joined."

Beth turned around, her face blank, emotionless. "Sam, why don't you tell her how you betrayed me?"

"I betrayed you? That's rich." Sam's hands tightened into

fists. It wouldn't solve things to smack Beth across the face with a right hook, but it would sure feel good.

Before she could take a step, the air became heavy, hard to breathe. Ghosts were nearby. She didn't have time for this. No more Bargains. Not now. She wasn't even sure if she could fulfill the one she'd already made.

But no one appeared. No one asked for help. No one sucked her dry.

Instead, they gave. Like a rush of fresh water, their energy drowned the animosity bubbling inside Sam. The pain around her temples soothed, the tension in her arms and legs eased, and the last of her anger slipped free, leaving behind a still calm, like a beach after a storm had been pulled back to sea.

She could breathe deeply again. The fury wasn't gone for good, but she wasn't consumed by it any longer. "I can't believe it."

"Sam, what just happened?" Kate's voice rose up at the end with an edge of fear.

Beth looked worried too, but when Sam met her gaze, it quickly slid into practiced disdain.

Sam gestured around them. "Ghosts."

"You were blazing as bright as a roman candle," Beth commented and placed a hand on her hip. "That's new."

"What?" Sam said. The ghosts claimed she glowed. Beth shouldn't be able to see that.

Kate crossed her arms. "I didn't see anything. How come Beth did?"

"I've got skills you don't have, Red."

Kate didn't look satisfied. "That bottle of wine in the kitchen is calling my name. So are you two good for now? Not going to try to kill each other on the way inside?"

"No promises," Beth sang and then breezed past Kate to enter the manor.

"Wow, this is going to be fun," Kate muttered. "You okay with the whole glowy-thing I somehow can't see?"

Sam gripped her shoulder. "I'm not sure how I feel about Beth seeing it. But I'm feeling . . . centered. The ghosts took away my anger. Helped me get control again."

Kate gave her a quizzical look. "Okay, am I just imagining it, or are the ghosts being awfully good to you? It's not like it used to be."

Sam looked off into the horizon, feeling older than her years. "Robert's with them now. Maybe that's the difference." He was kind to her when they first met. Compassionate too. The sliver of sun in the distance became a tiny line of gold against the purpling twilight.

Kate turned and went inside, pausing at the door. "You coming?"

"In a minute." Sam waited until she disappeared into the manor and then whispered. "Thank you," to the ghosts she still felt around her. Their energy dissipated in the breeze.

A loud crash shattered the air, coming from inside. Sam's legs pushed her into a full sprint into the manor.

BETH HEADED DOWN THE HALLWAY TOWARD THE SOUND OF the crash. Her gait was quick, but controlled. She paused for a moment at the room's threshold and listened. No breathing, no footsteps, just a soft chinking noise. Easing slowly around the doorjamb, she scanned the interior. Just like she'd trained herself to do in juvie.

At the far end, a big-ass fireplace spewed light throughout the room. The coffee table lay ruined, dead center. Thick pieces of glass hung askew like broken fangs. In the middle of the debris lay the base of a snow globe, the bottom half of Santa still wedged inside. Water and tatters of fake snow soaked into the Turkish carpet.

No way this was an accident. She didn't see anyone, but given the high windows and the fact she stood near the only exit, if they were here, she'd find them.

Kate and Sam burst into the room. *Seriously, could they be any more loud?*

"Don't bother, it's just—" Kate began to speak, but Beth's hand slashed through the air, silencing her.

Beth moved forward quietly on the balls of her feet and grabbed a poker from the fireplace. She had two knives, but those required closer proximity. The poker would give some distance, yet pack a deadly punch.

Though the iron should have been warm being so close to the flames, it burned her skin like she'd picked up an icicle. She ignored the pain.

Padding slowly toward the large couch and chairs in the back, her gaze darted around, scanning for movement.

Kate cleared her throat. "Like I was trying to tell you, it's just the friggin poltergeist again."

Beth stumbled. "What did you just say?"

Kate turned back to the hallway and yelled over her shoulder. "Couldn't be satisfied with the bookcase, huh?"

"Kate's got a poltergeist." Sam's words were dry, but anxiety pulled at the corners of her eyes.

Poltergeist.

Beth remembered the last time she'd faced one. Sam lying at the bottom of the staircase, her arm twisted behind her. Blood everywhere. Beth pulling her outside. Heavy dark laugher chasing their steps. They'd only been twelve.

Skin sweaty, Beth's grip on the iron slipped, but she held on. Iron was good against that type of beast.

She stalked back toward them, pointing at Sam. "If Kate's got a poltergeist, then you're on the first plane home."

Sam stared at her like she were a splinter she needed to pluck from her finger. "I didn't know you cared."

Beth leaned the poker against a chair and wiped her hands on her jeans. "You almost died the last time we faced one of those things. Kate's got enough on her plate without having to deal with your corpse."

Kate's glance ping-ponged between them. "What's she talking about, Sam? You told me the poltergeist left you with a broken arm and some bruised ribs."

"Only because she was lucky." Beth enjoyed the pissed-off look on Sam's face. Screw whatever Sam wanted. Kate deserved to understand the danger. "The homeowner died.

Broken neck. It also killed his wife. Rammed her into the wall over and over again until she was just a mess of bones, a meat sack."

Kate paled and gripped the side of the nearest chair. "Sam, you need to go."

"I'll go if you go."

"We should *all* leave," Beth said. "None of us should be dealing with this poltergeist shit."

"I'm staying. Ray hasn't done anything really violent," Kate said.

Sam pointed at the ruined snow globe. "I don't think Santa would agree with you."

Beth snorted a laugh. She couldn't help it.

Sam sobered. "You can't have it both ways, Kate. Either it's too dangerous for me and we all go. Or Ray's harmless and I stay."

"If I run, I'll be giving up on Paul's dream."

Beth shook her head. "Paul wouldn't want you hurt because of him. I know all your money is tied up in the B&B, but what if I give you a loan, just to get you into a new place? Then you can sell the manor and pay me back."

Kate's eyes narrowed. "I am not giving up on this place. And besides, there isn't another B&B within a hundred miles."

Sam touched her arm. "So, you move. You could even come back to the States."

"No."

There was so much weight behind the word that any protest

from Beth stalled before it reached her lips. "Something else is going on, isn't it?"

Kate walked away from them and stopped in front of one of the windows, staring out. "I've always felt a connection to this place. Not just the manor itself, but the grounds." Her voice was quiet, but held steel. "It's helped after I lost Paul. Like there's a reason I need to be here."

Sam looked at Beth with a raised eyebrow. Beth shared her confusion. What kind of connection could Kate have to this place?

Beth finally spoke before the silence lengthened too much further. "At least have the girls bunk with Stu and Aggie for a while. Just to be safe."

"That's a good idea," Kate said. "And don't feel you need to stay if you think it's too dangerous."

Beth hugged Kate. "Are you kidding me? I wouldn't leave you to fend for yourself. Given Sammy's track record, she's not going to be able to get that shit done by herself." She saw Sam tense out of the corner of her eye.

"Are you sure you're staying for that reason?" Sam said. Her voice was pleasant yet laced with land mines. "The great Beth Marshall facing off against a poltergeist would give spice to your show."

Beth stepped away from Kate. She'd forgotten how much of a bitch Sam could be. "At least I'm helping people with my show. All you do is entertain them because you can't face your ghostly baggage. You deal in fiction."

Sam grabbed her arm. Beth had forgotten the strength that

had always been underneath that willowy frame.

"My abilities are as real as yours," Sam said. "I just don't choose to flaunt them."

Beth yanked her arm back. "Because you don't have to." She pushed into Sam's space until they were almost nose to nose. She gave Sam points for not backing up. "And because you hate who you are."

"I don't hate who I am." Sam's voice wavered just enough Beth knew she'd scored a hit. "I just couldn't believe in gifts that didn't believe in me."

"You wanted *this* gone way before the accident." She pointed to Sam's heart. "This thing that makes you special. Lets you talk to the dead."

Sam's eyes filled with tears. Beth wrapped an extra layer of I-don't-care around herself, but it had holes in it. When they were kids, she'd always been the one crying, not Sam. Never Sam.

"You didn't see them," Sam whispered. A single tear spilled over her lashes and down her cheek. "You didn't hear them. You didn't suffer when they reached inside you, making you feel every horrible thing they'd experienced." Sam brushed the tear away with the back of her hand. "If you had, you wouldn't question my choice."

Beth blinked, hoping no one saw the moisture in her eyes. She wasn't totally unfeeling, but it didn't change what had happened in the past between them.

"Then stop questioning my choices and what I do for my career." Beth turned away. "I get enough crap from folks who call me a bullshit con-artist. You know how *that* feels."

"Beth—"

She didn't wait to hear what Sam was going to say next. She stalked off toward the kitchen, her heels clicking loudly on the hardwood floors.

She'd wanted to help Kate, but seeing Sammy again . . . it had been a mistake.

S AM STOOD IN THE HALLWAY, TRYING TO GET CONTROL OF her tears. She listened to Beth and Kate in the kitchen, their conversation just a faint buzzing in the air.

She kept seeing the pain on Beth's face. She'd been the one betrayed by Beth, but Sam always felt she could have handled what happened at her parents' funeral better.

Her parents. She missed them so much. She'd always been able to talk with them.

She placed her hand against the wall, the plaster cool underneath her skin. "I know you can't hear me, Mom, but I could sure use your wisdom right now." Her whisper was swallowed under the hiss of the heaters kicking on.

"Is there anything I can do to help?" Robert said from behind her.

Sam nearly jumped out of her shoes. She whirled around and pointed a finger at him. "What are you trying to do, kill me?"

Robert frowned. "Why would I kill the one person who

can help me?" The frown disappeared. "You have been crying. Pardon my manners."

Sam took a breath. "No, you should pardon mine. I bit off your head for something stupid."

"Beth vexes you, that much is evident. How long have you been friends?"

"We're not friends. Not any more."

He raised a dark eyebrow.

"We met when we were eight, but we haven't been close for a long time."

Robert put his hands behind his back and paced the hallway. "It is obvious that the loss of your friendship has wounded you both deeply."

Sam opened her mouth to protest, but found she couldn't utter the words. "It's been difficult," she said finally. "Though I think Beth could care less."

He stopped pacing and gave her a stern glance. "When you are not looking, she gazes at you as if she never thought to see your face again."

"That's ridiculous."

"And when she is not looking, your eyes follow her as if you are afraid she will disappear."

"I don't—"

Robert waved a hand in her direction, looking imperious. "I was raised by my father to read people. It assisted in negotiations. You both mourn the death of your friendship. There is no point denying it."

"You ghosts are a nosey bunch," Sam grumbled. "Always

seeing things I wish you wouldn't."

"Ghosts," Robert repeated, a wash of sadness softening his features. "Sometimes I forget I am such." He shook his head, sending a glossy curl of hair brushing against his jaw.

Sam could imagine how he'd been when he was alive. His whole life ahead of him. Plans made, dreams to fulfill. All that taken away. "I'm sorry your life was stolen."

He glanced at her, surprise in his eyes. "Thank you. They talked of your power, but not of your compassion."

"They?"

"The other ghosts. The ones you helped before."

Sam took a step closer to him. "But they shouldn't have been in the Rinth if I'd helped them." Had she done something wrong? She shook her head. Why should she care? She'd been a conduit, a tool, used by the ghosts and the Universe. Nothing more.

"No. They were not in the Rinth. But if you remember, I mentioned the Rinth exists next to Entwine. I heard stories." He lifted his hand toward her and then dropped it. "You did a great service for many years."

"A great service? I did what I had to do to make them go away. They wouldn't leave me alone. Day and night. Bloodied, desperate, demanding my help." She hugged her arms to herself. "It was a nightmare."

Robert took a step toward her, bringing them within touching distance. "A nightmare which caused you to bond with Beth and Kate?" Robert's breath brushed against her face.

"That was a long time ago. What we had is lost." How did

he seem to know what was inside her? Know her better than the living? "Why do you have to be dead?" She hadn't meant to speak the words.

He reached out a trembling hand and held it near her cheek. Not touching her, but she felt his essence just the same. A warm vibration danced against her skin.

"In this moment, with you, Samantha Eveline Hamilton, I wish I were alive." He touched her then and Sam swayed toward him, but caught herself.

"I can't." She took a step back. "Once I help you and Kate, I'm getting rid of this curse." Her voice shook, sounding uncertain, but it didn't matter how attracted she was to Robert or the empathy he showed. "There's no point to any of *this*." She waved her hands back and forth in between them.

"This connection between us might be temporary." Robert came closer. Sam backed up further until she hit the wall. "But I am unable to deny it."

Sam's hands went to his face, cupping his cheeks. She couldn't seem to help herself. Her mind screamed at her to stop, but her body wasn't listening. "This doesn't mean I'm accepting my powers."

He nuzzled her right ear. His hands gripped her waist, pulling her toward him until no space remained between them. "Of course not." His breath sent tingles through her much like the fireflies from the Bargain.

"I hate ghosts." Sam's protest was a bare whisper.

"Duly noted. I have enough interest for the both of us." He kissed her before she could say another word.

Blood rushed through her, waking all her senses. His soft hair between her fingers, the primed tension in his body, his ghostly energy mixing with hers and racing along her skin. She was drowning, dissolving in the kiss. Every hair, every pore, every piece of her felt Robert's touch. The hallway disappeared, the manor, everything, until only they remained.

Robert finally pulled away. Slowly. He moved back a step. Sweat slicked his brow. "This makes me wonder just how you would kiss if you truly *liked* a ghost."

Sam laughed softly. She'd never been kissed like that before, never lost herself so fully. "Thank you for getting my mind so completely off Beth."

Robert bowed. "One must help the Necromancer so she can continue in our quest."

Sam's smile turned into a grin. "You are truly like no other ghost I've ever met before."

"Perhaps you are simply seeing ghosts with older eyes." Robert took a step forward and brushed aside a strand of her hair. The touch of his fingers on her temple sent heat through her again.

The sound of Beth and Kate's laughter rolled through the hallway. "Maybe I need to see others with older eyes too." Sam held his stare.

Robert kissed her forehead. "As one who died before my time, I will tell you it is never too late to mend something which has frayed. The real question is how much are you willing to risk? There is always a price."

"Thank you," she whispered. "Thank—"

He disappeared, leaving her alone in the hallway.

She'd asked for her mother's wisdom, but got Robert's instead. Hadn't she come back to Scotland to face the past? She squared her shoulders. Time to find out if Beth's friendship was worth saving.

CHAPTER 12

"WHAT ARE YOU TWO TALKING ABOUT?" SAM JOINED Beth and Kate in the kitchen. She took the glass of cabernet gratefully from Kate and enjoyed a deep sip. Beth's gaze was drier than the wine.

"We were talking about hunky hunky Robert." Kate did her wiggle dance again, but with more power. She looked like novice burlesque dancer having an itch down below.

Sam almost spit out her wine.

"I've heard he's a super hottie," Beth said.

"He's Lord Robert Grenning from the 18th century, and I'm going to help him clear his name." Sam kept her tone light, not wanting to give Beth any ammunition.

"18th century, huh? So, he's butt-ugly then." Beth sat down on one of the stools by the kitchen island. "Big wart on his nose and bad teeth?"

Sam grabbed some grapes from a bowl on the counter. "He's actually quite attractive and surprisingly kind."

Beth gave Sam a shrewd look. "Wait a second. Isn't Robert

the name of the ghost in your book?"

"Yes." Sam knew what Beth was going to say. She'd wondered about it herself.

"So, just like your book, the ghost is gorgeous, named Robert, and is in love with the blonde heroine. The only one who can see him." Beth gave Kate a pointed look. "Quite a coincidence."

"Robert's not in love with me." If either of them ever found out about that kiss in the hallway, they'd never let it die. Now it was her turn to shoot a stare at Beth. "I didn't know you read my books."

Beth leaned back, swirling her wine in her glass. "Kate gives them to me as Christmas presents. I read a few before I donated them to the library."

Kate slid a plate of cheese and crackers between them. "I think Sam's gifts were already coming back *way before* she saw her Robert."

Sam needed to head off this line of discussion before Kate got into the it's-who-you-are argument. "So, how's your show going, Beth? That last one on the missing necklace was really interesting."

Beth paused with a cracker half-way to her mouth. "You watch my show?"

Sam bit back her first immediate response—only when nothing else was on. "When I have time, I try to catch it."

"I really hate the host, Hanna." Kate wiped her mouth with a napkin.

"I'm stuck with her," Beth said. "But to be fair, she's very sweet and doesn't realize how she's coming across. No one tells her because she boosts ratings."

"She definitely boosts something." Kate yanked down her v-neck shirt to expose the top of her chest and black bra. Her voice turned sultry in a good imitation of the host of Beth's show. "Ooh, tell us more about your dead father. It's okay, you can look at my boobs, everyone at home is too."

They all exploded into laughter, and it was like they were in Kate's basement again sharing stories after school. *This is what I miss.*

The mirth drained away from Beth's expression as if she'd felt the same thing Sam did and hadn't like it. "I suppose I should tell you what I found. What brought me here. It's a smoking pipe."

"Who asked you to find it?" Sam said.

"No one. I was compelled to find it."

"What?" She looked at Kate and found surprise there as well. "But someone has to ask you to find the object. That's the way your powers have always worked. Have they changed?"

Beth glanced at both of them. "Haven't yours?"

Sam played with her wine glass, shifting it in her hands. "I'm not sure yet. My abilities have only been back for a short time. But I have a feeling things have evolved." Like touching Robert.

Kate broke a few crackers onto her plate "Do you still get the cord of light thingy, Beth?"

Sam remembered Beth's descriptions when they were kids.

"The cord is what attaches you to what you're searching for, right?"

"Yup. It's still the same," Beth said. "I'm able to find older things now though. Close to one hundred and fifty years old, and it continues to rise."

"When you're compelled, does it feel different than the usual?" Sam watched Beth closely. Like Kate's gifts, she had the feeling Beth's abilities had changed for the worse.

Beth played with the cracker crumbs pushing them down on her plate with her finger. "It does feel different. It's like I have a grappling hook shoved inside me, yanking me forward."

Everything felt closer, hushed around the three of them. For an instant, it was like they were under a sheet in Sam's old treehouse with a flashlight between them and a bag of Cheetos.

"That sounds horrible and painful." Sam realized Beth might now understand the pain Sam went through with ghosts. What else didn't she know?

Beth's voice was soft. "The first time I was compelled, I expected to see my stomach ripped open, insides on the outside. But that's not the worst part. The longer it takes to find whatever it is I'm drawn too, the worse the consequences."

Kate's eyes were wide. "What consequences?"

"First, it's extreme exhaustion, like I haven't slept in days. Then, it moves into something like the flu, all aches and pains." Beth's eyes grew unfocused. "This last time with the pipe, my assistant, Lacey, threw me into the hospital when I collapsed and wouldn't wake up."

Sam gasped. What would happen to Beth if she couldn't find something she was compelled to search for?

"That's awful." Kate's face was pale.

Beth touched a drop of spilled wine on the countertop, swirling it this way and that with her finger, not looking at them. "My parents used me to steal things since the time I could talk. Maybe these consequences are punishment for not turning them in sooner."

"You were the bravest person I ever knew when you stood up to them." Sam meant every word. "This compulsion thing, whatever it is, has nothing to do with your parents. Our powers have changed. That's all."

Beth shook her head, like she didn't want to believe what Sam said. Kate took her hand. "Listen to her. It's the truth."

Sam knew what Beth was feeling. She lifted her glass in a toast. "We can't let the past stop us from living, really living. Here's to the future."

Kate nodded. "I second that. Here here."

Beth gazed at Sam for a long moment. "Speaking of the past, I've been thinking lately about the night we performed the ritual."

"At my treehouse." Sam remembered that night clearly. It had never faded from memory.

Beth leaned on the countertop, cradling her chin in her hands. "No one understood what we were going through, not really. No one knew how it felt to be who we were."

Kate held up her thumb, the scar still visible in the flesh.

"Remember how you thought the safety pin wasn't sanitary? You didn't want to go through with it."

Sam nodded. "It wasn't that. Not really. I was just scared shitless at what we were doing. I knew it was bigger than what we thought."

Beth looked at her own thumb, her own scar. "You'd just seen Mr. Clemins, Sammy. Remember that?"

"He wanted me to tell his family he had another son." Sam took a sip of wine. "They wouldn't believe me. Almost called the cops."

Kate leaned forward. "I had just had that premonition—"

"About Tony McCalister," Beth and Sam said in unison.

"He was going to get into a horrible car accident, but no one would listen to me." Kate swallowed. "I knew he was going to get hurt."

"I'd been brought in for trespassing on school grounds after hours." Beth's voice was hushed. "My cousin, Jerry had passed out. He needed his inhaler, and I'd tracked it to the school. Given my parents' history, the cops didn't believe me."

"Everyone thought we were crazy," Sam said. "Everyone but my parents."

"They were the only true parents I ever had," Beth said. Then she cleared her throat. "To Mr. and Mrs. Hamilton. Taken from us way too soon." She lifted her glass finally.

Sam's grip on her wine glass tightened to almost crushing. How could Beth make that awful dig about her parents when they'd been outside and then suddenly be nice? The glass warmed under her grip. Wine sloshed over top, wetting her sleeve.

"Hold on, Sam." Kate got up and ran to the sink, wetting a towel.

Beth held Sam's gaze. "What's between us is between us. I shouldn't have brought your parents into it earlier. I'm sorry for what I said."

Sam didn't know what to say. Since that day of the funeral, Beth had never apologized for anything. Was Robert right that there was hope?

Kate wiped Sam's sleeve. "Okay, did Hell freeze over, because I just heard Beth say the 's' word."

"It won't be a habit." Beth sniffed.

Kate laughed, but didn't look at Beth. She sat again and raised her glass. "I love my parents, but they still don't accept the truth about me. Sam's dad was the one who encouraged me to believe in myself. To never give up. He was a great man."

"I miss you, Mom and Dad," Sam said. "I hope you know I would have said goodbye if I could have." She put her glass down and gripped the counter. Memories of that night, sitting by the car, calling for them, filled her mind. They'd never come. Tears swam in Sam's eyes and her vision blurred. "The one time I would have welcomed my power, and it abandoned me." The last was said almost in a growl, but it broke apart into a sob.

Beth took Sam's hand. Her grip was light, tentative. "I'm sorry you had to go through that, Sammy."

"We're here for you." Kate held Sam's wrist, tears on her cheeks.

Then, something she never thought would happen again,

did. A surge of power, like touching a live wire, raced down Sam's arms toward Kate and Beth.

They gasped, but didn't let go. For a long moment, the current of energy ran through them, between them, joining them.

Beth was the first to pull away, tears rolling down her cheeks. "It's that stupid energy thing." She stole a tissue from the box Kate held out to her. "It's the only reason I'm crying. I didn't think that shit would happen again between the three of us."

"No one knew 'that shit' was still there anymore until you showed up." Kate's eyes sparkled. "I love watching the two of you bawl like babies right now. Further proof I'm not the only emotionally fucked up person here."

"You watch it, Shorty," Beth threatened, but ruined it by sneezing.

Sam waved a crumpled tissue at Kate. "Yeah, Pip. Be quiet."

Kate raised an elegant eyebrow. "I do not answer to Shorty or Pipsqueak any longer, but it's good to see you two have recovered enough to be grouchy." She picked up her cell phone. "I'm not up to cooking tonight, so I'm going to order us some food. Catch Beth up on the poltergeist, the dead girls and the serial killer, 'kay?" She walked past the table and out into the hallway.

Beth's mouth hung open, her gaze following Kate. She turned back to Sam. "Craziness ensues. Just like old times, eh?"

Sam laughed, but it was thick, still moist with tears. "That's just what I'm afraid of." She blew her nose again and took extra time wiping her eyes. "But I'm really glad you're here."

Beth's face shifted into neutral. "Of course you are. You need someone to boss around and do your heavy lifting, right?"

"No. I thought earlier . . ." Sam realized she'd believed, just a little, that things could go back to the way they were as kids. "For a moment I thought I saw a glimmer of my best friend, but I forgot how good an actress you are."

Beth got up and poured more wine. "Takes one to know one. Now, fill me in on what's been happening. We don't have to be besties anymore to help Kate."

Sam did as Beth asked, her voice a monotone. She'd allowed herself to hope. Hope lead to trust. Trust led to betrayal.

She had her answer. There was nothing to save.

ROBERT ARRIVED IN SAMANTHA'S BEDROOM. HE WANTED to know the outcome of her discussions with Beth. After her comments about "nosy ghosts", he had deliberately made himself scarce during the exchange.

He found her already preparing for sleep, kicking off her shoes and slipping off her trousers. He turned his back, but not before catching a glimpse of her shapely calves.

Though he had kissed her earlier in the hallway downstairs, it could not happen again. Beatrice's warning loomed loud in his mind. And what had happened to his resolve that this was a business relationship? Somehow seeing her so fragile in the hallway had dissolved his convictions.

The sound of Samantha's nightgown sliding over her head drew his attention. How he longed to be that nightgown, caressing every naked curve. He tried to calm his breathing.

Clenching his hands to his sides, he counted to ten and then peeked back over his shoulder to find her suitably covered underneath the sheets. He waited another moment before materializing, as Beatrice called it.

"Good evening, Samantha. How did everything transpire with Beth?"

Samantha didn't appear startled, instead she looked relieved. "It didn't go like I had hoped."

She adjusted the pillows behind her back, and the movement sent her blonde hair cascading over one shoulder. Robert willed himself not to look at the swell of her breasts underneath the thin sheets and turned instead to gaze at the chest of drawers.

"I am sorry it was not what you had wished for. But I have heard from the other ghosts that she can find anything she chooses. Perhaps she can discover a way back to your friendship?"

"I'd like to think she could, but I don't believe she wants to. It takes two, remember?" Sam patted the bed. "Sit down. Looking up at you is straining my neck."

Robert hesitated. Carefully glancing around, he didn't see any other residents of Entwine.

"Who are you looking for?"

"Beatrice and any other ghosts who might be around."

Samantha smiled. "Why, she wouldn't approve of you sitting on my bed even though you're fully clothed and I'm underneath the covers?"

Just thinking of what Beatrice would say if she did see them in such close proximity sent a wave of unease through Robert. "She would not approve of me being within touching distance."

"What does she think about what we can do? I can't touch any other ghosts, I tried earlier, so I'm not sure what's going on."

He walked over to the bed and sat down gingerly. Upon the very end. "She does not appear to have any ideas as to why we are able to interact as we do. But she has cautioned me against continuing the practice."

Samantha leaned forward. "Why?"

Robert rested his hands on his knees. He did not wish to worry her. "She believes we should concentrate on the matter at hand. You will clear my name. Nothing else should distract from that purpose."

"Partial lie."

"Excuse me?"

Sam touched her breastbone. "Ghost lie-detector. I know when you're fibbing, and only a piece of that was the truth."

Robert frowned. He was not sure how he felt about a woman knowing when he lied. There were some small falsehoods that were vital when dealing with the fairer sex. "Do you know about the Wardens of Entwine?"

"Vaguely," she said. He could almost see the wheels in her mind turning. "Several ghosts have mentioned them."

"Beatrice is concerned they might take an interest in me if they knew about our touching."

"So, when we kissed in the hallway, that could have caught their attention?"

He stared at her for a long moment. There was no point lying. Leaning in, he lowered his voice to barely a whisper. "I tried to resist, I truly did. But something inside you calls to me."

Samantha looked down, laughing softly. It had a dark sound. "This all feels like another jab at me from the Universe."

"A jab?"

She traced the paisley pattern on the comforter with her finger. "The one guy I've met who I finally have a spark with and he's dead." She looked up at Robert. "No offense."

"I am confused," Robert said. "Are you saying you have not felt this spark with one of the living?"

Samantha shook her head. "Not that rush of excitement, that heat they say you feel when you connect eyes with someone. When *you know, they know,* exactly what you're hoping will happen next."

Robert wondered if she could read him right now. Of what he wanted to do and what he wished would happen next.

He didn't deserve any more moments of happiness. Not after what he had done to his family. He stood. "I came to find out if you were all right, and now that I know, I should leave." He headed for the door.

"Would you mind staying?" Her words stopped his steps. "I don't really want to be alone right now. I feel raw after everything with Beth."

Robert turned around slowly. "I do not think it wise."

"We could just sleep." She patted the pillow next to hers. "Wait, do ghosts sleep?"

He knew he should go, but her gaze was so vulnerable. He did not doubt she needed the company. That much he could do in return for her help in clearing his name and wiping the stain of murder from his family legacy.

"Ghosts do not sleep." Robert walked around to the other side of the bed and took off his boots. "However, I will stay until *you* fall asleep."

He stayed on top of the covers. Samantha turned off the light and snuggled into him, laying her head on his chest.

"We should not touch." Robert moved, but Samantha pulled him back.

"No one is here. I would sense it. And the lights are off."

She grabbed his arm, wrapping it around her, and nestled up against his side. The weight of her head on his chest felt comforting. Right. If Robert closed his eyes, he might forget he was dead.

"Were you married before you died?" Her words were soft.

He stroked her hair. "No. I always thought I would have time for that. Many of my choices seem foolish now. Have you been married?"

"No." She toyed with the seams of his shirt. "Never met the right guy. You know, the one with the—"

"Spark." Robert kissed the top of her head. Her scent swirled around him. Vanilla, caramel, and something darker. He buried his face in her hair, breathing in deeper. "I never found that either until I kissed you." He should not have admitted that, but could not seem to help himself.

Her fingers slid under his shirt, dancing across his stomach. "How can I like you? You're a ghost."

"Perhaps you are changing?"

"I don't want to change. Not about that."

He captured her hand before it dipped too low. Already his

thoughts tumbled with the possibilities of her skin against his. "Hush now and go to sleep." His words were gruffer than he intended, but his control was hanging by a thin thread.

"No." Samantha rolled on top of him, her legs straddling his waist. "I don't understand this, not what I'm feeling, not why you're different. But at this moment, I don't care." Her green eyes glowed in the dark, and he couldn't look away. "I just want to feel what it would be like to be with someone I have that spark with. I don't care if it doesn't last. We have now."

"But the Wardens." This was the last attempt he could make. Beatrice's disapproval, his being unworthy of this dalliance, no matter how fleeting, all other protests fell away. His body already hardening, already demanding he do what he had wanted to all along.

She leaned down, her long hair caressing either side of his face. "We're safe. No ghosts. No Wardens. No Beatrice. Just you and I." Samantha kissed his forehead, his nose, his cheeks. Each touch left an imprint of heat on his skin. "And if they want to punish you, they'll have to deal with me. I'm the Necromancer."

Her glow brightened until she blazed like a phoenix before him. The rest of his protests burned away under her light.

He pulled her to him, finding her lips. They were soft, but with steel underneath. The satin length of her tongue slid into his mouth, and Robert tightened his grip. He wanted her clothes gone. Now.

She seemed to read his mind. Her nightgown came off quickly. Robert covered the swell of her breasts with his hands, her nipples hardening under his touch. He drew them into his mouth, one after the other, reveling in the taste of her.

He flipped her onto her back and rid himself of his shirt and trousers. Still bathed in her inner light, with her hair flowing out across the bed, Samantha looked like a masterpiece, each brushstroke, perfection.

His hands slid up her thighs. The skin was smooth under his touch, her strong muscles flexing underneath. He nipped at her calves, kissing his way upwards.

Her hands wound in his hair. She was strong, but he held back. Taking time by her hip bones, delving his tongue into her bellybutton, until she bucked underneath him.

His fingers found her wetness. He slid them into her, then out, faster and faster. His tongue flicked against her sex until she began to writhe. His thumb replaced his tongue, and he kissed his way up to her breasts and then her mouth. She clung to Robert, rocking against him. Their kiss grew wild, ravaged.

She screamed into his mouth. Her glow grew blinding. For a moment, everything was pure white. Samantha shuddered whispering his name.

He cradled her in his arms. His sight gradually came back, but for a moment, it looked like he shared Samantha's glow, his skin a golden pearl.

"That was . . . I've never felt something like . . ." Samantha said in between hard heavy breaths. "Robert, I—"

An icy wind blew through the room. Beatrice stood there, fury on her face. Without a word, she grabbed his arm and he lost shape, substance, hurtling downward.

CHAPTER 13

ROBERT PACED ALONG THE ENTRANCE TO THE GARDEN, still fuming from what Beatrice had done to him last night. Though she had asked him to meet her here, she tarried inside the manor with several ghosts. He must have words with Beatrice about her actions during his encounter with Samantha.

Encounter? Though he could not feel the sun's warmth like the flowers around him, heat coursed through him every time he thought of last night. It was folly what they had done. She had made him hope, had made him almost believe he deserved some happiness even in death. Whatever he felt for her was more than a hunger brought on by years of isolation.

"What is the point?" he asked, not caring if the flowers heard him talking to himself. "Even if I believed in forgiveness for my actions, she is alive, I am not." He paused, his fingers sliding completely through the leaves of a rose.

"Don't torture yourself," Beatrice said from behind him. "You can't touch them."

He turned. "I can still appreciate their beauty and hope for something more."

Beatrice walked through the ivy trellis toward him, carefully avoiding the rusted iron planter between them.

She smoothed her apron, her face losing its harsh lines, softening. "Do not hope for what can never be, my lord. It will only lead to heartbreak. We need to go after the geist, get the location of the journal, and send you on your way."

"Who were you talking to inside the manor?"

"Informants. I had hoped they might have a clue to the journal's whereabouts so we didn't have to take on the geist." Her shoulders dropped. "Alas, they don't know anything of value."

"You were also verifying if they had witnessed my visit to Samantha's room." It wasn't a question. He knew Beatrice well enough that she would leave nothing to chance. Not when she was protecting someone.

She frowned. "I did. No one knows a thing. We're lucky. Your mistake could have been costly."

"It was my mistake to make. I am a grown man, not the babe you once raised." The anger flared easily inside him. The leaves on the trellis shook in the wind.

Beatrice's jaw tightened. "Are you willing to risk Samantha's life for your mistake?" She dropped her voice. "Who knows what the Wardens would do to her to get your cooperation."

The anger drained away under the real threat in her words.

He knew she was right, yet it did not change the way he felt about Samantha. "We are connected in a way I have never known." He heard the raw emotion in his voice.

He remembered how they had lost themselves in that first kiss, how she had felt nestled in his arms, how her heart had clamored underneath his hand, and how she made him feel alive.

Beatrice grabbed his hands in both of hers. "Besides this connection you say you feel, what else draws you to her? Is it because she can touch you?"

"No, it is not that." Robert thought for a few moments about Beatrice's question. "Her compassion for others, even for the ghosts she is sworn to help though she despises her gifts. The way she comforted Patty though she herself was frightened. Her strength in returning to a place which holds such misery for her." He brushed her cheek with his fingers. "You both share those admirable qualities."

Any response Beatrice would have mustered was drowned out by the sharp peals of children's laughter. The pounding of footsteps on the stone were muffled, but still promised the arrival of a small army.

Patty and Riley raced into the garden. An army of two.

With her dark stockings bagging around her knees, laces missing from one shoe, and her brown hair curling madly about her face, Patty embodied wild nature trapped in a seven-year-old frame.

Riley was much like the boys Robert had grown up with. Clean shirt, dark trousers—he believed they were called jeans—

and a blue jacket with a stiff collar. Short hair neatly groomed and trimmed. Very presentable.

They ran around a stone bird bath and hunkered down behind a bench nearby, peeping toward where they had come from.

"I'll find you," Emily bellowed, her voice coming closer. She paused near Beatrice and Robert. "For I am the witch of the manor, and I like to eat little children." She made a horrible groaning sound as if she were already sampling a prior victim.

Patty squealed, but Riley's hand over her mouth caught most of the sound. Emily cocked her head and waited a few more seconds before stomping away. She called out her threat again further on. Emily's hunt had moved back toward the house.

Robert remembered playing such games when he and Lillian had been children. He touched Beatrice's shoulder, and she smiled at him, tears creeping into her eyes.

"You almost gave us away," Riley said, removing his hand from Patty's mouth. They both stood.

"Sorry. She just sounded so scary."

"Don't worry, Pats, I'll always protect you."

"You will?" Her eyes widened.

"Of course. When we grow up, we're getting married." He nodded his head with such strength, Robert did not doubt his intent.

"And we'll live here with your grandparents and my mom," Patty said. Her smile moved from pleased to exuberant.

Riley's mouth flopped open, seemingly flummoxed by the sight. His cheeks reddened. "Come on, let's make a break for the woods. That's where we'll find the magic branch to fight her with."

Patty curtseyed. "Lead on, my prince."

Riley pretended to get on a horse, pull Patty up behind him, and then they galloped past Robert and Beatrice and out the far end of the garden.

Robert grinned, he took a few steps towards their retreating backs. "I am the warlock . . ." His words trailed away and his feet slowed. For a moment, he had forgotten they could not hear him. He mattered nothing to the world of the living.

"My lord," Beatrice said softly.

He had always thought there would be time to be a father. Tears warmed his eyes, the heat traveling down his cheeks and catching in his throat. "Why find such a woman after what I have done? Alive, I could have tried to be worthy of her. But I do not even get that chance now." He shook his head. "Samantha complains of the Universe's perverse sense of humor." He laughed, but it brimmed with darkness. "This must be some cruel jest upon my soul."

The iron planter near the trellis beckoned, seeming to reach for him, tilting forward. If he grasped its chilling surface and did not let go, everything would fall away. He would be ripped apart, ceasing to exist. She would be free and not ensnared in an infatuation with a dead man.

Robert took a step toward the planter, but Beatrice tugged him back before he could move any further. "That's not the answer, though I have been tempted myself over the centuries.

Seeing everyone you love die. Being alone. It shakes even the most formidable soul." She gazed up into his eyes. "I didn't expect you'd fall in love with the Necromancer."

"Love? I hardly know her." But the thought of leaving Samantha when she cleared his name sent despair tearing through him. It hooked its claws upon his bones and sliced his tendons with the sharp snap of its beak. Beatrice yanked him into a fierce hug. It was the only thing that kept him upright.

Her words were muffled against his arm. "Oh, you poor dear. I forgot you've never truly been in love before."

"It cannot be. Can it?"

Beatrice looked up at him. "It took your parents less than a day."

"But that was different."

"Why, because they were both alive, and you're a ghost?" She shook her head slowly. "I should have seen it before. It's why you disregarded all my warnings. You couldn't help it. The heart will not be denied."

He wanted to put up argument after argument, but he could not. When had it happened? The first time he had seen her, radiant like a star plucked from Heaven, or when they had nestled together like he had been made for her? It didn't matter. Beatrice was right. He was in love.

"What do I do?" His words were a ragged whisper. "I do not deserve someone like her."

"Hush now about being deserving or not." She wiped the tears from his cheeks with the edge of her apron. "You were the best man I knew in life, and you continue to live up to that promise in death. You need to forgive yourself."

"I cannot." For a moment, there was a fluttering of light in the darkness of his regret. It reminded him of Samantha's glow. But it quickly died. "So how do I get past this? Being in love."

"Well, if you were a lass and alive, I would suggest a large bowl of ice cream to drown your sorrows in." Her voice had a forced cheer to it, almost shrill. "But for you. For you, the best we can do is get this over with quickly so you can heal. You won't do that until you're away from her."

Away from her. Beatrice's words echoed like a pronouncement of doom. But she was right. The longer he remained, the more he would be tempted to coax that flame inside him, to believe he might be able to be happy again.

In another life, another time, things could have been different. But there was no hope for them. Even if he believed in Beatrice's words, he could never offer Samantha a life, children. "The sooner I am on my way, the better."

"And to move you on your way," she said, "we need the journal's location from Caleb, which means we need to get rid of the geist." Beatrice's face smoothed out and became more focused.

Finally here was something he could do. Something he could affect. "Ray will either leave this manor willingly, or I shall destroy him."

Sᴀᴍ sʜɪғᴛᴇᴅ ꜰʀᴏᴍ ꜰᴏᴏᴛ ᴛᴏ ꜰᴏᴏᴛ ᴏᴜᴛsɪᴅᴇ ᴛʜᴇ Cʀᴏꜰᴛs' front door and noticed Kate also seemed nervous, though Logan and Beth were unaffected. Logan had already shared the information about Sam's abilities with all the families. They had agreed to see them.

She knew she had to concentrate on why they were here, to get something from Ellie to use in the memory journey, but Sam's mind kept returning to what had happened last night with Robert. He'd tried to put her off, but she'd pushed it. Drawn by that damn connection he mentioned. Even now, her hands ached to touch him again, to snuggle in his arms.

He's a ghost, Sam. A ghost. Get a damn grip on yourself. It'd just been some fun. Okay, admittedly the most amazing orgasm she'd ever had, but she needed to put an end to it. Didn't she?

You could stall clearing his name and finally have some mind-blowing sex. The voice had a sly quality to it. Her starved libido was being devious. Did he want to pick up where they'd left off? Was he being truthful about not being able to resist their bond?

This was utterly ridiculous. She was obsessing about a ghost.

"Earth to Ms. Perfect," Kate said, waving her hands in front of Sam's face.

Sam frowned. "I hate when you call me that."

"But it got your attention."

Logan knocked on the front door again, and it was opened by a plump woman with short brown hair, clutching a photo album. Caked foundation and the heavy weight of grief added about ten years to her face.

Logan stepped forward. "Good afternoon, Mrs. Croft. These are the ladies I told you about."

Her bloodshot eyes regarded them with hope. "The ones who can talk with the dead? With my Ellie?" The words exploded from her lips as if she'd been holding onto them for hours.

Sam smiled, still seeing Ellie in her mind. The strength in her jaw, the strong determination in her eyes, the life cut short. "I spoke with your daughter just this morning."

"Is she here now?" Mrs. Croft looked around and then up like Ellie would suddenly swoop down on angel wings.

Sam shook her head. "She misses you so much. It's too painful for her to be here right now, but she told me to tell you she loves you more than Tunnock's Tea Cakes."

"Those were her favorites." Several tears spilled down Mrs Croft's heavily powdered cheeks. "I love her more than macaroni pie. You'll tell her that, won't you? And that I miss her? And that I'd like her to come see me even if I can't see her? I'll know she's here."

That was something Sam *could* do. Some small way to help the Crofts through this tragedy. She took her hand and squeezed it. "I will. I promise."

"May we come in?" Logan said, his tone soft.

"Of course, of course." Mrs. Croft moved aside. She wiped her cheeks with the side of her hand. "You said on the phone you needed her things? They're in the spare room in the back." Her wide shoulders began to shake, a small tremor threatening to build. "I haven't had the heart to go through anything from her apartment. My girl. My baby girl." A sob escaped up her throat, coming from someplace dark and deep.

Kate grasped her arm. "I can only imagine what it's like losing a child. When my husband died, I thought my whole world ended." Her eyes were bright, close to tears.

Logan looked like he'd eaten something that disagreed with him, but it quickly disappeared under a small smile. It must be hard to compete against the memories of Paul. But if Kate wanted to create new memories, she had to let someone in.

Sam followed them inside. The entry way led into a small living room to the right and stairs to the left. Everything looked wan in various colors of brown from the walls down to the carpet. Near a small table by the window was the only sign of color.

A shrine.

A large framed photo of Ellie sat in the middle of yellow flowers. Standing guard around the display were pink and purple stuffed animals, from Ellie's childhood by their wear. Candles on the sill saturated the air with burnt vanilla.

Kate sat with Mrs. Croft on one of the couches. "We'll wait here while you go look at Ellie's things." She gave Sam a go-on look.

"The last room on the left," Mrs. Croft managed weakly.

"Now we don't have much new information," Logan began.

"But we're hoping Sam can help us with our investigation."

Sam retreated down the hall. After just a few steps, she heard a scuff on the carpet behind her and realized Beth had followed her.

Sam turned around slowly. "I can manage on my own," she whispered, pleased it sounded neutral. That seemed to be the best way to deal with Beth until she was gone. "Ellie already gave me the description of the pendant we'll need."

"I can find it quicker," Beth whispered back. This close, even in the weak hall lighting, Sam could see the flares of gold in her brown eyes.

She thought about protesting, but then realized it would only be out of habit.

"Good point. Let's go." Sam enjoyed Beth's stunned face for a moment, and then headed down the hall again.

Sam stared into the room Mrs. Croft had mentioned. It looked like a craft store had exploded. Not a speck of surface showed on any of the tables that had been shoved along one wall, heaped full with scrapbooking supplies and paints and sequins and fabric. A mirrored cabinet commanded the wall in front of them. The large window to the side barely let in gray light through its filmy pane.

A huge mound of boxes sat in the center of the room next to some rickety-looking chairs.

Sam walked in. "This might take forever even with your abilities. We're looking for a silver Tree of Life pendant, so it could be anywhere."

"I'm much faster than I used to be with the small stuff."

Beth cracked her knuckles loudly. "Step aside. I work better without anyone too close."

"Since when?"

Beth gave her a long look. "A lot has changed. I need some space."

Holding up her hands, Sam took several steps back.

"Ask me," Beth said.

Sam thought about why they needed the pendant. It would help them find the killer. They needed to stop him before he killed again. Before he tried to kill Kate. Without a true need to find the item, Beth's ability wouldn't respond. "Please find Ellie's Tree of Life pendant."

Beth closed her eyes and breathed in deeply. A second later, she jerked to attention in front of the boxes.

"Yup. The pendant's definitely here." Beth smoothed the air in front of her as if she cleaned an imaginary window.

The air grew cloying, reminding Sam of when ghosts were nearby. Something settled over Beth's skin in a gauzy haze, but there wasn't any face. It couldn't be a ghost.

"There you are." Beth's voice dropped into a deeper range. There was an echo to her words, like someone else spoke at the same time. That was new.

"Beth?" A small spurt of adrenaline filled Sam's chest, moving to her stomach.

"It's in the bottom box on the right." Beth turned toward Sam, her eyes completely black.

Sam stumbled back. She knocked over a box, releasing a flood of porcelain figurines, clinking together. "I thought the black eye thing was just a TV trick on your show. It's real?"

"Relax. This is how it works now."

"Are you okay in there?" Kate called out from the front of the house.

"We're fine," Sam shouted back, though her voice lacked conviction. She tried again, sounding stronger. "Nothing broke. We just jostled a few boxes. Clumsy."

"You're the clumsy one," Beth muttered.

Sam watched the blackness in Beth's eyes disappear like it had been sucked down a drain, dissolving into her pupil. The tatters of white lifted from Beth's skin and faded like bits of ash on the wind.

Sam lowered her voice. "What the hell is going on?"

Beth attempted a shrug, but it never quite made it past her tight shoulders. "Just another change in my abilities." Her voice was back to normal.

"You looked like a demon."

"You say the sweetest things."

"No, seriously. I'm worried."

"You don't have to pretend to care. Kate's not around."

Sam didn't bother arguing further. It wasn't like it would make a difference. She bent to dig out the box Beth had pointed to.

"I can get it out." Beth pushed her to the side, but wobbled on her feet. "I'm fine." She stumbled.

Sam caught her just before she hit the floor. She eased her into one of the chairs. "You are not fine."

"Just a bit woozy. That's all. No big."

"Here." Sam dug into her jacket pocket and gave Beth an

energy bar. "Kate stashed some of these for me. With the rate I've been going through them, I should buy stock."

"Humor has never been your strong suit."

"Accepting help has never been yours."

Beth gave her a long look before tearing open the wrapper of the bar and taking a big bite. "It kicks my ass for a bit, but it doesn't last," she said mid-chew.

Seeing Beth weak like this, fragile, brought back memories. Bad ones. Memories of the nights she'd bandaged her up after her parents had beat her. There was a time she would have done anything to protect Beth.

Sam walked back to the stack and freed the box in question out from under the pile. She put it on one of the chairs.

The top layer of the box contained framed photos of Ellie. Baby pictures on up through college. Sam picked up a recent photo and gazed at the gorgeous vibrant woman looking back at her. Her hands trembled. Someone had ended her life, her chance at a future. Sam didn't have to like her curse, but if it helped stop this psycho, she'd use it.

She put the photos down on the floor and glanced over at Beth. Her eyes were drooping closed.

"You're falling asleep. Go out to the car," Sam said. "Stretch out in the back."

"I'm not falling asleep, I'm squinting against that damn glow you have." Beth held up a hand in front of her eyes, peeking through her fingers. "It's brighter than before."

Sam gazed down at her arm, her chest. Everything seemed normal. "What does it look like?"

"I'm not sure how to describe it." Beth got to her feet slowly, but her balance seemed restored. She walked around Sam studying her. "It's like headlights are pressed up against your skin, coming out your pores. And your eyes are glowing like emeralds. You know, the really deep deep green ones." She paused, like she'd just realized she might have said something nice. "The fake ones."

Sam frowned. Heaven forbid Beth ever gave her a compliment. "I glow to the ghosts in Entwine."

"Then how come I can see it?"

"No clue. But I saw something around your body when you were looking for the pendant. It broke apart and drifted away when you were done."

Beth froze in place, only her eyes searching Sam's face with worry. "What *something* around my body?"

"That's never happened before?"

Beth crossed her arms and then let them fall stiffly to her sides. "Are you fucking with me?"

Sam sighed. "Like I have time for that. We're here for Ellie, remember?" She turned back to the box and took out a small zipped bag. It clinked when she lifted it. A quick peek inside showed jewelry. She handed it to Beth. "Go through this while I dig some more."

Beth took the bag and sat on the chair again. "Patty told me about her premonition."

"She did?" Sam didn't realize Beth was close to the girls.

"That kid's really powerful. Something bad's gonna happen to Kate unless we stop it."

"Then we have to stop it." Sam dug back into the box and her hand closed around a metal container in the shape of a heart. She pulled it out. The latch on the side was tight, but she managed to open it with her nail. A tangle of necklaces sat inside, hopelessly entwined and hooked.

On the top, as if it had been waiting for her, was a silver Tree of Life pendant on a long chain.

Beth inhaled sharply. "That's it. The one Ellie told you she wore on the night she died."

Sam held up the innocuous pendant. She already felt the killer's hands tightening around her neck.

CHAPTER 14

KATE OPENED THE DOOR TO SCOTTISH GLAMOUR, THE local mystical and apothecary shop, and ushered Beth and Sam inside. A gust of wind almost slammed the door shut behind them. The day had turned darker. Stormy.

They'd managed to get what they needed from the visits to the victims' families without Kate bursting into tears. Just the thought of her own daughters not laughing, not snuggling her, not complaining about something, made her feel hollow.

She took a deep breath and cleared her thoughts. They'd made it just before closing. Sam should be able to get the supplies she needed for the memory journey with the ghosts.

Sage and rosemary twitched at her nose, almost making her sneeze. She didn't see Yasmin, Stu's niece, but then again, it was difficult to see very far inside the crowed shop. Sam and Beth had already effectively disappeared into the magically-inspired chaos.

Cluttered shelves clung to the walls, heaped full with herbs and tarot cards and gems. In the middle section, rows upon rows of books were loaded onto low tables that seemed to stagger under the immense weight.

The pathways between the tables were so narrow, Kate had to turn sideways to make it through. She wondered how many search parties had been dispatched to find missing patrons.

Perched on either side of the back counter like a pair of vultures overlooking their prey, speakers emitted the sounds of frogs and rhythmic drums. She heard Yasmin's voice coming from the room behind the counter, which was concealed by a heavy purple curtain. Though her tone was soft, it still managed to cut through. She must be giving a reading.

Kate decided she should find Sam and Beth before they killed each other. Though they'd been civil on the way here, Kate still felt the tension between them. Hers weren't the only emotions close to the surface. Apparently.

Kate made her way down a narrow trail in between two statues and ran into a guy's chest. "I'm so sorry," she managed to get out before realizing who she'd run into. Graham, Logan's brother.

"Watch where you're going there, Katie," he said, the smile already in his voice. Dressed in khakis and a leather jacket, he looked like a mixture of approachable neighbor and borderline bad-boy. His brown hair was shaggier than his brother's and windblown.

"I take that back. I'm not sorry." She punched him lightly on the shoulder. "You're taller than I am. You should have seen me coming." Her words were tempered by her smile.

"You're so tiny, you should have a warning bell," Graham

said. He touched the side of her neck gently where her necklace hung. "I'm sure we could get one from Logan. His cat must have a spare somewhere."

Kate knocked his hand away and gave him a quick hug. "Hush you. No one's belling anyone." The faint scent of something woodsy and green wafted in the air. "When did you shave your beard? You didn't mention it last week when I called you."

He rubbed his smooth cheeks. "I didn't realize I should consult with you on my grooming decisions. I was considering waxing my chest." He began to lift up his shirt, and she smacked his hand, laughing.

"You just want to show off your abs. Claire not giving you enough compliments?"

Graham's smile drooped. "We broke up three months ago."

Kate thought about hiding behind one of the statues. "Graham, I didn't know. I'm so sorry."

"I've kept it quiet. You know how this town is." A shallow laugh escaped his mouth. "I didn't want to be peppered with questions every time someone got in my cab."

Kate completely understood his concern. Small towns had a way of jumping on the bandwagon of opinion. Even the wrong one.

"In fact," Graham leaned in closer and lowered his voice. "I've heard it from the gossip train you've been out to see the families of the dead girls. Is that true? What are you up to, Katie?"

The gossip train. Why was she not surprised? "We were trying to keep it hush-hush." Kate realized she was clenching her hands into fists. She uncurled them slowly.

"Which part were you supposed to keep secret? Talking with the victims' families, or the fact your friend can see ghosts?"

"Both," Kate squeaked. Suddenly it was hard to breathe. How many people had seen through her cover-up at the cafe? "Sam's going to kill me. I brought her to Scotland to help me, not be a sideshow."

At least Graham didn't know *why* they were visiting the families. Logan wouldn't have shared that with anyone, especially his brother. They had never been close.

He leaned a hand on a nearby table. "Well, Mrs. Carmichael from the bakery has already told her sister, my receptionist, that they're going to hit up Sam to talk to their Aunt Mabel. There's some question about their brother's paternity."

Kate ran a hand over her forehead. It came back sweaty. "Oh. My. God."

Graham leaned back, his laughter ringing out through the store. "Katie, I'm joking. Well, at least I hope I am. Though you never know what might be brewing behind closed doors."

"I can't believe you worried me like that." Her words were short.

"I'm sorry, but you're just so easy to tease. It's hard to resist." He had the puppy-dog look down pat.

She gave him a hard glare, but felt it unravel in front of his earnest gaze. "So, I've been told. But don't do that again, Graham. She's working through some . . . issues with her gifts."

Graham glanced over his shoulder toward the back of the

store. "I sensed a core of steel in that one. Or iron, if that set of daggers is any indication. She's more than meets the eye, isn't she?" When he turned to face Kate again, all teasing was gone.

"She is. Though I can't believe she showed you her daggers."

"She didn't. I saw them when she dropped her purse. Where did she get them? They look old."

"They are. From a relative." Kate's words blurred at the end. She shook her head, suddenly woozy, but it only made things worse. "Daggers," she murmured.

The store grew hazy around her. The woodsy scent of Graham's cologne intensified. No, not his cologne. Her forest. At night. Near an old oak tree surrounded by beeches.

The familiar rush of ice, slid along her arms. This would be a vision of the future. Heavy mist coated the air, but she saw a sliver of light cut through the darkness. She recognized the shape. One of Sam's daggers.

Kate ran toward it, but it danced away, leading her. A rumble echoed through the night. Crying escalating into screams that were suddenly cut off.

The dagger stopped moving.

There was someone up ahead. A man's shape through the mist. The killer. Her breath caught in her chest, her lungs in a vice grip. If she saw his face, they could stop him.

Kate crept toward the man slowly, pushing through the branches as quietly as she could. Visions were tricky. She was never quite sure what she was supposed to see, but it wouldn't end until she did. Unless someone interrupted her.

"Katie." Graham's voice sounded like it was oceans away.

She ignored the pull. Another few steps and—

Someone gripped her shoulders. Warmth chased away the frost. Graham's face loomed inches from hers. "Katie," he said again, his breath hot on her cheeks. "Wake up."

The shop snapped into focus like a stretched rubber band rebounding. She found herself clinging to Graham. "Dammit. I almost had it." She could have ended this whole thing. It was right there in front of her.

"Almost had what?" Graham's words were worried. "What just happened?"

No one knew about her visions and she wanted to keep it that way. "Sorry about that," Kate said briskly, trying to sound like nothing was wrong. "I get light-headed when I don't eat enough in the morning. Low blood-sugar." She pushed away from him to stand on her own.

"Hello," Sam called out from the back of the shop. "Is there someone who works here that can help me?" Her words were inquisitive, but with a bottom layer of frustration. Kate saw her and Beth through an opening between two skyscrapers of books.

Kate sighed. "I have to get going, Graham."

He shook his head. "I should tell your friends—"

"No." Kate patted his arm, feeling the tense muscle underneath. "Don't worry them. I don't need anything new they can argue over."

Graham moved back, watching her as if to see if she could

continue to stand on her own. "Are you sure you're all right?"

Kate nodded. "I will be after I eat this energy bar." She fished one out of her purse.

He studied her for a moment longer and then finally nodded. "If you need anything."

"I'll call. I promise."

"Put the purple ones away," Beth said loudly. "You need the blue ones to center you." She dropped a set of long blue tapers into Sam's basket.

"Blue's not going to work." Sam dumped the candles back into Beth's basket. "And just like the last five suggestions you made, I know what I'm doing, so back off."

Beth grabbed the candles and tossed them into Sam's basket again. "No one is accusing you of being stupid, Sammy. Just believe what I'm telling you. Blue is the one you want. You need to be fully in control for the memory journey."

"I do know how to do research." Sam grabbed the candles and held them in her hand. "I'm a writer, remember?"

"Oh Lord." Kate rubbed her temples. "And I thought my girls were bad when they fought."

"Should I stay?" Graham offered.

Kate pushed him toward the door. "No, I'll be fine. Get out while you can."

He smiled and clasped her shoulder lightly before heading to the front door. Kate made her way back to her friends.

"It's good you're a writer," Beth said. "Because no one would pay to see you on TV moping around and complaining." Her voice took on a wheedling quality. "I hate my rich life, I hate my awesome career, I hate that I'm so special I can speak with the dead." She paused to flutter her eyelashes. "Don't you feel sorry for me?"

Sam threw the blue candles at Beth, and the molded wax smacked her nose with a loud *fwhaap*.

SAM STOOD THERE A MOMENT, STUNNED BY WHAT she'd done. She hadn't even thought about throwing the candles, but they were smashing into Beth's face before she'd realized it.

Beth rubbed her reddened nose with the back of her hand. She crouched into a fighter's stance, balancing easily on the balls of her feet. "That's all you got?"

Sam reacted on a primal level. She mimicked Beth's stance. The store basket slid from her arm and hit the concrete floor.

Fear and anticipation poured through her. This was finally going to happen. Either way, they were going to have it out. Once and for all.

Kate threw herself in between them, arms outstretched. "No, no, no. You're not brawling in Yasmin's store. But you two need to talk. Now."

"Stay out of this," Beth said, her gaze never leaving Sam's.

Sam had never played chicken before, waiting for the other person to break first. Her eyes felt chapped from trying not to blink.

Kate waved her hands in front of their faces, shattering their withering stares. "No one is punching anyone. What are you, ten?"

Sam's body still hovered in fight mode, but the moment was gone. Squashed by a tiny redhead. Though she'd really wanted to get in at least one swing.

She stared at Beth for a few seconds more and then straightened from her crouch. "Kate's right. It's time we got this settled."

"So, you're ready to tell Kate how you called the cops on me?"

"Cops?" Kate tilted her head toward Sam.

"We really should start at the beginning, Beth. When I caught you stealing my mom's jewelry." She paused for a moment. "At her funeral."

Sam's thoughts raced back in time with what she'd seen that day. Beth, framed by the backdoor, the afternoon sun glinting on the bagful of her mom's jewelry in her arms. The silken threads of betrayal had woven tightly through Sam that day, cocooning her heart.

Kate's mouth dropped open. "Stealing at the *funeral*?" She looked at Beth. "She's joking right?"

Beth didn't shift her gaze from Sam. "I was grieving. I wasn't thinking straight." Her eyes looked like smoky quartz, hard and unyielding.

This was the first time Sam had heard any excuse. Beth had just run that day. Run away with Sam screaming for her to come back.

"Beth." Kate's one word held the weight of disappointment.

"Don't you 'Beth' me." She dismissed Kate with a flick of her hand. "You weren't there."

"Who cares? In what universe do you steal anything at a funeral?" Kate shook her head.

Sam's arms finally relaxed, the tension eased by Kate's words. She'd never told Kate because secretly she'd been worried Kate would somehow take Beth's side. Now she saw how foolish that had been. A weight shifted and slid from her shoulders.

Kate turned to Sam, her voice still brittle. "As for you, since when is it okay to call the cops on your best friend? Especially with her parents' history."

The weight snapped back into place on Sam's shoulders. "I waited three hours before I called them. I assumed Beth would come back after she'd thought about what she'd done. But once it got dark, Bronson convinced me otherwise."

Beth gave her that same unreadable look as she had all those years ago, like Sam was a stranger. "Bullshit. You called them right away."

"You have connections now in law enforcement, right?" Sam shrugged. "Check the police report and see when it was filed. And why am I the bad guy for reporting my mom's things stolen?" She couldn't believe Beth was still trying to pin their lost friendship on her.

"I was going to come back." Beth's voice cracked and then steadied. "I just lost track of time."

Anger flared inside Sam. Beth's excuses were the flint. "Of course you lost track of time. It must have taken you hours to price every piece of jewelry."

"I hadn't planned to take it all." Finally a thread of pure anguish wormed its way into Beth's tone. Sam couldn't tell if Beth was trying to convince them or herself. "I just needed *something . . .*"

"Well, I guess you didn't take it all." Sam crossed her arms, her heartbeat quickening, dancing to a dangerous rhythm. "Unless you somehow pried my mother's wedding ring off her cold dead finger." Her voice slowed, and she filled it with the venom she'd held back for so many years. "I never checked."

Beth rushed Sam, hands outstretched like she'd claw her to death.

Sam needed a weapon. She grabbed one of the heavy books from a nearby table. The slippery book cover slid out from under her grip. Out of time, she crouched low, bracing for Beth's impact.

Robert's back materialized in front of her. Between her and Beth.

Beth rammed into Robert's shoulder and staggered back. "What the hell? Did you summon back-up?" She gave Sam a wary glance. "You can't use a ghost army in a fight. That's rule #85 in *my* handbook."

"My handbook is the only one that counts." Sam took a step forward to stand beside him. "And, it's not an army. It's Robert."

"I would not risk interfering," he said, glancing quickly around the store. "However, I believed she meant to harm you." His expression was cordial and businesslike. "And then you would not be able to clear my name."

"Oh, of course." *Of course?* What was going on? She'd worried how he'd feel about what they'd done, but she hadn't expected this. Had it all just been a means to an end to ensure her help?

She stared at him, her chest feeling hollow, empty. *He's just a ghost. You'll leave him behind soon enough.*

"How can Robert touch Beth?" Kate said. "Is he a poltergeist like Ray?"

Beth rooted around the pencil cup on the counter. "You know what we do to poltergeists." Her words were coated in menace.

"No," Sam said. "You threatened me, and he stepped in. He's not a poltergeist. I would know the difference."

Kate gave her a shrewd look. "You're not freaked out at all that a ghost can touch a living person. He's been able to touch you too, hasn't he?"

Sam took a quick step forward. "Yes, and please keep your voice down." She didn't sense any other ghosts, but they shouldn't take any chances. "What Robert can do needs to stay between us."

Beth shook her head. "Wow, you're getting it on with Casper. That's the only reason you'd be protecting a ghost. You hate ghosts."

She stole a quick glance at Robert. He was flushed, looking everywhere but at her. Did it make him uncomfortable to think about last night?

Sam's emotions shifted from confusion, to anger, to sadness, then back to confusion. "It's complicated, Beth."

Beth held up a letter opener in the shape of a sword. "This should uncomplicate it."

Sam smelled the iron. The metal scent froze the inside of her nose. "You'll have to go through me." Regardless of his reasons for last night, she'd protect him. Iron would be deadly.

"Children." Kate's voice rang through the store. "No one is stabbing anyone with that disgusting thing. Ghost or human." She held out her hand to Beth. "Give that to me. Now."

"He's dangerous," Beth said. "He leaves. Then I'll give you the letter opener."

Kate looked at the air above Sam's shoulders. "Robert, I promise to protect Sam. I won't let Beth hurt her physically." Her words were steady and filled with conviction. "Can't promise anything on the emotional front as these two are pretty fucked up. But I'll stop them from beaning or stabbing each other. You have my word."

"She is definitely of Beatrice's blood," Robert said, his eyes lighting with a smile. "I will trust her with your wellbeing, Samantha." He bowed to Sam, his gaze lingering for a moment on her mouth, eyes heating, and then he disappeared.

Sam's heart danced in her chest. She'd seen in his gaze what he'd been thinking, and it wasn't about a business arrangement. She remembered this feeling from sixth grade. She had a crush. Only this time it was a crush on a ghost. This was absurd.

"He's gone." Sam gave Kate a nod.

Beth slapped the letter opener into Kate's palm. "No more friggin dead white knights coming to Sammy's rescue. Time for her to admit how she screwed me over."

"Fine," Sam said, tired and wanting this all over. "I'm sorry you had to suffer through a night in jail."

"Night in jail?" Beth said. "Don't try to whitewash what happened."

"I'm not. You weren't in jail the next morning when I checked." She suddenly had a very bad feeling about what Beth was going to say next.

Beth's hands balled into fists, her knuckles white. "You gave the cops the perfect scapegoat for the unsolved robberies in town, given my parents' rep. You sold me out before I could make things right. *You* sent me to juvie."

Kate looked at Sam. "What's she talking about?"

Sam had no answer for her. "Bronson's friend on the force said you'd just get a slap on the wrist. A warning."

Beth's smile had an oily, dark quality about it. "Our friend, Bronson. Isn't he just always looking out for me? I was released all right. To prepare for sentencing."

Sentencing? Sam tried to take a breath, but it caught in her lungs. Sparks flared in her vision. Beth had really gone to juvie?

"So, that's where you disappeared to." Kate took a few steps towards Beth. "I thought they'd finally taken you away from your parents. Placed you in foster care. I tried to find you, but no one would tell me anything."

Sam had thought the same thing. She'd been hurt when Beth had left without saying a word, but after what had happened, she'd been relieved not to see her again.

Beth eyes were bright with tears, though her face remained hard. "I lost everything I cared about. Two years of my life wasted. My gift was the only thing that saved me, though it didn't stop everything that happened." She faltered on the last word. Her gaze latched onto Sam. "I threw in my lot with the gang who ran the place. Finding things is pretty useful to the right people."

Sam's vision cleared, her dizziness gone, burned away by the naked hurt in Beth's eyes. "I had no idea."

"And you never cared to really find out. Bronson could have discovered what happened if you'd asked him." Beth shoved her hands into her leather jacket. "You knew how I felt about your parents. All I wanted, all I needed was something from your mom, something to hold onto, for when things got bad at home. I never meant to take everything." Her shoulders drooped, her voice sliding into a harsh whisper.

Sam's body felt numb. "I didn't understand," she whispered, but Beth ignored her.

"I was gone for hours because I holed up in your treehouse, crying." Beth shook her head. "I don't know why I'm telling you this. You don't care. You turned your back on me then. You'll do it now."

The truth of what Beth said was in every line of her face, in the stiffness around her mouth, in the haunted shadow in her eyes. The years of silence, the animosity when they spoke, the passionate defense of her business. It all made sense now.

Sam had made mistakes, but Beth's actions had started it all. If she hadn't stolen, she wouldn't have ended up in juvie, but any voice of reason drowned under the onslaught of guilt.

Who knows what they'd done to her in juvie. *Oh god, what*

if they'd beaten her like her parents had?

Like an elevator in free fall, she dropped to her knees, unable to stand. "I failed you both. You and Kate." When her friends had needed her the most, she'd bailed. No wonder she hardly had any friends in her life.

Kate walked over and stood in front of Sam. "We already talked about our friendship. That's done. Handled. As for you and Beth, it sounds like you both royally messed things up." Her words weren't harsh, but they were insistent. "But no relationship is perfect. Goods and bads, ups and downs."

Beth favored her with a sour look. "Sammy's been responsible for a lot of the downs. *A lot.*"

Kate's head turned toward Beth like a dog picking up the scent of meat. "And she did a lot of good. Who stood up to the bullies? Who bandaged your wounds? Who finally got your parents to stop beating you?"

"It ended because I threatened to tell someone," Beth said. "That's why they stopped."

Sam stood. Kate was right, they'd made their peace. She couldn't go back and change what happened with Beth. Maybe they'd never find their friendship again, but the time for lies between any of them was over. At least on her end. "Your Aunt Marie gave me some leverage over your parents."

"My dead Aunt Marie?" Beth's voice rose at the end.

Sam nodded. "I blackmailed them to leave you alone."

Beth took a few slow steps toward Sam, but then stopped. "An eleven-year-old against my parents? They could have killed you." Her voice held a tremor.

For the first time in the shop, Beth's expression was open, like someone had cleared away a layer of dirt from a window. Her best friend looked back. Only for an instant, and then she was gone.

"It was worth the risk," Sam said. "They broke your wrist, Beth. Snapped two ribs. Things were escalating. I had to stop it."

Beth ran her hands through her hair. "Yet two years later, you still betrayed me."

Kate lifted her arms up as if in supplication to the dragon mural on the ceiling. "Juvie wouldn't have happened if you hadn't stolen her mom's stuff. Take some fucking ownership already for your actions. And given how your life has turned out." Her voice became as dry as the old books behind Beth. "What do you have to whine about?"

Beth's mouth opened, froze in mid-snarl and then closed again. After a few seconds, she said. "I think you're a worse nag now than you ever were as a kid."

"You're just pissed because you know I'm right." Kate pointed at both of them. "We all agree there were mistakes on both sides. Move on already. We've got bigger shit to deal with." She fixed them both with the evil eye. "Like a poltergeist and a serial killer."

Sam nodded. "Protecting you is going to take all hands on deck."

"I still don't believe the killer is after me, but we do have to catch him." Kate looked at each of them. "Now shake hands on the 'we're moving past this' pact."

Sam held out her hand. "Beth, I'm sorry for my part in

things. I take full responsibility for not understanding what was really going on." She hoped Beth heard the sincerity in her voice.

Beth stared at her hand and then finally took it, gave it a quick shake, and then dropped it like Sam had a disease. "I'm sorry for not having my shit together enough to simply ask for something from your mom. It was stupid." Her words sounded like they'd been yanked from her lips.

A sharp scuff sounded behind them and something fell with a loud crash.

Sam whirled around, already pulling her steel-core hair sticks from her french twist. She reached to push Kate behind her, but Beth had already done so. The blade in Beth's hand gleamed like it had been freshly polished.

They closed ranks in front of Kate, protecting her, like they'd rehearsed it a thousand times. And found the threat was a heavily pregnant woman wearing leggings, a flowing blouse and a bemused smile.

CHAPTER 15

"Yasmin, sorry for the little melodrama here," Kate said. "Move out of the way, Sam. I know her. She owns the place."

Kate's fingernails were sharp pokes in Sam's back. "Sorry." Sam stepped to the side, letting Kate pass. "We're all on edge with the murders," she said to Yasmin.

Sam wrapped her hair back into a french twist and slid the iron hair sticks into place. She wasn't sure what caused her to immediately move into protect-mode. Though the vibe she got off Yasmin was anything but threatening.

Beth slid her knife back into her boot sheath. "Yeah. Sorry if we scared you."

"Do not worry, my friends," Yasmin said. She was about Kate's height with dark curly hair and skin that reminded Sam of the color of desert sand. Her words didn't have a Scottish accent. Instead, they were very crisp, with a British flavor to them.

Large eyes tilted up at the edges, giving her an air of

inquisitiveness, like she wanted to find out everything about you. Probably why she did so well in the fortune telling business.

Kate shimmied past a buddha statue to hug Yasmin. "How much did you see of their antics?"

"Enough," Yasmin said lightly. "I fought with my sisters all the time, and still do. It is nothing."

"Sam, Beth, this is Yasmin, Stu's niece," Kate said. "She owns this shop."

Sam nodded. "Nice to meet you. I apologize for the weapons. Just a tad overkill."

"Not overkill," Yasmin said. "Instinct, was it not?"

Beth rubbed her nose. It was still red. "It was. I moved without thinking about it." She gave Sam a rueful look. "Considering our past, I'm surprised we worked so well together."

"Old habits and all that," Sam said lightly. Though she remembered all too well how they used to have each other's backs. It seemed like a lifetime ago.

Yasmin's face grew serious. "It's good Kate has you around. She refuses to see the danger."

Kate stiffened. "How're you feeling?" She patted Yasmin's pregnant belly, heading down her favorite road of deflection.

"And again, we change the subject," Beth muttered.

Sam couldn't agree more. Eventually Kate was going to have to face the truth.

Yasmin gave both of them an indulgent smile. "We'll have to wait a bit longer for Kate to see what we do." She turned back to Kate. "I'm doing well, though this little one has been kicking up a tornado lately. Sometimes I wonder if she has my gift, and what she might be seeing. Do either of your daughters have the sight?"

"Her youngest does," Beth said.

"No she doesn't." Kate gave Beth a confused look. "She and Emily like to play pretend."

Beth shot Sam a look that said, *Do you break it to her or should I?*

Kate had more than enough on her plate without knowing her daughter had visions and blamed herself for her father's death. Sam shook her head at Beth, willing her to let it go for now.

"It's not pretend, Kate," Beth said. Sam was surprised by her gentle tone. "Patty's told me about her premonitions. I believe her." She shot a pointed look at Sam. "She deserves to know."

Kate's face struggled between a smile and disbelief. "No, Patty's still suffering from Paul's death. It's been extra hard on her."

Sam took her hands and rubbed her chilled skin. "It's more than that, Kate. Beth's telling the truth."

Kate stared at her for a long moment as if waiting for someone to say this was all a joke. Then anguish seeped into her eyes. "I'm not—she's not—she can't have . . . Oh God, why didn't she tell me? How long has this been going on? Has she been scared?"

Sam answered her questions patiently, like she did with Emily. "She blames herself for Paul's death. I don't know. Yes."

Kate stood there frozen. Sam grabbed her purse from the nearby table and dug out her flask. She pressed it into Kate's hand. "Take a sip. It's going to be okay."

Beth whistled. "A flask? Maybe there's a bit of the old Sammy still in there yet."

"Patty blames herself for Paul?" Kate shook her head slowly. "It wasn't her fault. And they've both seen how bad things are when I have a vision. No wonder Patty never told me. She's probably frightened out of her mind."She took another long sip, color seeping back into her face. She handed the flask to Sam.

"I'm sorry, Kate." Beth fidgeted, then caught herself. "I thought you needed to know so you could help Patty."

Kate blew out a breath through her nose. "Just another fuck-up to add to my list. Letting my daughter suffer with her gift all alone."

Sam walked over and put her arm around Kate. "You're a kick-ass mom. Remember your 'no one's perfect' speech, that goes for parents too. Patty will be fine. This is fixable."

Kate looked up at her, determination replacing the anguish. "Let's get the herbs you need so I can go home and apologize to my daughter for being such a lousy mother."

Picking up her fallen basket, Sam found the blue candles she'd hit Beth with, albeit a bit banged up. She shot a quick look at Beth, but only received wide-eyed innocence. Sam glanced at Yasmin. "You don't happen to have any bistort incense, do you?"

Yasmin smiled slowly and reached into the pocket of her pants to pull out a small box. "It came last week. For you."

"Last week? I didn't even know I was coming to Scotland until a few days ago."

Yasmin handed her the box. "I sometimes have feelings or visions of the near future. Of course, nothing as mighty as Kate."

Sam scrutinized the postmark. The date matched Yasmin's claim. And it was addressed to Sam. "How come you can't do that for us, Kate? I'd like to know what's going to happen when we do the memory journey later."

"Memory journey?" Yasmin asked, interest brimming in her eyes.

Kate frowned at Sam. "Is there someone in the back, Yasmin? I thought I heard you doing a reading."

"Oh, don't worry, my friend. He left through the rear entrance. We're alone for now." Yasmin shifted her position so she could see all of them equally. "Now what is this you're doing with memories?"

Sam put the box of incense into her basket and set it down on one of the tables. It teetered against an oil burner and a statue of Vishnu. "I'm going to try to experience the last memories of three ghosts who were murdered."

Yasmin closed her eyes for a moment, said something under her breath, and then opened them again. "Ah yes, you are the Necromancer. I see you with Entwine's eyes now. You shine so brightly, it's difficult to stare too long."

Sam glanced at Beth. "She can see me like you can."

Kate squinted at Sam. "Why am I the only one who doesn't see it?"

"Because you're not tied to Entwine." Yasmin nodded toward Beth. "But she is."

Beth didn't look pleased by the news. Instead she looked mildly ill.

Yasmin grabbed Sam's hand. "Don't give up on your heart's desire. Fate has a way of righting things."

"Do you mean Robert?" Sam's words stumbled out of her mouth in a rush. Why had she thought of him immediately? "Forget I said anything," she added quickly, but she couldn't forget her feelings. Whether she liked it or not, she was falling for a ghost.

Beth jabbed a finger at her. "I told you. Sammy's got it bad for a ghost."

Kate shook her head. "Even if she did, there's no way for them to be together, and Sam's not going to kill herself."

"Holy hell," Beth muttered. "She's not an imbecile. Why would you even bring that up? Besides, she might not stay in Entwine even if she died." She tilted her head toward Sam. "But hey, if the sex is great, there's no reason you need to stop enjoying that."

"I am not having sex with Robert." This was true, but only because Beatrice intervened.

Beth thrust her hips forward and back. "How is it with a dead guy?" Then a look of disgust twisted her lips. "Eeew, that's not like necrophilia, is it?"

"Only if she were having sex with a dead body. Robert's a ghost." Kate sounded like they were discussing something from a clinical study.

Sam held up her hands. "My sex life is not up for discussion."

"Someone is a wee bit embarrassed by her ghostaphilia

habits," Beth said with a wicked gleam in her eye.

A bark of laughter escaped Kate. "Sorry."

Beth sobered. "Heart's desire. As if that isn't cryptic. It could fit a lot of things." She gave Yasmin an appraising look. "Maybe someone heard Sam talking about the bistort at the manor, and this could all be a sham."

Yasmin frowned. Though it was just a slight depression of her lips, her entire countenance changed. A rumble of thunder outside shook the shop walls, and a few items danced toward the edges of the shelves.

Beth glanced at the shelving and then back to Yasmin. Sam sensed the tension in her body, just like before when they'd almost come to blows.

"She's the real deal, Beth," Kate said. "But let's concentrate on the living, shall we? Stopping this killer, saving lives. You know, the important stuff."

In a flourish of bejeweled scarves, Yasmin bowed. "As always, your counsel is wise, Kate." She turned back to Beth. "Forgiving your sharp accusations without merit, what benefits do you bring to the Triumvirate of Pluthar?"

"What did you just say?" Sam waved her hand at Yasmin. "Not the Beth part, but the Triumvirate of what?"

Beth let out a snort. "She said Pluto. I heard that wasn't a planet any more."

"Pluthar," Yasmin said in a patient tone.

"Riiiiiight," Beth said in a drawl. "Sounds like something you googled to look important. Are we supposed to be impressed?"

Yasmin cocked her head. "It means sister. I didn't realize you had no idea of your power together. Of how your shared blood binds you." She plucked one of the books from a nearby table, and flipped it open. "You see here and here and here." She flipped through page after page showing pictures of three people, three objects, three creatures, the pattern repeated. "Three is a mystical number. It's the perfect balance."

"Everyone knows that three is a special number," Sam said. "No disrespect," she added quickly. "But I wouldn't call us a triumvirate or even bound together. Some of us are barely back on speaking terms."

"So that's why you don't know of your unified power." Yasmin nodded her head as if everything suddenly made sense. "That will soon change."

"What do you mean?" Sam said. "Are you saying we can join our powers?" The thought of having visions or being compelled to chase after objects didn't sound enticing.

"Much will be possible for your Triumvirate," Yasmin said.

Kate held up her thumb, the scar visible even in the murky lighting inside the shop. "When you say binding and shared blood, are you talking about this?"

"Yes, you performed a joining ritual, long ago," Yasmin said.

"It was just something silly we did as kids." Beth rubbed the scar on her thumb.

Sam thought back on the ritual. Kate had come up with the words. Beth had found the safety pin. And Sam had tried to talk both of them out of it. Now years later, she found out she was right. They'd done something that day. Something big.

Yasmin gestured to them with open hands. "You gave a

piece of yourselves to each other at a time when you were changing, developing, still coming into your gifts. That gives you power. And the ritual was done out of love, increasing that power."

Beth crossed her arms, hugging them to herself. "That sounds an awful lot like witchcraft. We don't cast spells. Hell, we can barely do what we do without killing ourselves."

"I don't want my visions to get any more powerful." Kate's face was somber. "They're bad enough as they are."

Sam planned to get rid of her powers after she left Scotland, so she wasn't worried about the potential of the Triumvirate. It wouldn't matter.

"No no no, my friends," Yasmin said. "Soon you'll need each of your strengths to face the coming troubles. You must count on each other."

"Great," Beth muttered. "Cryptic crap about 'coming troubles'. Looks like we're already set up for failure."

Kate slapped her shoulder. "Would it kill you to have some hope?"

Sam focused on Yasmin. Even if she wasn't going to be a part of this triumvirate in the long run, it made sense to find out more. "There have been other Triumvirates of Pluthar, haven't there?" She couldn't imagine they'd made something new with their slipshod ritual when they were kids.

Yasmin spread her arms wide. "Alas my friends, it's closing time." She ushered them toward the front door.

"But you haven't answered my question," Sam said.

"Come back tomorrow." Yasmin prodded them toward the

door. "And don't worry about your purchases. We can settle up later."

Stumbling out into the night, Sam saw Yasmin shut the door and flip over the sign to read "CLOSED" in the window. "She's not telling us everything she knows."

Kate said, "She might not know anything more. Visions are tricky things."

They huddled under the tiny awning. The skies overhead opened up, spewing heavy drops of rain. The wind whipped around them with a cold bite.

Sam looked at both of them, a shiver working its way through her shoulders. "So can we count on each other again? At least through catching this killer?" She held out her hand toward them, palm down, like they used to do.

"You can both count on me," Kate said. "Always." She put her hand on top of Sam's. It felt toasty in the cold air. They both looked at Beth.

"I came here for Kate, so I'm in. Besides, together we've kicked some major problems in the balls."

She placed her hand on top of theirs, and a charge ran through Sam like it had in the kitchen. But it felt more like subtle heat than electricity this time. Something shifted inside Sam, like chains stretching toward Kate and Beth. Chains which had rusted from years of disuse, being forged again with new energy, new power, new determination.

No one said anything, but from the worry on Beth's face, and the satisfaction in Kate's eyes, Sam knew they felt it.

For better or worse, they were in this together.

"WHAT IF HE DOES NOT COME?" ROBERT'S VOICE WAS hushed. He glanced over at Beatrice. They had been waiting together in the upstairs hallway for the geist to appear.

Samantha, Beth and Kate were out with the children procuring milk shakes, whatever those were. The manor now held only the dead.

Beatrice paced the hallway. "He's a show-off like Caleb. Just holding out for the right moment."

The day had turned rainy and restless through the windows, echoing the unease Robert felt inside. Caleb had promised the location of the journal if they rid the manor of the geist. They had no choice but to face a dangerous and unpredictable foe. They needed to succeed, but finding the journal and clearing his name meant he would never see Samantha again. He ignored the pain in his chest at the thought of leaving her. She had gazed at him with such sweetness at the apothecary earlier. Perhaps she cared for him too?

Speculating over matters of the heart at this juncture was fruitless. He stepped closer to the wall. "I will tear the wallpaper with my bare hands if needs be to force this fiend into showing himself."

Beatrice pointed a finger at him. "You'll do no such thing. His mere touch could kill you."

"What?" Robert grabbed her arm. "I will not have you put your existence in jeopardy. You must watch over your family.

We will find another way to secure the journal's location."

"I've got a plan." She looked calm, determined.

Robert crossed his arms. "A plan you have not told me of. Why am I not surprised?"

Beatrice tightened the bow on her apron. "There are *ears* everywhere, my lord."

Logic demanded they leave at once, but his heart told him to trust Beatrice. She would not lie about something so grave. If she had a plan, he must believe her word. He leaned down until they were eye to eye. "At the first sign of danger, we abort any such plan of yours. Agreed?"

"Agreed." Beatrice sounded reluctant, but she had given her word. That was all that mattered.

"You're wasting your time." The voice came out of nowhere and everywhere, heavy with malice. "You'll only fail."

Out of the corner of Robert's eye he saw the images on the wallpaper slide along the cream background. The vines looked like snakes seeking their prey. The flower buds loomed large, as if preparing to leap off the walls and smother him.

"Stop your antics," Beatrice said loudly, just under a shout. "We all know what you can do, Ray. We're here to talk."

"You're here to get rid of me. I won't go. I . . ." The strength in Ray's voice withered, and the vines on the paper turned brittle, brown. "I can't."

Hearing such sorrow in Ray's voice, Robert found pity welling up inside him. Pity and empathy. "It is your time to move on." He stretched his arms wide. "No amount of pain you inflict on the living will fill the emptiness in your heart."

A rocking shudder lifted the floorboards under Robert's feet, the wood protested in creaking, quavering noises.

"You don't know me," Ray said in a long growl. "Go away. Or you won't like what happens next."

"We can't go, Ray," Beatrice said. "We've made a deal with Caleb. At least hear us out. This could be a good thing for all of us."

One of the flowers on the wallpaper expanded to the size of a face, the petals growing into cheeks, a nose, a forehead, and forbidding eyes. "I warned you."

The bulbs overhead shattered. The nearby windows blackened as if someone had drawn a heavy curtain over them.

"Close your eyes, my lord."

Robert squeezed his eyes shut. Behind his lids, a gleaming grew. He cracked his eyes open, blinking against the bright light spilling forth from Beatrice's hand.

In the radiance escaping through her fingers, Robert caught his first true sight of the geist. His form in constant movement. Running, sitting, standing, crying, screaming. It was like nothing Robert had seen before. As if the same man were captured in different moments, struggling for dominance.

"Caleb has something we desperately need, and you're the price." Beatrice lifted up the light a bit higher and the shuffling images of Ray scuttled back a few feet. Her face held confidence, but Robert hoped he was the only one who noticed the trembling in her hand. "This isn't your home. I know you didn't die here. It's time to move on."

Harsh cackling broke through the air. "Move on? I'm already

in hell. I don't need to go anywhere else to suffer."

The radiance in Beatrice's hand highlighted all the careworn lines on her face. She suddenly looked older, more tired. "Don't you want to see the ones you love? I know a Runner who can help. You just have to be willing to let go."

"I don't have anyone waiting for me," Ray said. "Not where I'm going."

"What is holding you here?" Robert said.

The spinning shuddered to a stop for a moment, and Ray peered out at them from the maelstrom of images behind him. Dark eyes hooked Robert's gaze. "If you really want to know why I'm here, ask the Seeker, the Oracle, and your Necromancer."

The Necromancer would be Samantha, which meant the Seeker was Beth since she found things, and the Oracle had to be . . .

His thoughts struggled to connect. The oracle must be . . .

Weakness pulled at Robert's limbs. "What is happening?" he managed to croak. He staggered back a few steps, and then his legs buckled. Energy seeped from his hands, his feet like he bled power from his very pores. Ray's shifting motion slowed. He looked more solid, more stable.

Beatrice thrust her hand toward Ray, the light flaring. "Leave him be." She stepped in between Robert and the geist, but the drain upon Robert's energy continued.

Robert tried to build a barrier around him like they had done for Samantha, but nothing held, siphoned away by Ray. The only option was to attack. Beatrice had warned against touching the geist, but if he did nothing, he would be destroyed. Pulling himself to his feet, Robert stumbled forward, pushing Beatrice aside and careening toward Ray.

"No, Robert," Beatrice cried out, but he did not slow.

Ray's eyes opened wide. He did not move or try to evade Robert's charge. With his last ounce of strength, Robert's hands closed around the geist's throat.

Images attacked Robert, chased by sounds and smells. A man crying. Hands slipping through hands. A girl tumbling into darkness. Voices raised in argument. A sharp crack. The pungent smell of pipe smoke.

The visions fled. On their heels, emotions leapt into him, wrenching apart his insides.

Anger swelled through his skin until he thought he would burst, then regret dried him to a husk, and finally sorrow bled from his eyes until all he could do was curl into a ball. He needed to end the anguish. It was all his fault. There was no forgiveness.

"You don't belong here."

Ray's voice reached him across the desert of despair in his mind. Robert opened his eyes and found himself in a small room he did not recognize. Wood paneling covered the walls. His chest felt as bruised as if a horse had galloped over his body.

"Where am I?" Robert's voice cracked as if he had been screaming for days.

"My hell." Ray's voice matched the creak and the cadence of the rocking chair he sat in. Tired and slow. "It happens over and over again. What I've done. I deserve this. You don't."

Robert managed to stand, using the paneled wall as support. "Surely you have suffered enough. Let us free you."

"What I *need* isn't possible."

"Tell me," Robert urged. "Tell me what you seek."

The ceiling of the room shuddered, small cracks widening into deeper chasms. Light blazed from each seam.

"My lord, follow my voice," Beatrice shouted from above. Robert felt small, like a puppet inside a child's dollhouse. "We have only a few moments."

Robert expected the geist to stop him, but Ray just sat there, rocking in his chair, his cheeks seeming to sink further into his hollow face.

"We will find a way to help you," Robert said.

"There's no forgiveness." Ray looked away.

"Now, my lord." Beatrice's voice rose with alarm.

The floor broke apart under his feet, furniture tumbling into the unknown depths. Robert leapt up toward the ceiling, his hand reaching for the glow. He was suddenly back in the hallway, clinging to Beatrice.

She wavered on her feet, the faint embers of light extinguishing in her hand. Her skin looked chalky, ashen. She leaned heavily on Robert, and he helped her toward one of the windows. The pale afternoon light and raindrops had returned.

Ray was gone.

"Was this your plan?" He kept his words gentle, not used to seeing her so weak. It reminded him of being a boy, helpless while his mother took ill.

Beatrice touched his shoulder. Her gaze darted over him. "Are you sure you're all right? You should be dead after running at him."

"I am already dead."

"Don't you smile at me. You know what I'm saying." Some color had returned to her face. "That was a foolish thing to do." Her voice shook.

Robert took her hand from his shoulder and kissed it. "It was either attack or be consumed. I had no choice."

"I didn't know he was powerful enough to hurt you from a distance." She shook her head slowly. "I should have been more prepared. I'm sorry."

Robert kissed her temple. "If you had prevented Ray from attacking me, I would never have discovered some of what made him a geist."

"You know why he is what he is?" Beatrice sat up straight. "Why he won't leave?" She scanned the hallway quickly. He knew she looked for other ghosts, but it was deserted.

"There was an accident of some kind, and I believe someone was shot. I think there was a girl." What he had done reminded him a bit of what he had heard Samantha share about the memory journey. "How is it possible I saw into his past?"

Beatrice gave him a considered look. "I don't know. I've never heard of a ghost seeing another's memory. You seem to be making a habit of the unusual lately."

"I am surprised he let me go," Robert said. "I felt he had the means to bind me to his prison."

"There might be more hope for him than I originally thought."

"What do you mean?"

Beatrice's gaze sharpened. "Just like for the living, ghosts can be scarred by tragedies. When they don't face the emotions around those events, they turn into geists."

Robert nodded. "Inside his mind, it was like winds of emotion protecting the eye of the storm at its center. The center is what Ray is hiding. Why he is the way he is."

"Even at their worst, there's a piece of every geist who wants to heal. That's why we see them the way we do, in constant movement. They can't settle." She placed a finger on the side of her nose and tapped it twice. "But Ray gave us a clue to help him when he mentioned our girls. I'm not surprised at Samantha's involvement, but I'm not sure how the other two factor into this."

"Even if we do discover the reason for him being here, I do not think it will be an easy matter to get him to depart."

Beatrice winked at him, looking again like her usual self. "He could have killed you back there, but didn't. He wants our help."

Robert hoped Beatrice was right. However, wanting their help and accepting it were two different things.

CHAPTER 16

"WHY ARE YOU HERE?" SAM SAID TO ROBERT. THEY stood at the entrance to Kate's bedroom. Through the open door, Sam saw the others already preparing for the memory journey ritual. "This doesn't have anything to do with clearing your name."

"You are still important to me," Robert said. "Of course I would be here to help on such a perilous venture."

Sam nodded. "Ah, so you're worried something might happen to me and I won't be able to help you."

"No," Robert almost grabbed her arm, but pulled back. "I mean, yes, I do still want your help and I am worried, but that is not the only reason I am here."

She didn't want any more mixed signals. Was this business to him or something more? Her mind told her to let this go. What did it matter what he wanted when this arrangement would all be over soon? But her heart pushed her on.

"Did I imagine something between us?" Sam said. "Something like a friendship, something more?"

Robert ran his hands through his hair. "Questions like this will only make things worse. I am doing this for you."

"Doing what?"

"Turning away," Robert said. "It is for your own good."

Partial lie. He was hiding something. "My own good?" Sam moved further into the hallway, hopefully away from Kate and Beth's prying ears. "You're a ghost. I'm a means to an end. Why not have your fun while you can?"

Robert straightened. "You insult me at the deepest level." Disappointment filled his eyes. "I might not be deserving of someone like you, Samantha, but I would never treat you as less than you are. Never."

He turned to go, but Sam grabbed his hand, not caring who saw. The need to wipe that awful look from his face overrode any concern.

"I've got trust issues. Huge ones. I like you. A lot." She pushed on, for once saying exactly what was in her heart. "And it confuses me. Number one, you're a ghost."

"And you hate ghosts." He let out a short sigh.

"Two, we just met." She swallowed. "Three, I'm falling for you hard and it makes absolutely no sense." His grip tightened on her hand. She didn't look at him, couldn't. "I can't stop thinking about you, wanting to be with you, everything. Just like in my books." She finally took a breath. "Four, I'm scared. Because I know I'm going to lose you, lose this feeling, when I get rid of my abilities."

Robert brought her hand to his cheek. "You could keep them. Continue to be the Necromancer."

"I can't," Sam whispered. "What kind of life would I have if I did?"

"One without deception. One without lies." He kissed the palm of her hand and her knees wobbled. "One where you could be exactly who you were meant to be."

"Would you be there?"

Robert dropped her hand and for a long moment, they just stared at each other. "I was pulled from the Rinth for one reason, to repair the damage to my family's name." He touched her cheek again, his fingers trembling. "You would be a prize I could never hope to claim. You deserve much more than me."

"Are we going to do this or what?" Beth said from the bedroom.

"Coming," Sam yelled. She leaned closer to Robert. "If only I had met you in another life, another time."

Robert's eyes widened and then burned with an intensity she'd never seen before. "In another life, another time, I would have loved you with everything I possessed. I would have been worthy. I would have been the man you needed."

Sam's heart stopped, everything stopped. He spoke the truth. Her lie detector stayed green. He loved her?

"Sammy, come on." Beth grabbed her shoulder. Robert was gone. "It's almost midnight."

Sam nodded, not trusting herself to speak, her mind still racing about Robert. But she needed to put that aside for now. She had to be focused for the memory journey.

She followed Beth into the bedroom. They'd decided to use a small round table and had set it up by the fireplace. An olive green cloth covered the table's surface. Beth put the blue candles in their holders and arranged them around the edges.

Beth's cream colored night-shirt looked designer-made. Nothing slouchy, nothing messy, just clean lines fitting her body perfectly over a pair of black yoga pants.

Kate came out from the bathroom, balancing a full bowl of water in her hands. She took slow, careful steps toward the table. Steam misted into the air above it.

The air shifted, becoming thick.

"We're here, Necromancer," Ellie said. All three ghosts had appeared near the windows. Robert was with them. He gave her an encouraging smile.

"They're here," Sam said. She was glad Robert had stayed. He made her feel safer somehow, though there was nothing safe about what she was about to attempt. She walked over to the table. "Let's get started."

Beth gave her a sharp nod. "Which do you want first? The rosemary oil or the incense?"

"The rosemary oil. We should purify the area first." Sam took the bottle from Beth. "Thanks." She twisted off the seal and poured several drops into the water. The scent of mint and citrus filled the air. "It'll also help me focus my intent. I'll need the incense next."

Kate handed her the small boxes filled with frankincense and bistort incense cones. "What will these do?"

Digging out a cone from each of the boxes, Sam then placed them on the metal dish. "Combined together, they'll help with divination and improve mental strength."

She noticed Beth didn't make a crack about her mental strength. Both her friends were serious.

Beth leaned her elbows on the table, chin resting on her fists. "So, you haven't done this since we were ten?"

"Nope."

Kate handed Sam a lighter. "You did a memory journey when we were kids?" Her flannel shirt looked like it had been Paul's, and it clashed with a different pattern of flannel on her pajama pants. With her hair up in a tousled bun and glasses, she looked like a librarian with a lumberjack fetish.

Sam shoved her hands in the pockets of her robe. "Remember when you were in that coma for a month when you were ten?"

Kate nodded slowly. "After my bicycle accident."

"The doctors didn't know if you were ever going to wake up," Beth said.

"What did you do?" Kate's voice grew softer.

Sam touched Kate's arm. "We both had this bad feeling you were never coming out of it. We decided to try to have a vision."

Beth tucked her hair back behind her ears. "We thought, hey, with the right herbs we might get lucky and see how to save you."

Kate's body stiffened. "What happened?"

"We met at my treehouse," Sam said. "Beth went first, but nothing worked. So, I tried it. Instead of having a vision that would help you, I somehow went into Andrea Guthrey's memory."

Kate's eyes opened wide. "Wait, you mean Andrea who lived

on our street? Andrea who was stabbed to death?"

"The same one." Sam's hands fluttered over her stomach. "I felt the knife plunging into me, and Andrea's pain and fear when she realized it was her uncle underneath the mask."

Kate breathed out. "Holy crap."

"But that wasn't the worst part." Beth's face looked ashen. "Sammy started screaming. It wasn't like anything I'd ever heard before." She swallowed. "Then, the skin on her stomach just exploded with blood. Gushing everywhere."

Wendy gasped, and Sam looked over at the ghosts. Monica looked worried, Ellie's mouth hung open, Wendy swayed on her feet, and storm clouds gathered in Robert's eyes. Sam hadn't told any of them about the potential danger. Until it was too late for anyone to talk her out of it.

Kate's hand flew to her mouth. Her fingers shook. "You two are telling me that not only did you see Andrea's memories, *you* actually physically experienced what she did?"

"I did." Sam's stomach throbbed in memory.

"Mrs. Hamilton was home," Beth continued. "She helped me get Sammy to the hospital."

Sam looked over at Beth. "You said if I died, you'd find my ghost and kick my butt for leaving you alone."

"Yeah, well, I was scared shitless. I didn't want you flatlining in my arms."

Sam took Beth's hand and held on, even when she tried to pull away. "The pain was so bad, I wanted to let go. You saved me."

Sam saw a spark of hope in the depths of Beth's eyes. Then,

it was gone. Beth pulled her hand away finally. "It was no big deal." Her tone was flat.

Kate let out a breath, looking too pale. "There's no way I can convince you not to do this, right? Getting strangled three times is insane. What if it's too much? What if—"

"I've got to do it. The Bargain, remember?"

Kate opened her mouth and then closed it. She stared at Sam for a few long moments and then finally glanced over at the clock on her dresser. "It's a few minutes to midnight."

Sam gestured to the ghosts. "Please." She took out the three items they'd collected from the families.

The ghosts moved closer. Ellie's eyes brightened at the sight of her pendant. She leaned forward, and her long hair slid over the front of her burgundy top. "My Ma gave me that. Was she okay when you saw her?" The sharp lines of her face muted.

"She's strong," Sam said. "I gave her your message, and she said she loves you more than macaroni pie."

Ellie's eyes filled with tears, but she just gave Sam a quick nod, not saying anything.

Sam looked over at Wendy and Monica. "Wendy, your parents are finding great comfort in your sister. They all miss and love you." Wendy clutched at the fabric of her yellow sundress, her face crumpling.

Robert touched Wendy's shoulder. "Do not fret, lass. Though you may have died too soon, you are not alone."

Sam cleared her throat and looked at Monica. "Your dad has decided to move back to America now that you're gone. He told me that he hopes you'll visit him there." Monica's bottom lip trembled, and then she tugged on her navy blazer, straightening it again.

Ellie took a deep breath. "So, doing this memory thing means you're going to be choked?"

Wendy's hands went to her own neck in a nervous gesture. "No one should feel that. Especially not someone trying to help us."

Sam wasn't used to having ghosts care about her. First Robert and now Wendy? "I'm hoping I can skip from memory to memory before it gets to that point."

Beth tapped her arm. "Can you do that? Zip between the memories?"

"I don't know. I hope so."

"Thank you for helping us," Monica said. Her long face grew even more serious. "We've asked a lot of you."

Sam smiled, though she felt its fragility on her lips. "I just wish you didn't need me to do this. That you were all still alive." Even with everything she could do with her powers, she could never bring them back to life.

Picking up the lighter, Sam looked at all three ghosts. "I can only see the moments right before your death. I'll try to memorize everything I can about what he looks like. Think back to that day."

Sam lit the incense. The pungent scent of the woods joined with the rosemary. "Hold hands and remember." Her words slowed. "See it. Feel it."

She closed her eyes and took several deep breaths in and out. Her heartbeat slowed with her breathing. Beth and Kate's fidgeting in their chairs, the hiss of the incense as it burned, all the sounds in the room fell away.

When the ghosts joined hands, she felt it. The bond between them and that link to her strengthened, pulling tight. Light began to swirl behind her closed lids.

Sam reached to her left, remembering where she'd left the first object. It was Monica's key card. She felt along the edges, the sharpness of the plastic. The flashes of light behind her eyelids dimmed. She opened her eyes.

The forest arched up around her. The twilight sky seeped around the trees' dark skeletal limbs.

Her lungs thundered. Monica's lungs. She'd made it into Monica's memory. She took a step and felt wobbly on her feet. Woozy. She needed to go deeper into the woods. Away from him.

A heavy weight slammed into her back. She went down hard, teeth smashing against the cold ground, mouth filling with blood.

Sam's entire body shook, flooded with adrenaline. Wait, this was Monica's body, not hers. Monica's memory. Sam gripped onto that awareness tightly.

She was here to find information about the killer. This had already happened. She couldn't prevent it.

"Please, Paul," Monica slurred her words. "You don't have to hurt me."

Paul flipped her over onto her back. Pain lanced through

Monica, through Sam. For a moment she almost blacked out.

Paul crouched near her, his face shaded in the dimming light of the setting sun. Sam pulled herself away from Monica. It was like trying to free herself from a marsh of sticky mud, but she was finally able to focus and take in what details she could. Beard, green eyes, oval face, baseball cap. She couldn't tell height at this angle, but he had an average build.

"It's too late. You ruined it." His words were filled with regret.

Then his hands were around her neck. She inhaled quickly, barely getting in a breath. The rocky ground dug through her blazer, slicing her back. Blood slid down her skin. Hot in the cool air.

He squeezed harder. The pounding of her heart thundered through her head.

Monica dug her nails into his gloves. Paul grunted in pain, but his grip only grew stronger.

He climbed on top of her. She tried to buck him off with her hips. He rammed his knee into her stomach. A heavy burn seared through her deflated lungs.

This was not how she was supposed to die. Monica's despair weighed Sam down, igniting her own memories of loss. The car accident, her parents' death. Sam pushed that night away.

Got to focus. Have to see. Kate could be next.

Monica's eyelids fluttered, flailing to stay open. Sam threw all of her energy into those last images the dying woman saw. Anything that could identify the killer.

There. Above the edge of his glove. A small tattoo. Part of it was faded, but the upper piece looked like a compass. Like the one she'd used at school to draw a perfect circle. A surge of hope raced through Sam. A clue. Something to catch this psycho.

Paul leaned in close and whispered in her ear. She couldn't hear him through the pounding in her head, but this had to be important. If she could just make it out . . .

"Sam!"

Sam's eyes flew open. Her cheek stung, burning. Beth loomed above her, much like Paul had over Monica. Sam scrabbled back, nails scraping on the hardwood floors until she hit the footboard of the bed. Her elbows ached from the impact, but the pain in her chest outweighed everything. Her heart clawed its way up her throat like a rat trying to escape a flood.

She couldn't breathe. Her lungs were squeezed tight.

Kate yelled, "She's turning blue again. Do something." It sounded like it came from a long distance.

Beth's reply sounded equally faint. "You slap her this time, then."

"No one is touching her again." The command in Robert's tone broke through Sam's confusion. She knew if she could reach him, she'd be okay. She crawled toward his voice.

"You are safe, lass." He crouched in front of her. "Just the remnants of a horrible memory. No one will hurt you." His words were soothing, lulling.

He slid his hand close to hers on top of the hardwood floors until only a breath separated the tips of their fingers. The imaginary corset around Sam's chest eased, and she sucked in a quick breath, and then another.

Robert pulled his hand back and stood, though the look on his face said he would have grasped her into his arms if he could have. She knew the feeling. Knew it deeply.

Beth walked over to her gingerly. "You stopped breathing, Sammy. Scared the shit out of us."

Kate followed behind and kneeled next to Sam. "Sorry about the slapping bit. We needed to revive you. I was this close to calling the paramedics and starting CPR."

"I'm okay." Sam's throat felt rough, but not raw like she had expected. Sam got to her feet with Beth's help and walked over to the mirror on Kate's dresser. The skin on her throat looked like a nasty sunburn. She touched her neck gently with her fingertips and a dull ache answered. And this was only the first strangling.

She looked for the other ghosts. Wendy, Monica, and Ellie were by the window. Tears streamed down Monica's face. Ellie and Wendy comforted her.

Beth handed Sam a glass of water. "I thought you were going to skip to the next memory when shit got real. What happened?"

"Killer Paul whispered something to Monica right at the end. I was trying to hear it."

"Did you?" Kate dug out a notebook from her dresser.

Beth held one up. "Way ahead of you, Red." She clicked her ballpoint pen and opened up a page. "Spill."

Sam sat down and told them what she remembered. "I didn't hear what he said to her."

"I didn't either," Monica said quietly. "I'm sorry." She wiped the tears from her face, but more fell.

"It's not your fault," Sam said, wanting to comfort her. For the first time, she wished she could touch a ghost other than Robert. She'd felt every moment of Monica's last minutes alive. Her hands shook.

"You almost died," Kate said. "You can't do it again, Sam."

Ellie nodded. "She's right. Even if it means we have to find a different way."

"There is no other way," Sam said. "We have to stop him before he kills again. This is our best chance."

Beth frowned. "Neither of us has to like it, Kate, but we have to let her do it."

Robert stood there, looking like the captain on the bow of his ship ready to wage war. "I do not like it either."

Sam smiled at him, but his scowl didn't waver. "I promise I'll do everything I can to be safe." But would it be enough?

Kate remained silent, though mutiny glimmered in her eyes.

Sam turned to the ghosts. She picked up Wendy's flash drive and looked at her. "Ready?"

Wendy nodded. A look of determination had replaced her earlier nervousness. Ellie and Monica flanked her and then they all joined hands.

"Be careful, Samantha." Robert's voice held a healthy dose of worry.

"I will," she said with more conviction than she felt, and then breathed in a deep lungful of incense. "Okay, here we go."

The tie between her and the ghosts hummed, snapping into place. Closing her eyes, lights flashed through her lids. The harsh odor of urine and manure burned her nose.

She opened her eyes, Wendy's eyes. She was in a barn.

Stumbling into an empty horse stall, her legs gave out, and she fell into a mound of straw. Whatever he'd drugged her with was strong. She needed to hide.

She turned over slowly and piled the straw around her. The prickly edges scraped her legs and caught on her sundress. She tried to slow her breathing, slow her squirming heart. The rafters above her spun in slow lazy circles like vultures. Waiting to pick her bones clean.

She'd been so stupid. Going off with a cute stranger had seemed perfect payback to her cheating boyfriend.

Footsteps sounded along the dirt floor. Measured and precise. He'd found her.

"I don't know why you ran from me," Paul said. The raspy voice that had captivated her now gnawed against her skin. "We're meant to be together."

The stall door hit the wall with a bang, and she flinched, the straw shifting, falling free. He yanked her up by her hair. She screamed and grabbed onto his gloved wrists. He threw her back to the floor. Like a cat playing with a toy.

"Don't," she mumbled, her tongue feeling too swollen in her mouth to speak clearly. "Please."

Sam dragged herself out of Wendy's anguish, the cold tendrils wrapped around her trying to hold her back. She pulled free finally and studied him. Long hair, past his ears, the same dark brown color as in Monica's memory. Scruff, but no beard. Average height and size. Brown eyes.

Wendy's fear sucked her back into the moment. She wasn't going to go down without a fight. She clawed at his face, but Paul reared back quickly, away from her reach. Then his fist slammed into her cheek. Once. Twice.

He gripped onto her throat like he couldn't let go, like he held on for his own life. Crushing her tendons. Her windpipe.

Sam needed to leave. Already her throat ached. It was hard to breathe. Wendy flailed and that's when Sam saw it. The same compass symbol on the inside of his arm, just above his wrist.

Sound disappeared, sucked away with the air in her lungs. His lips moved, but she couldn't hear what he said.

She'd seen enough. Sam pushed through the threads holding her in Wendy's memory. They clung to her, not wanting to give way. She needed to leap to Ellie's memory. She stretched her hand out and felt cold metal. Ellie's Tree of Life pendant.

Everything went black. A chill wind brushed the hair back from her sweaty cheeks. The smell of freshly cut grass warned Sam she'd entered a different memory.

When she opened her eyes, the bark of the beech trees was bright against the murky moonlight. Their limbs gleamed like bones.

Exposed roots hunched upon the ground. They were moving. Heaving toward her like they meant to drag her down, drag her under the wet soil.

She blinked her eyes and the images settled. He'd drugged her with something powerful.

In the distance, she saw the gardens and the manor house. If she could just make it there, Ms. Banberry would help her.

She used a tree trunk to steady herself, her mind replaying the night. They'd had dinner, and he'd kept her laughing the whole time. Paul was an amazing dancer. Light on his feet. Which probably meant he was fast.

Keep moving. She pushed herself forward a step. The world spun again, and she stumbled on one of the tree roots, falling face first to the ground.

"Dammit," she said, her lips coated in dirt.

Not trusting herself to stand again, she got to her knees and crawled. Her jeans grew wet from the grass. The lights in the distance beckoned her. Safety. Help.

"You always run." Paul's smooth voice said behind her. "I don't understand why."

Ellie stiffened, freezing. He was close.

What the fuck was he spouting about? She'd just met him to-night. In front of her, just a few feet away, was a tree limb. She'd have a weapon if she could summon the strength to use it. She dug her fingers into the cold wet soil and crawled, dragging herself forward.

"I love it when you get feisty." He laughed, like she'd done something adorable. "We did all the things you said you'd missed. I can make you happy. Just like he did."

A few inches more. Ellie's fingers closed on the tree limb, and she looked back over her shoulder. He stood behind her. "You're a lunatic."

Sam separated herself from Ellie's thoughts, though it was harder to do than with Wendy or Monica. The strands of memory were tighter, more like sticky ropes. She had almost forgotten she was a passenger and not really Ellie.

Sam memorized everything she could about Paul. Blond hair, clean shaven, blue eyes and glasses. Same tattoo above his wrist.

Then Ellie dragged her back inside the memory, and she swung out with the tree branch, catching Paul hard against the face. She'd bloodied him, though the scratch looked tiny in the moonlight.

She'd never be able to fight him off, but she could leave evidence for the police when they found her body. With everything she had remaining, Ellie threw the branch as far as she could. It whistled through the air, and the forest swallowed it whole.

Paul wiped the blood from his face with the edge of his shirt. When he looked down at her only coldness remained. Death.

Ellie crab-crawled backwards, afraid to turn away from him. He leapt on her, pinning her to the ground. She pummeled him, ripping his shirt, twisting left, then right, anything to get away. But her movements were small, weak.

He didn't budge. He stroked her neck almost lovingly and then began to squeeze.

Paul leaned in close and whispered.

Sparks danced in front of her eyes. But she'd heard him. She knew . . .

She'd stayed too long. Ellie's memory bound her, the strands constricting around her essence. She fought to break free, but only made it through a few layers before exhaustion stalled her efforts. If she didn't make it out of Ellie's memory, she didn't know what would happen to her. Maybe she was already dead on the floor in Kate's bedroom.

Kate. Beth. They could help her. Yasmin had called them the Triumvirate of Pluthar. Said they were strong together. "Can you hear me?" Sam shouted in her mind, picturing both women. "Beth, I need you. Kate, help me. Please." She felt a jolt of connection with Kate and Beth. She saw herself in their eyes. Passed out. Barely breathing. Then the connection was gone.

Ellie's memories lulled her backwards. *Let go*, they seemed to whisper.

Sam reached out, trying to touch another object in her world. Anything that might jump her into another memory. Someone gripped her hand.

She knew who it was. Felt his essence rush down her arm and into her mind. Robert.

"Samantha."

Her name roared through the air, sounding as if Robert screamed it with every ounce of his being. Ellie, Wendy, and Monica's voices joined in. A burst of energy yanked Sam upward.

The sky brightened overhead to white. There was a ceiling fan, cracks in the plaster overhead. She was on the floor of Kate's bedroom again.

"Holy crap," Beth yelled. "We'd thought we'd lost you."

Sam tried to speak, but her throat hurt too badly. Kate helped her sit up. "I'll get you something hot." She rushed from the room.

Ellie, Wendy and Monica, sagged against each other. Their

forms were almost transparent. By comparison, Robert looked more solid than ever.

"Ghosts helped," Sam whispered. "Thank you."

Robert nodded, his gaze brimming with something she hadn't seen since her parents were alive. He looked at her like she was the most important thing in his world.

"I will see them safely to Beatrice for healing." He wrapped his arms around the three ghosts. They disappeared.

The clock on the wall said three a.m. She'd been under for over an hour this time. Her connection with Kate and Beth hadn't helped. Maybe they weren't as connected as Yasmin thought? Maybe they weren't a triumvirate of anything?

Kate came back into the bedroom with a steaming cup in her hand. She handed the tea to Sam. "Are the ghosts gone?"

Sam nodded. "Gone."

"I heard something," Kate said as if she couldn't believe her own words. "When you were under. Your voice in my head." She slid to the floor next to Sam and nudged her with her shoulder.

Beth looked at Sam sharply. "Me too, but I thought I imagined it. Were you calling for us?"

"Yup." Less words were easier for her to manage with her throat.

"And we fucked up." Kate looked so guilty, Sam reached out and took her hand. "If it wasn't for the ghosts . . ."

"S'alright," Sam managed, though it was anything but. A chill swept through her body. She'd almost died.

Beth sat across from them. Her plush slippers were in the shape of pigs with devil horns. "Looks like Yasmin was right.

We need to learn how to use our powers together. Or we're in trouble. God, I hate feeling helpless." The words were muttered, but Sam heard them clearly.

Sam took Beth's hand slowly, giving her ample time to pull away. She didn't.

Beth held out her other hand to Kate who grasped it immediately. The familiar warmth surged through Sam again like it had outside Yasmin's shop.

"We'll figure it out," Sam said, hoping she was right.

Beth's lips curved into almost a smile. Almost a real one. "What makes you so sure? I don't even like you."

"Don't like you either," Sam lied.

Kate dropped their hands and poked Beth's knee. "Well, I like you both, so that's enough. Remember, we're the Triumvirate of excellence. Or was it the Triumvirate of goodness? Oh hell, I can't remember what Yasmin called us."

"Triumvirate of Pluthar," Sam said, feeling a little better than when she'd first woken up on the floor. Whatever the ghosts had given her in energy, she was healing more quickly than she expected. It didn't hurt to speak now.

"So what'd you see?" Beth asked. "Did you finally hear what he said?"

"He said, 'You're not Kate.' Right before he murdered them."

"What?" Kate's hand went to her chest, fingers grasping her locket.

Beth's face grew serious. "So, Kate isn't just a potential victim."

Sam shook her head slowly. "No. She's his end game."

CHAPTER 17

SAM FINISHED HER SCRAMBLED EGGS AT THE KITCHEN TABLE, surprised she had any appetite after last night. The killer was after Kate. Playing like he was Paul, her dead husband. The other women had been an opening act. A murderous prelude.

The morning light blazed through the glass of the backdoor. All Sam wanted to do was curl up on the floor in front of it like a cat. For everything else just to go away.

She glanced at the text from Michael on her phone. He said he might come by Kate's place on his way to his parents' next week. She hadn't replied yet. While it would be great to have his support through all this, she couldn't tell him what was really going on. More lying wasn't what she needed right now.

Kate bustled over and slid a fresh pancake onto her plate and one onto Beth's. "These are nice and hot." She went back to the stove to turn the sizzling bacon. Cooking equalled coping for Kate.

"We need to get her to talk about it," Sam said quietly to Beth.

Beth didn't look up from her tablet. "We do. Before we end up so full of food, we can't speak. I think that's her master plan."

Kate joined them at the table, setting down more syrup and a plateful of bacon. A loud crash sounded from upstairs. The bookshelf again.

Kate slid down into one of the seats and held her head in her hands. "That little shit needs to go if I'm going to have any chance reviving this B&B." She crunched a piece of bacon like she could masticate it into submission.

"I promise you I'll deal with the poltergeist after we handle the serial killer," Sam said. "Your life first, then the life of the B&B."

Beth cracked a yawn and leaned back in her chair. "The local newspaper isn't online, is it? I want to see the latest on the murder investigation."

Kate shook her head. "Nope. But I get a copy every morning. It's probably still outside."

A sharp rap rattled through the back door. All three women jumped. Through the glass, a dark shape blocked the sunlight, casting a long shadow into the kitchen.

Beth slipped her hand inside her robe and came out with a gun, gaze calm. "Expecting someone Kate?"

"I don't think anyone's going to kill us in the kitchen," Sam said. "In broad daylight."

Kate's eyes widened. "I can't believe you had that around my girls."

"It's got a safety." Beth said. "I'm not taking chances anymore." She got up and headed toward the door.

"This discussion isn't over, Beth." Kate rushed forward, beating Beth there. "It's probably Max. Sam met him at the bakery."

Sam nodded. "He's infatuated with Kate, which means he's a suspect."

A second knock sounded. More insistent this time. "You're being ridiculous, Sam. Max O'Toole is not a killer of anything but weeds." Kate's words were a whisper. She pointed at Beth. "You are not going to shoot him."

Beth slid the gun back into her robe. "Who is it?" Her voice brimmed with brightness, but her gaze was dark.

"It's Max. I help with the gardens," a deep voice said through the door. "Is Ms. Banberry at home?"

Kate opened the door. "Come right in, Max." She turned back to Sam and Beth, a warm smile on her face. "You'll have to excuse Beth's caution. She lives in Los Angeles. She's not used to being neighborly." She shot Beth a sharp look.

Bits of grass clung to the bottom of Max's pants. He smelled of fresh dirt, though his hands were clean. Max's smile brought out a deep dimple in his right cheek. "Oh, no worries, Kate. It's good to have friends looking out for you."

He stepped through the door, and the sun caught in his dark curly hair, bringing out glints of red.

Beth's mouth hung open. Sam shot her a look, and she closed it quickly.

"What brings you by so early?" Kate took him by the arm and led him to the kitchen island.

"Just wanted to bring in your paper," Max said. "Didn't mean to intrude on your get-together." Max fished the paper out of the side pocket of his worn barn jacket. "The lad managed to miss the front door again."

"Well, I'm glad you stopped by. I've made too many pancakes." Kate took down a mug from the cupboard and went to the coffee pot. "The usual?"

Max leaned his hands on the marble. "That'd be grand, Kate. Just grand. You're looking mighty fetching with your hair back like that."

A blush filled Kate's cheeks, making her look years younger. Her fingers hovered by her loose red curls. They'd escaped her ponytail as usual. "You're too nice, Max. I look like a bedraggled mess."

Max took his jacket off. The long-sleeved blue plaid shirt brought out the tan on his neck. "Not to me."

The rest of their conversation buzzed in Sam's ears while she studied Max, comparing him to the ghosts' memories.

Beth walked back over to Sam and sat next to her. Neither Max nor Kate seemed to even realize they were still there. "Does he fit what you saw?" Her voice was low. Her hand back in her pocket.

Sam nodded. "He's in the right age range." Her voice was the same pitch. Almost a whisper. "Late twenties to thirties." She munched on a piece of bacon to look busy.

"What about the rest?"

He seemed a little taller than Killer Paul, but then she noticed his work boots had a slight heel on them. The killer had been wearing loose clothes, so any muscles would have been concealed. It was going to be impossible to tell unless they found the tattoo. Sam rubbed the skin above her wrist, knowing Beth would instantly get her drift.

"I can't think of a good excuse to get him to strip," Beth said. Her expression grew thoughtful, as if she'd come up with one if she thought long enough.

Kate walked around the kitchen island toward them. "You remember Sam, and this is my other friend, Beth, who you unofficially met at the door." Max gave them both a wide grin.

Sam stood, her face growing warm. Hopefully he hadn't noticed any of their staring. "Hi. Nice to see you." It sounded awkward and about an octave too high.

Max nodded. "A pleasure again." He pointed a finger at Beth. "Aren't you that Marshall gal? The one who can find anything? My Da loves your show."

Beth put a hand on her hip, looking poised in her pjs and robe. Sam bet she'd look calm and collected stark naked.

"I'm glad your father likes my show. What did he think of our recent jaunt into the cemetery in Nashville?" Her voice had gone smooth, like there was a camera hidden somewhere.

"We loved it. Though we were stunned you found the necklace in the wrong grave."

Beth laughed. "It was a surprise to me too. I'm loving my visit with Kate so much I'm considering filming a few of my shows here. Do you have anything you'd like me to find?"

Sam shot Kate a quick look. Kate mouthed, "What the fuck?" from behind Max. Maybe Beth was trying to get more info about Max since he was on their suspect list?

Max grinned, the skin at the corners of his eyes crinkling. "Nothing from our family. The only heirloom is the famous pancake recipe from my great great something, Shamus O'Toole. But my Ma already has that. Keeps it under lock and key, she does." He winked at Kate. "Though, your pancakes are quickly surpassing hers." He clasped his hand to his chest. "Say you'll marry me, and I'll soon be the fattest gardener in all the land."

Kate waved her hands at him, laughing. "I'm sure you tell that to all your clients."

"There's no one quite like you, Kate," Max said, suddenly serious. "Believe me, I've looked." The last part was said under his breath, but Sam heard it. A chill crept through her skin. Beth stiffened beside her.

Max grabbed a bag near the back door. Sam heard the clink of tools. "I'm going to concentrate on the weeds today, if that's all right. They're getting a foothold in the lawn, and if I don't beat them back, Aggie will have my head." He turned back to Sam and Beth. "Very nice to meet you and see you again."

They murmured the appropriate responses, but waited until the door closed before they both turned to Kate.

"I'm going to be really upset if he's our killer," Beth said. "His ass is amazing. Are you sleeping with him?"

The smile on Kate's face disappeared. "Excuse me?"

"Just checking to see how close he's gotten to you. From your reaction, the answer is 'no'." Beth's tone was clinical and precise like she was cataloging facts in her mind.

"You don't know Max. I get it." Kate paused and then crossed her arms. "But he couldn't have strangled those women."

Sam pulled the rigid Kate over to the table and pushed her into a seat. "No one is saying that Max is the killer. Until we narrow it down more." She looked at Beth. "Have your powers changed so you can find things like tattoos? That might narrow it down."

"Nope. That still hasn't changed. It's got to be a thing thing. Something that can stand on its own." Beth took a sip of coffee. "We'll have to search the old-fashioned way. Since it's not exactly shirt-sleeve weather, how about any local massage places or spas? You have to be almost naked for most treatments."

"If we could only trust people to be quiet about our questions." Sam sat back down at the table. "We know he's a local. All the women were killed around the area, and there'd be no need to disguise himself if he wasn't from here."

Beth tilted her head. "Unless we have multiple killers."

Kate shook her head. "No, Sam already shot that theory down. When the ghosts cluster, it's because they were killed by the same person."

"Nice to see you paying attention to the Rules," Sam said.

"Maybe Sam heard wrong and he didn't say my name." Kate pointed at her. "He could've just said 'great.' You're not great."

"He didn't." Sam hated the scared look flitting around the edges of Kate's face. "For some reason Killer Paul is using other women who look like you. Eventually he's not going to be satisfied with a copy."

Beth opened up her notebook. "Maybe he's practicing?

From what Sammy said, he's trying to do things to make the fake Kates happy."

The color drained from Kate's cheeks. "Does he think we're going to be together?" She grasped her coffee cup, the china chattering against the saucer. "If so, why murder the other women?"

"Because they aren't really you. They're inferior in his mind." Sam massaged her temples, feeling tired. "Who the hell knows? We're not profilers. We're just supposing what a psychopath's motive is."

"This is really happening, isn't it?" Kate's last two words stuttered slightly.

Sam gripped her hand, willing her strength into Kate. "That's why I'm here. My powers wouldn't have come back just because. They came back to help you."

Kate swallowed and then sat up a little straighter. "The girls need to be further away than Stu and Aggie's. The poltergeist is one thing. This killer is something else. I need to know they're safe."

Sam sat back in her seat. She was right. The girls needed to be removed from the killer's chessboard. Just in case. "Do Stu and Aggie have any relatives nearby? The B&B isn't open, so neither of them is needed right now. They could take the girls on a trip."

"Aggie has a sister in Aberdeen." Kate nodded. "If Riley goes, they won't ask questions. They'll think it's an adventure."

Beth touched Kate's shoulder. "Great idea. Aggie and Stu will take good care of them while we take care of you." Sam hadn't heard that caring voice in years.

"I know I suggested it, but we could be putting Aggie and Stu in danger," Sam said. "What if the killer tracks the girls down to use them as leverage?"

Kate shook her head. "Stu's ex-military, and Aggie can handle herself. She was a private eye. I'll talk to them today."

Sam exchanged a surprised look with Beth. She wouldn't have pegged the caretakers as anything other than a kindly old couple.

Sam got up and poured another cup of coffee for Kate. Beth already had out the cream and sugar to doctor it up just the way she liked it. Funny how well they worked together when they weren't at each other's throats.

"Here," Sam pushed the mug toward Kate. "Once we've got the killer handled and the poltergeist booted, the girls will be back and your B&B will be on the way to recovery."

Kate looked dazed. "I've never been targeted by a whack-job before."

"That's not true," Beth said. "What about Roger in the fourth grade? He named his hamster after you. Had a little shrine with your pictures around the cage."

Kate giggled and then froze. "Wait, why don't we talk to Logan about what we've found out? He knows the people here. He might know who has the tattoo."

"Have you seen Logan's arms?" Beth said.

Kate sat up straight like someone had rammed a rod against her spine. "Stop right there. Logan is not the killer."

Sam shot a quick look toward Beth. "Answer the question,

Kate. Does Logan have the tattoo?" Kate wouldn't hide something like that from them, not even if she believed they were wrong about Logan.

"No. Honestly, I don't know." Kate shook her head. "He doesn't wear short-sleeves often. I never looked."

"Then we shouldn't involve him any further in this." Beth held a hand up toward Kate. "Just until we know more."

Kate's gaze snapped back and forth between them. "We can't have the main criteria being anyone who's given me the time of day. That's ridiculous."

Beth flipped open her notebook. "Well, if we used that as our guideline, half the town would be a suspect. Case in point, the plumber yesterday could barely keep his eyes off you long enough to fix the pipes."

"And Logan is more than just someone who gives you the time of day, Kate," Sam said. "You can't deny that. Though the plumber is too old, and I saw his arms. No tattoo."

Beth lips thinned and then relaxed back to their natural fullness. "It was just an example. Kate is Miss Popularity in this town."

"So, let's make a list of the . . . potentials." Sam swallowed the word *suspects*, knowing what Kate's reaction would be. "We've got Logan."

Kate harrumphed, sounding much like Beatrice, but didn't say anything further.

"And Max," Sam continued. "We should add Graham too."

"Is that the guy at Yasmin's shop who was giving Kate the goo-goo eyes?"

Kate slammed her fist on the table. The sugar bowl lost its top. "He wasn't giving me goo-goo eyes. Oh hell, I'm not going to win with either of you. Fine, add Graham to the list."

"Anyone else?" Beth asked.

"Isn't that enough?" Kate said.

A ripple in the air moved the hair back from Sam's shoulders. Wisps of white and gray swirled just behind Kate like bits of cloth caught in the wind. It was a ghost, but it hadn't materialized yet. Sam's energy rushed out through her pores, siphoned by the ghost. She gripped the edge of the table, unable to stop the drain.

"It's a . . ." Sam's words fled back down her throat, chased by a sudden, choking fear.

The ghost was petite with porcelain skin and red hair. Another version of Kate. Bruises circled her neck. She stared at Sam with dark assessing eyes.

"Snap out of it." Beth shook Sam, breaking the line of her gaze, and she could finally breathe. "What's going on?"

Sam managed only a whisper. "There's been another murder." She looked between Kate and the ghost. "We're running out of time."

CHAPTER 18

"I'M SAM." SHE STARED AT THE NEW GHOST, HOPING SHE couldn't see the dread seeping through her. How many more would die before they could find the killer?

The air near the ghost shimmered, and then Beatrice appeared a few feet away followed by Robert. He gave her a small bow. "Pardon our intrusion, Samantha."

Just having him here gave Sam a jolt of strength. "I'm happy to see you, Robert. You and Beatrice."

Beth wrote in her notebook. "Okay, we've got Robert, Beatrice, and an unknown victim. Any other ghosts?"

Beatrice shook her head. "None that'll come near this lass for a bit. Not until she settles and accepts her death."

"No other ghosts," Sam told Beth.

Beatrice patted the ghost's shoulder. "What's your name?"

"Amber Peters," the ghost replied, her voice sounding like sandpaper against wood. She rubbed her bruised throat. "This isn't fair. He's got to be stopped." Her eyes flashed, reminding Sam of Ellie's when they'd first met.

"Her name is Amber Peters," Sam said. "She could be Kate's sister. Same color hair, pale skin, petite. And she's American."

Kate looked over her shoulder at the calendar on the refrigerator. "There's always been a few months between the murders. But Ellie's only been gone a month.

Beth chewed on the tip of her pen. "He's escalating. Let's get the details down so we nail him before there's another victim."

Amber swallowed and then winced. "Ellie and the others told me I should talk to you." Her voice sounded a bit less rough than before. It grew stronger. "One minute he was choking me and the next, I was with them." Amber looked around. "This isn't Heaven, is it?"

"No, it's not Heaven." Sam glanced at Beth and Kate. "It's definitely the same killer. Amber met the other three when she died."

Amber looked down. "I tried to fight him off. I did. Why did this happen to me?"

Robert took a small step forward. "It is all right now, lass," he said in a soothing voice. "He cannot hurt you any longer."

"You've got to stop him." Amber crossed her arms, pulling her leather jacket closer around her. "I had plans, dreams. I didn't get to have kids." Her voice rose with each word.

Robert took her into his arms and stroked her hair. "My life ended sooner than it should have too. It appears Fate has other plans for us. Ones we cannot foresee."

Amber gasped for breath, trying to speak in between sobs. Her eyes widened. "What are my parents going to do? I was all they had."

"What's going on?" Beth said.

"Robert's helping Amber." She hated she couldn't do more. Couldn't even comfort the victims. At least Robert was able to help.

Robert rocked Amber in his arms and sang. His words were of longing, of final acceptance, of there being a balance to all things, good and bad. Sam had never heard anything so beautiful. It felt like he sang not only to them, but to the Universe.

She'd never met a man who was so kind, so caring. Someone who thought about everyone else first. Who knew what she could do and thought it was wonderful.

He finished, and Beatrice sighed. "I can't believe you remember that. I used to sing it to you when you were a bairn."

Amber pulled back from Robert to stand on her own. She appeared calmer, but tears streaked her cheeks. She looked so much like Kate. Too much.

Kate waved her hand in front of Sam's face. "Can we have some close-captioning for the ghostly-impaired?"

Sam grabbed Kate's hand across the table. "I do not want to see your ghost before you're good and old, Kate. You hear me? Promise me you'll stop fighting and let us protect you."

Kate's skin flushed. "I promise."

Beth leaned back in her chair. "Finally."

"No one else should die like I did either," Amber said. The

haunted look was still there, but it was not as forlorn as before. "What can I do to help?"

"Did he have a tattoo near his wrist?" Sam asked.

Amber nodded. "Ellie asked about that too. The top part was a compass, but the bottom was faded."

"She confirmed the tattoo," Sam told the others. "The same one."

Beth wrote it down. "What else?"

"He didn't have a Scottish accent," Amber said. "That part doesn't match what Ellie or the others told me. I thought he was American, like me. That's why I went with him for coffee. Fellow compatriot and all in a foreign city."

"She thought he was American."

Beth sat up straight. "That's new."

"I know where you're going to go with this, Sam." Kate's head shook back and forth. "Lots of people can fake an American accent around here. Hell, they stream Beth's show along with other American TV. It's not unusual."

Beth looked at Sam. "Who're you thinking of?"

"Logan. He showed off his skill at the police station."

"Holy shit." Beth slammed her notebook shut. "I hoped it wasn't going to be him. You two are sugar-overload cute together, Kate."

Kate shook her head. "It's not him. It can't be."

Amber's form flickered, growing hazy. "Not good at this yet," Amber managed to say though she was just a bare wisp of shape. "I'll try to come back later. I—" She disappeared.

"She's gone." Sam's temples throbbed. She'd need to include

Amber in the Bargain soon. Otherwise, she'd be drained whenever she showed up.

Beatrice stepped forward, almost clicking her heels together when she stopped. "Now that the lass is handled, we need your help with Ray. If we don't get rid of the geist, we'll lose our best chance to clear Lord Robert's name."

"It's on my list already." Sam pinched the bridge of her nose, the headache traveling down to her sinuses. "I've promised to help Robert clear his name, but we've got bigger issues. Lives are being lost and Kate could be next."

Beatrice leaned in close. "You know very well Robert must cross over before *certain* parties become interested. If you care for him, you'll help us. Or is he just another ghost to you? Another nuisance?"

"That is unnecessary," Robert said. "And uncalled for."

Sam rose to her feet, pushed up by anger. She looked at Beatrice and Robert. "Both of you, the study. Now." They blinked out immediately.

"Why do we have to go to the study?" Kate said. "I need to get dressed and over to Stu's to see the girls."

Beth shook her head. "You were talking to the ghosts weren't you?"

"Yes." Sam headed for the hallway. "I remember again why I hated this so much."

ROBERT GLARED AT BEATRICE. THEY WERE SUDDENLY IN THE study. "Did you pull me along with you?"

"No." Beatrice's face was pale. "I believe it was the Necromancer. She willed it."

"She has such power?"

Beatrice swallowed. "I underestimated her."

Samantha stormed into the study. Her slippers slapped against the hardwoods. Beatrice backed up, out of her way. Samantha dropped heavily into an armchair by the fire and looked at both of them. Her eyes flashed, and for a moment Robert thought he saw the arc of lightning in their depths.

"What's this about you needing to get rid of the poltergeist?"

Robert stepped closer. "Please do not be upset with Beatrice. She thinks only of my safety."

Samantha leaned back in the chair. Weariness replaced the anger in her face. "Tell me what's going on."

He finally had a glimpse into the burden of her gift. She would always be called on, always be sought after to help others find peace. But where was her own?

He cleared his throat. "Ray will not leave the manor. We need your assistance."

Her gaze shifted to Beatrice. "And why are you two dabbling in poltergeist removal?"

"Another ghost promised us the location of my lord's journal." Beatrice's earlier unease had disappeared. "If we get rid of Ray."

"You hid a journal here?" Samantha said. "I knew there

was a clue here somehow to help you."

"I kept it during my relationship with Sarah." Robert walked over to the fire, staring into its depths. "She had many suitors besides me. One of them killed her. I am sure of it."

Samantha looked down at her hands. "Even with my iron daggers, I barely wounded Ray. I'm not sure how I'll get rid of him."

"We do not want you to kill him." Robert glanced toward the door to the hall. "Ray is in great pain. We want to find out what will make him let go and move on. That will accomplish the same end."

"I can't go into a poltergeist's memory," Samantha said. "I don't think I'd ever get out."

"That won't be necessary," Beatrice said. She paced in front of the fireplace. "Ray indicated we should consult the Oracle, the Seeker, and *our* Necromancer."

"So, you thought he meant Kate, Beth, and I?"

Beatrice nodded. "It made sense. My Kate can see the future. Beth finds things. Together you should be able to figure this out."

Samantha sat up straight. "Wait a second." She pointed a finger at Robert. "How do you know what Ray is feeling, his great pain?"

"I spoke with him." Robert sensed her rising distress. "I also managed to glimpse some of his memories."

Samantha stood, her entire body rigid. "Beatrice should know how dangerous it is for a ghost to face a poltergeist. She wouldn't have allowed you near that thing." Her gaze searched his face. "But you got close, didn't you? You'd have had to in order to get his memories."

"I did it for you," Robert said.

"Why would you risk yourself like that? Are you so anxious to move on?"

Robert's breath hitched in his lungs. The naked pain and longing in her eyes told him more than anything she said. The feelings she had hinted about were deeper than he realized. Maybe deeper than she realized. She knew what he had done, the pain he had caused his family, and still she cared for him enough to fear for his existence?

A small shoot of hope pushed its way through the regret and darkness inside him. Not blooming yet, but yearning for the sun of redemption.

"Rest assured, dear Samantha, I have no wish to leave you." He let his words hang in the air, knowing she would detect any falsehood. He was still uncertain how they could be together, but Samantha held the living and the dead in her grasp. Perhaps she could find a way for them?

She smiled at Robert, and it was like sunlight touched every inch of her face. Then she looked over at Beatrice and sobered. "Just promise me you'll be more careful."

"We will," Robert said. "You have my word."

"I'll ask Kate and Beth if they have any ideas on how to crack the mystery of Ray. But first and foremost is finding the killer." She gazed at Beatrice. "I refuse to have any more ghosts come my way as victims because we delayed. And there's the Bargain I made with them to consider. I won't break it. The poltergeist situation has to wait."

Beatrice smoothed her apron. "As it should be." Her voice was tight, and Robert detected a dose of contriteness. "I just didn't want you to forget about my lord. And the consequences of delay *there*."

Samantha gazed around the room, searching. "Some ghosts just came in. They're not materialized, so I can't see them. Who else is here with us?" She looked at Robert. "Is it the ghost you said is helping you?"

Robert glanced around. Several ghosts lurked in the back of the room, observing. They were too far away for him to make out much but dark clothing and morose features. Closer were two women from his time, judging by the cut of their dress, who stood by the window making a big show of looking at the wallpaper.

"Just riffraff." Beatrice fixed the ghosts with a fine glare. "Shoo, the rest of you, or I'll make sure a Runner finds your hiding spots." The ghosts did not appear happy, but they obeyed Beatrice one by one.

Robert clasped his hands behind his back. "The ghost who has agreed to assist us is named Caleb. He commands the woods on these grounds."

Samantha's brows drew together. "Commands the woods?"

"He *is* the woods." Beatrice's voice held a note of pride.

"I'd like to meet him, talk to him." Samantha seemed excited by the prospect.

"I can assure you an audience with Caleb is no pleasure," Robert said.

"You don't understand. Ellie was killed in the woods. She hit her attacker with a tree branch." She paced in front of the fireplace. "If I could find that branch, and it had his blood on it still, we could run DNA tests . . ."

"What are DNA tests?" Robert whispered to Beatrice, not wanting to disturb Samantha's train of thought.

Beatrice whispered back. "You can tell by the blood who the killer is."

The marvels of this time continued to amaze him. What was next? A machine that could see inside your body?

Samantha ticked off items on her fingers. "We'd have to get DNA samples from the suspects. Logan will be easy, and so will Max. We'd have to come up with some pretense for Graham. If it's not any of them, we're up shit creek again."

"So you believe this is all the work of one killer?" Robert said.

"It is." Samantha gave a quick nod. "I'm sure of it."

"I also thought the same with the murders in my time." For a moment Robert saw the journal in front of him and the notes he had left for Lillian. "I believed there was a connection with Sarah's murder and the others."

"You think her death was part of something larger?" Beatrice said. Her face paled. "You never mentioned this before."

Robert met her worried gaze. "I did not want to involve you. It was suspicion. I had no real proof."

Samantha grew still. "Did you go to the authorities?"

Robert nodded. "I pleaded with the Justiciar, but he would not listen to me."

"What if the reason we were brought together wasn't only to

help clear your name?" Samantha's gaze held his. "What if these two killing sprees are connected somehow?"

"How?" Robert said.

"I don't know. But we're working on two serial murderers that are somehow connected to people who've lived in this house. Unless it's a coincidence?"

Robert thought upon her question carefully. "I do not believe in coincidences."

Samantha looked grim. "I'll do some research on the murders from your time." Samantha slid her hands into the pockets of her robe. "When can I meet Caleb?"

"We should visit after the geist is handled, otherwise Caleb will not consider granting your request regarding the tree branch," Robert said.

"You should think of what you can trade for Caleb's information," Beatrice said. "Nothing's for free with that one."

Samantha lifted her chin slightly. "A ghost always needs something only I can give. The real question is whether or not his information is worth it to me to make a Bargain."

She turned and stalked out of the study. The ends of her robe flared out behind her as if she were wearing queenly garb. Robert felt as flummoxed as the boy, Riley, had appeared in the garden when faced with his love.

Beatrice snapped her fingers in front of his face. "You've changed your mind, haven't you? About her? About being worthy?"

"I have."

Beatrice glared at him, but it did not last. "I'm pleased

you've stopped punishing yourself, but this path will only lead to pain for both sides."

"This time I know what I risk. My gaze is clear, and I cannot falter." They walked out and down the hallway together. "A great woman taught me to never give up on what my heart most desired."

"Sounds like a foolish woman to me," Beatrice grumbled. "What happened to her?"

"She is still by my side." He slid his arm around her waist. "Advising me, guiding me, helping me."

"And obviously doing a terrible job of it."

He stopped and hugged her until finally, she hugged him back. "I would not have it any other way, dear Beatrice."

CHAPTER 19

"IF WE GET RID OF THE POLTERGEIST," SAM SAID TO KATE and Beth, "we can leverage that with Caleb and hopefully find the tree branch Ellie used to hit the killer."

Beatrice and Robert gave her approving nods. They stood by the kitchen island.

Beth took her chewed-up pen from her mouth. She hadn't moved from her earlier position at the table. "So, this crazy poltergeist thinks the three of us somehow know why he's here?"

"That's what he told Robert and Beatrice."

Kate tapped the outside of her coffee mug with her fingers. "I don't like that we're just titles. Like who we are doesn't matter, only *what* we are."

"Destiny is not going to shackle us, if that's what you're getting at." Beth looked at both of them. "We control our lives."

Sam had never believed in destiny. Hell, she'd ignored her own power for years. But there were too many intersections for all this to be completely chance.

Robert leaned in slightly. "Perhaps if I recounted what I gleaned from Ray's mind, it would help?"

"Yes, please." Sam turned to the others. "Robert's going to tell me what he remembers."

"I saw a young girl in his memory. She seemed to mean a great deal to him." Robert's gaze grew distant. "There was a sense of falling. The crack of a firearm. The heavy scent of pipe tobacco."

Sam repeated everything Robert said. At the mention of the pipe, Beth jumped to her feet.

"The pipe." She rushed from the room and returned moments later. She placed the pipe in the center of the table. "It's the reason I came here."

Sam studied the pipe closely. The amber swirls of wood lightened toward the bowl, much like cream mixing with coffee. A bright square of silver bisected the stem, stamped with the initials, RMP.

Robert nodded. "That appears to be the one I saw."

"Robert recognizes it from his time with Ray." Sam gestured to Beatrice. "Do we show it to Ray?"

Beatrice stared at each of them, seeming to mull things over. "Beth found the pipe. I think that's her piece done. You're going to have to talk to Ray and get him to move on. That's your part as Necromancer."

Sam looked at Kate. "So, that leaves you."

"Leaves me, what?" Kate straightened, looking nervous.

"You're the only one who hasn't done anything yet." Beth lifted her coffee mug and gestured toward Kate. "I brought the pipe, Sam will do her mojo with Ray, but you still need to play."

Kate inched back in her chair, away from the pipe. "What if I don't want to play?"

Sam saw something resembling waves of heat rising from the pipe. They floated in the air toward Kate. "Do you see anything funny, Beth?" She pointed at the pipe.

Beth squinted her eyes and then sat back. "I do."

Beatrice and Robert stared at the pipe as well. "I see Ray's essence around it," Beatrice said slowly. "He must have had this a long time."

"The ghosts see it too," Sam said.

"You're all crazy." Kate got up, looking like she was going to bolt.

She'd never seen Kate interact with an object, but something was off. And if Beth, Beatrice and Robert saw it too, it was definitely happening. Sam stood and walked around the table to her. "It's affecting you, isn't it?"

Kate's face was white. "How do you know that?"

"Whatever I saw headed right for you." Sam looked down at the scar on her thumb. "Maybe our connection is growing stronger. What are you feeling when you look at it?"

Kate pushed past Sam and sat at the table again. "Scared. That *thing* is screaming at me." Her voice was strained.

"Hey Sammy, can you do your memory thing with Ray?" Beth crossed her arms. "Maybe Red's part is something else?"

Sam shook head. "I won't be any help with Ray's memories. I barely escaped from the other memory journeys, and those were just ghosts, not poltergeists." Sam got the coffee pot and refilled their cups. "And I can only see the moments before their death. That might not be the moment we need."

Kate dumped cream and sugar in her coffee. She slid the creamer carton in front of the pipe, blocking it. "This is a waste of time. My visions are never connected with objects. They just happen."

Beth shook her head. "Our powers are changing, remember? That thing is talking to you. As much as I hate to admit it, it's gotta be a sign."

"You don't believe in signs." Kate frowned.

"I do when they're screaming at you."

"We should not risk your friend in this endeavor," Robert said. "We will find another way." Even when it meant putting his own goals on hold, here he was again, thinking of others first.

Sam touched Kate's hand. "Robert feels we should try something else, but I think you know what you have to do, don't you? Like I know the Rules?"

Kate clutched her hand, so hard it hurt. "What if I don't want to?" Her voice was tiny, reminding Sam of when they were kids.

"We'll be here for you." Sam nodded toward Beth. "We've got to keep trying this team thing until we get it right."

Kate didn't say anything for what felt like forever to Sam. But she finally hung her head, her shoulders drooping. "Fine, I'll do it. But I might get stuck and come back with Ray in my mind." She raised her head and pinned each of them with a stare. "If I do, you'll need to stop me from doing anything awful. Who knows what's going on in his head?"

Beth picked up a nearby wooden spoon and swung it toward Kate, stopping an inch from her nose. "Consider us warned. I'll bean you if necessary."

Sam looked at the concern on Beatrice's and Robert's faces. "We'll take care of her."

They disappeared. Beatrice was the last to go, her eyes fixed on Kate.

Kate's hands shook slightly as she held them open toward Sam, cupping them together. "Bring it on."

Sam picked up the pipe. Kate gave her a quick nod, and Sam dropped it into her hands. Kate froze. Limbs stiff, muscles clenched, eyes glazed over in white.

THE PIPE HIT KATE'S PALMS, AND THE KITCHEN disintegrated around her, disappearing. Suddenly she was in an unfamiliar wood paneled room.

Fireplace, old couch, thread-bare carpet, tiny kitchenette to the side, and a window in front of her. The smell of burnt toast sat heavy in the air, mixing with the vanilla plumes of smoke coming from the pipe in her hand. The heavily-veined hand in front of her wasn't her own.

So far, this seemed the same as her visions of the past. Which meant she knew what was coming next. She hated this part.

Her vision grew fuzzy, as if acid devoured the edges. Ray's

memory rose through her, sliding cold fingers against her skin, wrapping her tight. Kate didn't fight, didn't struggle, didn't hesitate. She might not like the drill, but she knew it. In seconds she'd cease to be herself.

She'd become Ray. She'd think like Ray. She'd—

Ray stared at the window, watching the mountain in the distance rise up and then fall with each movement of his rocking chair. The rhythm used to soothe him, but now it was merely a reminder of how useless he'd become. Sitting all day with an aching back.

"Here, Dad." Phyllis handed him a pillow. His daughter looked tired. Not surprising. She'd been working two jobs since his accident. "You know you're getting too old to sit on that thing without some support."

"What would I do without you?" he said and sincerely meant it. He'd been nothing but a burden to her. Would have been better if he'd have died at the factory. At least then she'd have his insurance money.

He slid the pillow behind the small of his back. The tight muscles released their grip on his spine one finger at a time.

"You were there for me and Mom, Dad. It's my turn now." Phyllis smiled and for a moment, she looked like his dear Doris. He took the pipe from his mouth, unable to inhale past the tears in his throat.

She grabbed her coat from the hook by the door. "Dinner's in the fridge for later. Mary's still out playing. Make sure to call her back in when it starts to get dark."

He nodded. "Will do." He saluted her, knowing it would

make her laugh, which it did. At least he could still do that much.

A chill climbed its way through his sweater. The fire only warmed one of his legs. The other had been so badly mangled, he'd lost feeling from the knee down. They didn't have money for a wheelchair ramp, and it didn't make much sense on a farm anyway. So, he hobbled along so slowly the seasons changed before he made it twenty feet.

Exhaustion slipped through him, as it did most days. His rocking slowed, his eyes drooping, closing. There were hours left of daylight still. He'd just take a quick nap, and then call for Mary.

The frigid air on his face startled him awake. A sharp wind blew through the open window, rustling the papers on the coffee table. The fire had just about gone out. The room was dark, matching the gloom outside.

Dark. His head whipped around to the clock on the wall and then back to the window. It was nine o'clock.

"Mary, honey. You here?" he shouted, though he knew she wasn't. She would have woken him when she'd come in. No doubt his granddaughter was chasing fireflies and had lost track of time.

He got to his feet slowly, using his cane. With a shuffling gate, he made it to the door and opened it. The frail moonlight barely dented the night. He flipped on the outside light, flooding the front yard in a yellow glow.

"Mary," he yelled. "It's time to come home, darling. I've got dinner waiting for you."

The only sound was the creaking branches of the nearby trees moving in the wind. Usually she shouted back right away. She never strayed far from the house. The skin above his upper lip grew slick with sweat.

"Mary," he bellowed again. This time, it wasn't the wind who answered.

It was the sound of wood breaking. And a scream.

Fear slammed a spur in his ass, pushing adrenaline through his body. He rushed down the stairs and almost fell flat on his face. His legs still thought they could move as they once had. "I'm coming, Mary."

He knew where she was. Knew she was in danger. He didn't have time to call anyone to help.

He half walked, half dragged himself through the field toward the old well.

"Help me!"

Mary's voice sliced through him.

A flash of white up ahead confirmed his fears. She'd been playing on top of the old boarded-up well, and the rotted wood had given way.

"Lord, don't let her fall. I'll promise anything you want." *She's only ten years old. Please don't let her die.* He wasn't sure whether he spoke the words aloud or in his heart, but he prayed they'd be heard.

"I'm coming girl," he shouted and urged his old limbs to move faster. He went down several times in his rush to save her, but pulled himself up again and again. Somewhere along the way, he lost his cane, but he couldn't afford to go back.

He reached the well, and saw her whitened fingers gripping the stone lip.

"Grandpa," she cried. "I can't hold on."

Bracing himself against the base of the abandoned well, he leaned forward and saw Mary dangling over the blackness below. Her white shirt was torn, and there were scratches on her hands, wet with blood.

"Hang on," he said and grabbed her wrists. The full weight of her body nearly pulled his arms from their sockets. His granddaughter scrabbled with her feet against the wall, trying to climb, but the movement just pushed her back out, further into the center of the well.

"Keep still." Ray pulled back. He managed to raise her up an inch or two, but she was so heavy and kept wriggling. His grip slipped on the blood from her hands.

He jammed his knees against the stone lip, bracing himself to lift her up the rest of the way. Something cracked inside his body. His right leg gave way. Her weight yanked him up and over the well's edge. His belt buckle caught against the stone, jerking him to a stop.

Mary's wrists slipped free. He grasped at her skin, her shirt, anything to hold onto her, but she plummeted.

"Grandpa!" Mary screamed, her hands clawing the air toward him. The oval of her face stretched long, eyes widening, mouth open. Then, the darkness devoured her.

Ray lay over the well's lip, hands still thrust forward, blood dripping down his fingers. He listened for a sound, for anything that would tell him Mary had survived the fall, but he knew she hadn't. There was no water left in the bottom, only sharp rocks.

Why had his body failed him? Why had he let her slip? Why had he survived?

The thoughts repeated in his brain. Each refrain like a nail piercing his skin. He inched forward, closer to the dark chasm below. It would be easy to join her. He deserved a dark and lonely death.

But someone had to tell Phyllis what happened. They might never find Mary's body otherwise and he wouldn't have his daughter thinking Mary ran away or got kidnapped. He owed her that much closure at least.

His remaining strength dried up. He slid back, away from the well, hitting the ground hard. Hot tears rolled down his cheeks, breath hitched in his throat, hands clenched and un-clenched, heart so constricted he barely felt the beat of it in his chest.

After what felt like hours, Ray used the cracked brick of the well to pull himself up to his feet. He'd go home and tell Phyllis, and then he'd figure out a way to kill himself. To pay for what he did.

But what would happen to Emily and Patty if she killed herself? The thought of her daughters jolted through Kate. She felt like she'd wakened from a horrible nightmare.

She'd found out what she needed. What secret poor Ray harbored. What he had gone through was horrible and it was all her fault. How could she go on living after letting Mary die?

Mary? No, Emily and Patty. Kate tried to shake Ray's

thoughts, to free her mind, but he clung to her like gum wadded up on her shoe. Her thoughts her own one moment, then coated in regret and despair. His emotional cling wrap smothered her. No matter which way she wriggled free, he clasped onto her again.

If she didn't break loose, she could come back in her body as Ray and kill herself before Beth and Sam knew what was happening.

She couldn't always break free, which is why she hadn't wanted to do this. Usually thoughts of Paul and her kids grounded her. She pictured her husband, the way he would smile at her when he first woke up. How they'd try out new recipes together and make a mess.

Her breath came easier. The laughter of her daughters chasing Riley echoed in her ears.

She'd never hear Mary laugh again, though. Someone needed to pay.

Holy crap. Adrenaline shot around her ribcage and pooled in her stomach. This was bad. Time for Plan B. The Triumvirate card.

"Sam, Beth. Get me out of here. Now." She repeated the words in her mind.

Like the moon in the distance, she sensed them, but couldn't reach them. Something blocked her.

Kate found herself in the wood paneled room again. Notepaper in front of her. A suicide note. Her hand shifted from smooth and white to old and gnarled. *No, no, no.*

Okay Plan C. A barrier. Something to stop Ray's memories.

Sam used barriers for ghosts. How had she done it? A wall. She'd built a wall inside herself to block out the emotions, but Kate couldn't focus on something that structured. Something easier. Strong, but manageable. A bubble.

Kate pulled her essence in tight and pictured a clear bubble around herself like the ones the girls would blow from a pink wand in summertime.

Mary used to blow bubbles. She'd run through the grass, chasing them. No. She had to stop thinking of Mary. Kate poured her love for the girls, her love for Paul and her love for her friends into the bubble. Her breath grew harsh, labored. The membrane was thin, but she felt it there.

The wood paneled room shimmered and disappeared. She was Kate. Her bubble was suddenly out in the middle of a vast ocean. Except the water wasn't water. Dark waves slammed into her bubble, each moaning with Ray's toxic pain, sparking against the membrane. Tiny cracks appeared along the top.

She needed to kill herself for what she'd done. Mary was dead because of her. *All her fault.*

Kate jerked away from Ray's thoughts, scrambling back, but there was no escape. His desire for death seeped in through the cracks.

Fear pulsed through her chest with each pained beat of her heart. She squeezed her eyes shut. What was she going to do?

"You're going to take a breath," said a voice she didn't recognize. A Scottish accented voice.

She cracked an eye open and found a red-haired older lady

in a dark dress with an apron and a white cap on her head. The bubble wasn't that big. They were almost eye to eye. Was this part of Ray's memory? But as soon as she had the thought, she knew it wasn't true. Maybe it was her own hallucination? "Who are you?"

"I'm Beatrice."

"You mean hunky hunky Robert's Beatrice?"

Beatrice frowned but it fought to be a smile. "Yes, Robert is very dear to me. But we're not here to talk about him. You need to get out of here now."

Kate realized she couldn't feel Ray's thoughts or emotions. When she looked outside the bubble, the water had stopped, waves frozen in place. "Are you doing that?"

Sweat dripped down Beatrice's forehead. "Yes, but I can't hold it for long."

Even though she was in dire circumstances, Kate couldn't help the huge smile stretching across her face. "I'm seeing a ghost. I'm seeing and talking to a ghost."

Beatrice laughed and patted her arm. "Oh yes, you are definitely one of my own kin. We tend to see the humor even in the darkest moments. But that's not why I'm here. I felt you struggling against the pipe."

"You did?"

"Yes. You already have all the power you need to separate from Ray and get yourself back to the kitchen."

The longer Kate looked at her, the more she could see a bit of Emily around the eyes. And Patty's mouth had the same firm set. This was her relative. Her blood. "Just tell me what do."

"You're the Oracle. Start acting like it." Her words were firm, matter-of-fact.

"What does that even mean?"

Beatrice leaned in close, starting to fade away. "It means get your ass in gear. Now." Then she disappeared.

The top part of the bubble shivered, reminding Kate of what an egg must look like from the inside before a baby chicken hatched.

She'd run out of options. There was no more time. Beatrice said she could do it on her own, so that meant she could. But how? What would the Oracle do?

She thought of the myths about oracles, the TV shows she'd seen, books she'd read. Oracles were all powerful. And strong. She'd been trying to be normal for her girls, not give in to her changing powers. But now was not the time to hold back.

If she was the Oracle, she controlled this landscape and everything that happened here. Kate didn't hesitate any longer. She punched the top of the cracking bubble, shattering it. She didn't need to be afraid. This was her construct, her world.

She placed her hands on her hips in her best superhero pose, wishing for a cape, but her t-shirt and jeans would have to do. "I'm running the show here and you can't do shit to me," she shouted into the blackness. "So, back the fuck off. I'm going home."

The waves vibrated for a moment as if they still struggled to reach her, and then with a cry they broke apart, pieces of Ray's memory falling around her, dying in the ocean of her mind.

The surface calmed, and Kate didn't feel Ray any longer.

Her body shook, and she found herself back in the kitchen. Beth stood in front of her, brandishing a wooden spoon, aiming it right at her head.

CHAPTER 20

"How many eggs go into your pancake batter?" Beth said, her hand clenched around a wooden spoon.

She didn't want to hurt Kate, but she'd knock her out if she was trapped in that whacko's memory.

"What are you talking about?"

Sam cast a worried look at Kate. "Just answer it. If you're really Kate."

"Fine. Four eggs. Now put that down." Kate gave her a mom-worthy stare. "That's my favorite spoon for cooking custard, and if you break it I'll . . ."

"It's her," Sam and Beth said at the same time, and then exchanged a relieved glance. Beth hated to admit it, but it was nice not being in the middle of a shit storm alone while they waited like nervous parents for Kate to wake up. She put the spoon on the table.

"What was I doing?" Kate raised an eyebrow at the duct tape they'd used to secure her wrists to the chair.

Beth took out her Kershaw pocket knife and cut through Kate's bonds. "You were pretty agitated. Kept repeating that everything was your fault. We didn't know what would happen, Red. But after the warning that you might not come back as yourself, we didn't want to take any chances."

Sam helped pull the tape off Kate's sleeves. "Just a precaution."

The small lines on Kate's forehead looked deeper, and her eyes were bloodshot. "I was worried I wasn't going to make it back as *me* for a while there. Did you hear me shouting for you?"

Sam pulled up a chair and sat down next to her at the table. "Nothing."

Kate looked at Beth and rolled back her sticky sleeves. "What about you?"

Beth leaned against the counter. "Nada. We kept waiting."

"I screamed for you when I couldn't get out," Kate said.

"You both heard me when I called." Sam's eyes unfocused. "But we didn't hear Kate. Why?"

Beth lifted herself up to sit on the kitchen island. "I think you're our main link, Sammy. The whole buzz-down-our arms thing starts with you. You're the anchor."

Kate nodded. "You're the strongest of us all, Sam."

"You're both strong," Sam protested. She fiddled with her blonde hair like she'd always done when they were kids. Sammy never seemed to like compliments.

"Not in the way you are." Beth shook her head. In the way Beth had always wanted to be. "When you believe in something, when you know it's right, nothing stops you. Even if it means you almost get yourself killed by my parents."

She turned away, not wanting Sam to see what she knew must be on her face. Fear. The thought of what might have happened to Sam twisted her insides. Her parents weren't above murder.

"It's okay, Apple Fritter."

Sam's use of their silly name game made Beth turn around. For a moment, they were back at Sammy's place. Beth hiding out after a beating. Sammy making her laugh until her tears finally stopped. "Thanks, Pork Chop."

Sam smiled, and Beth almost forgot they weren't best friends any longer. "Besides the anchor theory," Sam said. "I also think it's an issue of trust."

"Then we're screwed." Kate rubbed her eyes. "If I hadn't been able to get myself out of there, things would have been bad. Ray wanted to kill himself, and I would have come back with that desire burning its way through me." She shivered.

"We're the problem, not you, Kate," Sam said. "You trust us both already. Always have." Beth recognized the look she threw her way. A dare was coming. "We've got a truce, but this needs something more. I'm willing to work at repairing what we broke. What about you?"

Beth's heartbeat doubled, then triple timed. Her hand slipped into her pocket and gripped the comforting shape of her gun. You could count on weapons, not people. But Sam was right. They needed to work together, otherwise Kate's life could be over.

"I don't know if we can repair it," Beth said. "But I'm willing to slap some duct tape on and see what happens." Was she real-ly going to let Sammy back in? That usual protest came slower this time.

She gazed at Kate and Sam, seeing them as kids again. Kids she'd loved. She got up and busied herself at the sink washing her hands. There was no way she'd let them see her cry. She blinked, feeling the tears run down her cheeks. She bit her lip to keep it from trembling. Getting soft would get her hurt.

"So how did you get out, Kate?" Sam said.

"Well." Kate drew the word out. "I used the 'back off, I'm the Oracle' war cry, but I did have a ghostly crutch. Beatrice." She smiled. "She's my relative. I think that's why I felt the connection to this place."

"Beatrice was there?" Sam said. "How?"

Beth dabbed her face and eyes with the dishcloth. "You sure you don't have a fever, Pip?" She turned around and grabbed some cookies from the island and brought them to the table. She slid into a chair.

"I'm fine. I think where there's a Beatrice, there's a way. She wanted to talk to me, and nothing was going to stop her."

Sam cocked her head, and then laughed. "Robert's back, and he agrees with you, Kate. He says Beatrice is a force of na-ture." A smile softened her lips, and it only solidified what Beth suspected. Sam was in love with a ghost. Whether she wanted to admit it or not.

And Beth had no doubt Robert loved Sam. No ghost had ever helped Sam as much as he had. Ever. The green serpent of envy coiled around her lungs, constricting them. Sometimes, she felt the only way she would ever find love is if it became a solid object she could seek out with her powers.

"All right, let's talk about Ray," Kate said.

Beth took out her notebook and clicked her pen. "I'm ready."

Kate pinched the bridge of her nose. "Dammit, I'm going to have one hell of a headache shortly."

"I've got some Vicoprofen in my room," Beth offered. "And some Percocet, too, depending on what you think might work best."

Sam gave her a long look. "Is there a reason you brought narcotics with you? Everything okay?" Her tone was neutral.

The muscles in Beth's face tightened though she tried like hell to relax them. She had the urge to slid her hand into her pocket again.

"Depends on your definition of okay," Beth said. "I fell down the stairs at a location we used a few weeks ago. Strained some ligaments and muscles around my spinal cord." She rubbed her lower back for effect. "It hasn't been fun."

Kate patted her hand. Good ole Kate, always wanting to believe the best in people. But Sam wasn't convinced.

Beth set her pen to paper and looked at Kate. "So, what did you find out about Ray?"

Kate told them about the house, Ray's injury, his grand-daughter, and the accident. "I can almost taste the pipe tobacco still." Kate smacked her lips together. She reached for the pipe, but Beth picked it up before she could touch it.

"I don't want you handling this again," Beth said. "We've got what we came for. Let's not take any chances."

Sam took the pipe from her and studied it. "I understand why Ray turned into a poltergeist. He couldn't forgive himself for what happened. But how does knowing his story help us to help him?"

"He's obviously seeking forgiveness." Beth looked over at Sam. "We need to find his granddaughter. Once she forgives him, he'll see a door to Heaven and voila, problem solved. You've always said Entwine wasn't a permanent stop for ghosts. They move on."

Sam shook her head. "I assume they move on. But if Mary's left Entwine, I can't help. Let me ask. Beatrice, do you know if Ray's granddaughter is in Entwine?"

Beth stared at Sam. The late morning sun picked out the lighter blonde streaks in her hair, almost matching the glow Beth saw whenever she looked at Sam. She still wasn't sure how she saw with Entwine's eyes, as Yasmin had called it. And Sam's words about "something" covering her skin when she used her ability still creeped her out. What did it all mean?

"Beatrice says his granddaughter isn't in Entwine. She's checked with her connections, and Mary's not here."

Kate laughed and shook her head. "My great great relative has 'connections' in Entwine. I *love* it." Then she sobered. "But not good news Mary isn't reachable."

Beth leaned her elbows on the kitchen table. "Plan B then. A seance. We'll call up Mary's spirit so she can talk to Ray."

"No." Sam crossed her legs and then crossed her arms.

"You've only tried it once." Beth kept her tone soft. "And you admitted you didn't really know what you were doing.

None of us did. Hell, maybe we did it wrong? It could be different now."

Sam flashed her a look so filled with raw vulnerability, Beth had to drop her gaze. "I can't," Sam said. "If it doesn't work, I'm an utter failure, and if it does work, it means I screwed it up the first time."

And maybe Sam had lost her chance to talk to her parents again. Beth sighed. This wasn't going to be an easy sell.

Kate moved her chair closer to Sam and clasped her shoulder. "You were thirteen when you tried it last. You're thirty now. Look at how our abilities have changed. Before I touched the pipe, I didn't know getting visions from objects was even possible. Beth's being compelled to find things she isn't asked for. Who knows how your gifts are growing?"

Sam sat there, still bound up tight. Kate's entreaty hadn't made a dent.

Beth leaned forward. "I know how it is when you can't forgive yourself." She'd blamed Sam for so long, but part of juvie was her fault. Okay, a large part. She focused on Sam and Kate, hoping her face showed how serious she was. "Only Mary's absolution will free Ray."

Kate nodded. "She's right. I've been in his head."

"Come on, Sammy," Beth said. Time for some trust mending. "You would never let your own fear stop you from helping this poor guy and his granddaughter find peace. Regardless of how you feel about your powers, you're not going to punish Ray and Mary. I know you."

The clock ticked softly in the quiet kitchen. Still no movement from Sam. She might as well have been a tree rooted into the ground.

Okay—time to bulldoze with the trust. Beth took a deep breath. "I fought the urge to find the pipe in the beginning. Even though I knew I would get sick."

"Why?" Kate asked. Sam's gaze flicked to Beth and held.

"Because I saw your B&B in my head." Beth gripped her knees, her nails digging into her pj bottoms. "And I saw Sam. I knew if I found that damn pipe, I'd have to come here."

"You had a vision?" Sam spoke in the same quiet tone as Kate had.

Beth looked down. "I don't know. I guess? Maybe all of our powers are bleeding into each other as this Triumvirate gets closer to reality? What I'm trying to say is that I didn't want to do it, but in the end I knew I had to stop running."

Sam nodded. "From the past." She let out a long breath. "You're right. I'm not going to turn my back on Ray and Mary. I can't." She uncrossed her arms and legs. Her gaze flitted to a spot by the back door. "Beatrice said she knows a Runner who can help focus my power on finding Mary."

"Runner?" Beth glanced at Kate, but Kate gave her the I-don't-know-what-the-hell-she's-talking-about-either look.

"They take ghosts to and from Entwine." Sam glanced up at the kitchen clock. "We should do the seance tonight while everything is still fresh in Kate's mind."

Beth stood. "Well that gives us the rest of the day to do some research on the compass tattoo and see if we can narrow it down."

Sam also got to her feet. "I'm going to check out the local

library and see what I can find about the murders that happened when Robert was alive."

Beth shook her head slowly. "I hope this isn't some weird time-travel thing where Jack the Ripper is back. We already have enough crazy crap going on."

"No," Kate said, her voice hard. "Killer Paul is fixated on me personally, so it's someone in the here and now." She rubbed at the skin on her throat. "I'm finally admitting you both are right. It's only a matter of time before he makes his move."

Beth crossed her arms and felt the comforting weight of her gun still in her pocket. If the paranormal shit they could do didn't stop him, she would.

SAM SAT BACK ON THE CUSHY COUCH THAT FILLED MOST OF the space in the private reading nook of the town's library. It was more than a nook really. A sturdy door kept the noise from the main library at bay. The boisterous chatter of the schoolchildren on a field trip barely buzzed beyond the door.

Her neck twinged, no doubt protesting from the hours she'd spent looking through the microfiche records from the time Robert had been convicted.

A brush of energy against her skin warned her of a ghost nearby. Since she wasn't immediately fatigued, she knew who it might be. "Robert?"

He appeared in front of her, looking delectable as usual. "I did not wish to disturb your work."

Sam sighed. "Disturb away. I'm not finding a thing." She held up the printed copies of the reports about the seven murders around the time of Sarah's death. "No one connected these, even loosely. They all had dark hair, were around the same age, and had blue eyes."

Robert sat on the couch, at the opposite end. "They did not come from the same social background. In my time it meant they had nothing in common."

Sam leaned over and touched his arm lightly. "You can sit closer. No one is in here besides us, and the door's locked."

"We are truly alone?"

"Yes. Don't worry." Another sharp pain ran up her neck. "This damn kink. It's from looking down for hours at all that research." She rubbed a spot in between her neck and shoulder, trying to find the source. "We're having a seance tonight. We'll try to call up Ray's granddaughter and help send him on his way."

"A very sound plan." Robert pushed her hand gently aside. "Here, allow me. I have been told I have some skill in this area."

She turned on the couch, giving him access to her back. His thumbs dug under her shoulder blades. "Oh." She couldn't manage more words. She leaned back into him. He obliged. The tightness fought for a moment, his movements almost painful, then it released in a long line of relief from her shoulder up her neck and to her temples.

He moved to the center of her back, running his fingers and the heel of his hand, up and down her spine. She felt like jelly.

"Oh God, you are good. No wonder why you had so many mistresses." He stilled.

The papers had vilified his personal life, and here she'd added to the injury. "I'm sorry. It was thoughtless for me to bring that up when we're trying to clear your name." She looked back at him, noting the muscle in his jaw ticking in time with the clock on the wall. His gaze remained on the center of her back, not looking at her.

"I did have several mistresses." Robert's voice was gruff. "But I have since learned the value of finding one woman to love." He met her gaze finally, and she couldn't breathe for a moment. "And in pursing what I want no matter the cost."

Heat crept up her cheeks, through her whole body. She couldn't look away from the naked need simmering in his eyes.

Sam turned around on the couch to face him. Her heartbeat thrummed against her ribcage in anticipation. Any excuses or protests were silenced by the promise in his gaze. "And what do you want?"

He slid his fingers up her cheek, his thumb resting under her chin. "You."

"Not worried about the Wardens any longer?" Her body inched closer to him.

"I know it is dangerous, but I am unable to ignore what we have." He looked down, his long eyelashes dark against his skin. "You make me feel alive."

Sam touched his knee. His body trembled underneath her hand. "You make me feel . . ." She faltered. It sounded ridiculous to say he made her feel alive too, but he did. "You make me remember the lightness inside me. The joy." Now it was her turn to look down. "I'm not making any sense."

"You make perfect sense. You are in love with me."

To hear her own suspicion spoken aloud sent adrenaline through her chest. "But it doesn't matter what I feel. We're still in the same mess as before. Ghost. Living. Everything."

"Mayhap the great Necromancer can navigate us out of this mess."

Robert leaned forward. She thought he was going to kiss her, but instead, his lips stopped just above her neck. Though he didn't touch her, she felt his essence vibrate against her skin. His lips moved up to her chin, around her cheek, over her eyebrows, before they stopped, hovering over her lips.

Every cell in Sam's body felt like it rushed toward him. She didn't know what was going to happen in the future and right now she didn't care. Ridiculous or not, dead or alive, she wanted him. She kissed him, climbing onto his lap.

His arms wound around her, snaking up under her t-shirt. She slid her tongue into his mouth, and his grip grew almost crushing. His hands struggled with the clasp of her bra.

She pulled back. "Here, let me." She slid her top over her head and threw it. The bra came next. She helped Robert with his shirt, but before they could get to his trousers, his hands found her breasts. Her nipples puckered, hardening. Then his mouth followed his hands.

Sam held onto his shoulders, trying to stay upright after waves of heat flooded through her. His tongue teased one of her breasts, then moved to the other before she could recover.

Her hands moved from his shoulders to his hair. His thick delicious hair.

Through her khakis, she felt him long and hard underneath her. Sam moved back and forth matching the rhythm of his mouth on her breasts. Robert's hands gripped her hips, pushing her faster. His tongue grew more insistent, teeth nipping at her skin. Tension built inside her, coiling. Sam wrapped her legs around him, sliding his hardness up and down quicker and quicker.

Her head fell back. "Yes, yes," she groaned, not recognizing her own voice. It sounded primal, raw.

Robert took control, grinding against her. His lips found hers. They rocked together until her climax broke in a blinding rush.

She fell into his arms, sweaty. "I feel like a teenager who can't wait." She pushed a damp curl back from his forehead and kissed his nose.

Robert smiled, and it lit every part of his face. "Fortunately, *I* have excellent control." He bucked underneath her. She felt every inch of him. An echo of her orgasm slammed through her, leaving her breathless.

She slid off of him, dropping her jeans quickly. She was definitely up for seconds. His trousers were already past his knees.

The door handle rattled, and Sam's heart felt like it lodged in her throat.

"Miss. Are you done in there yet? This room is reserved in ten minutes for another party." The librarian's voice was insistent beyond the wooden door.

"Just about finished," Sam managed. "Be out in a jiff."

Robert stood, fastening his trousers and a frown firmly in place. "Timing does not appear to be in our favor, does it?"

She got dressed quickly. "I'm not letting you off the hook that easily, mister. You, me, alone, someplace very soon."

"I accept your Bargain, Necromancer." Robert kissed her so thoroughly, she felt it from the tips of her toes through the ends of her hair. Once again she forgot who she was, where she was, when she was. He released her finally, and she fell back onto the couch, none of her muscles working properly. He gave her a knowing smile and disappeared.

"Oh my." A huge grin spread across her face. The hunt for the serial killer, the poltergeist, helping Robert clear his name, could wait for a few minutes.

For the first time in what felt like forever, she was just happy. A ghost had made her happy.

CHAPTER 21

"THIS IS PRETTY BIG FOR WHAT WE'RE PLANNING," SAM said to Kate. She stared at the long narrow room with an equally long and narrow table in the center. Hopefully one day, the table would do more than sit empty, once the B&B was bustling again.

"I know it's a little large, but I didn't want to have the seance in the study. That's where the girls play." Kate frowned. "I'm so glad Emily and Patty are at Aggie's sister's. Even without Killer Paul in the wings, I don't want them to be exposed to all of this just yet."

Sam helped Kate lay the green tablecloth down. "Patty's already part of our world."

Kate gave her a brave smile. "I'm going to make sure she has a much better time of it than I did. Than we all did. We're planning a long talk when they get back."

"She's lucky to have you as a mom." Sam squeezed her arm. "Did Beth say when she'd be back?"

"Nope. But she's not going to miss the action or inaction,

depending on what happens. You know her."

Sam wasn't sure which would be the bigger draw for Beth—seeing Sam succeed, or seeing her fall flat on her face? "I'll get the treats from the kitchen while you finish setting up."

The kitchen was warm from all the stress-baking Kate had done. The scent of gingerbread still lent its spicy aroma to the air. Sam loaded up a tray with the cookies and muffins, but paused to look out through the kitchen window over the sink. The sun had dipped behind the far hills. Somehow it seemed right to perform a seance with the daylight dying, its glow being swallowed by the oncoming night.

She picked up the tray and headed back toward the dining room. They'd soon find out if this was going to work or if they'd have to figure out another way to get rid of the poltergeist.

"Gimme, gimme," Kate said before Sam took two steps inside the dining room. She grabbed an oatmeal cookie. "I'm famished."

Kate had already set ivory candles in ornate pewter holders around the table. Sam placed the tray in the center. It looked like they were planning a nice get-together with friends, not trying to call up the dead.

The front door opened and closed quickly like it had been caught and then released in a gust of wind. "I'm back," Beth yelled.

"Good," Kate shouted back, her mouth half-full of cookie.

Sam dimmed the overhead chandelier, so that the main light came from the candles. She smelled something in the air, dry and earthy. "Did you burn sage?"

"Well, that's what Google said to do for a seance," Kate replied. "You haven't done an official one before, and neither has anyone else."

"But I have," said a smooth voice from the doorway. A wave of relief washed over Sam. If she messed things up, Yasmin might be able to help get them back on track.

Beth stood behind the seer, looking pink-cheeked and proud of herself. "Got the expert," she announced with a flourish toward Yasmin. "Plan B."

Yasmin laughed and patted Beth on the arm, leaning in close like they shared a mutual joke. When had they become best buddies?

Yasmin slipped off her coat and handed it to Beth. Her vibrant red tunic over black leggings looked comfy. "While I do have some experience in these matters," Yasmin said, "I'm sure Sam will do just fine."

Sam pulled out the closest chair. "Please, sit down."

Yasmin sank into the chair with a grateful look on her face. Her hands closed over her pregnant belly and she sighed. "This little one is only a month away, but I feel like I could pop at any moment."

"Don't pop here," Beth said, her voice worried.

Yasmin smiled. "I'll try to hold back. Oooh, gingerbread muffins." Kate slid a plate with a muffin and fork toward Yasmin. She took a bite, and a look of nirvana smoothed out the lines on her face. "You're going to make some man happy again one day, Kate."

"Don't you start too." Kate fussed with setting out napkins.

Yasmin gave Sam a wink and then tugged on Beth's arm. "Come, sit. It's almost time. Is anyone else joining us?"

"Just us three, and now you," Sam said. "The ghosts who've been helping me, Beatrice and Robert, will also be here, and they're bringing a Runner friend of theirs."

"Ah, the infamous Robert." Yasmin gave her a knowing look.

Sam worked hard not to think about the library just hours ago. The memory of Robert underneath her. If she blushed now, Beth and Kate would be all over her again. "Yes, Robert needs my assistance to clear his name. Getting Ray to move on will help us find a journal we need to do that."

A slight tugging pulled at Sam's skin, more of a ruffling static electricity. Within a breath, Beatrice had materialized along with Robert and another man she didn't recognize.

"Beatrice, Robert, and their friend are here." Sam avoided looking at Robert directly, somehow feeling Beatrice would know what they'd done.

Instead, she studied the stranger. He looked somewhere in his forties with a lithe muscled body. Black pants and vest paired with a gray shirt. A silver band on his wrist caught Sam's eye. It had engravings on it that she couldn't make out clearly.

"This is Darrin, the Runner I told you about," Beatrice said. "When the time is right, Robert and I will get Ray down here."

"How are you going to manage that?" Sam said.

Robert and Beatrice exchanged a considered look. "We have an idea. Trust us," Robert said. "We will be careful."

Darrin gave Sam a nod. "I'm honored to meet you,

Necromancer. Have they explained how I'll be able to help?"

"Not exactly."

"Runners have a connection throughout all the realms. I'll channel your call so you have a better chance of reaching Ray's granddaughter."

"We really appreciate your help," Sam said.

Darrin smiled and looked years younger. "There's not much I wouldn't do for Beatrice. She's come through for me more times than I can count."

Sam turned back to the table. "The Runner's name is Darrin. He'll help me reach Mary. Once we have her, Beatrice and Robert will get Ray."

Beth let out a low whistle. "Oh, that's going to be fun for them."

A surge of anxiety rushed from Sam's stomach up to her chest. Were they really going to do this? A seance? Everyone stared at her.

"How should we start?" Sam asked Yasmin. "The last time I did this, nothing happened."

She remembered sitting on the floor of her room, calling for her parents over and over again for hours until Bronson, Beth and Kate had finally made her give up.

Yasmin gripped her hand. "It wasn't your fault then. Don't doubt yourself now."

"But then why—"

Yasmin cut off her words with a sharp squeeze on her hand. "Necromancers follow different rules. But I'm not the one to have that discussion with." She released Sam's hand. "First we all should clear our minds of everything other than our purpose here. To find Mary."

"Does it matter if we don't know what she looks like?" Beth asked. "Only Kate has seen her."

"And Robert," Sam added.

"It doesn't matter," Yasmin answered. "Merely thinking her name will suffice."

Thankfully Beth's research had gleaned Ray's full name and the name of his granddaughter, Mary Lynn Parsons. Everyone was silent for a few minutes. The only sound was the slight creaking of the manor in the wind.

"Next, you three join hands." Yasmin pointed at them. "As part of the Triumvirate of Pluthar, your power will help Sam."

Beth looked like she was going to protest the name again, but instead, she picked up her chair and moved it next to Sam and Kate.

"You ready to do this thing, Sammy?"

"No." Sam took Beth's hand. "But when has that ever stopped me." Kate grabbed both their hands. A warm buzz of electricity arced through them. They were joined.

"Finally, we'll need a focused call for the one we seek." Yasmin's tone was soothing. "Sam will begin, and we'll repeat what she says. All of us. Together."

Sam nodded. "Mary Lynn Parsons. We must speak with you." Her voice sounded weak even to her own ears. She tried again, louder this time. "Mary Lynn Parsons. We must speak with you." This time the air almost vibrated, as if her words were touching each molecule as the sound traveled.

Yasmin nodded at everyone, and they repeated what Sam said. Darrin walked over to Sam and placed his hand a few inches above her shoulder. This close, she could see the symbols on his cuff. The swirls cut into the metal appeared organic. They were beautiful. They looked Celtic.

Warmth built in her skin, right underneath his palm. Though he wasn't touching her, she felt his energy, joining with hers. It was different than when Robert did this. Darrin's energy felt foreign.

Darrin repeated the words, and his voice wove through hers until they were one call. She felt the call take on a life of its own, seeking, searching. The silver band on his wrist pulsed in rhythm with the words, spilling white light into the darkened room.

Beatrice and Robert joined in as well. More ghosts filled the dining room. Ten, then twenty—no, wait, too many to count. She should have passed out with this many ghosts materialized, but somehow she was fine.

The ghosts' voices rose, strengthening everyone else's. Their combined energy flowed against her skin, channeling through the connection she had with Darrin. She'd never experienced such power before. Her body felt light, almost as if her spirit could simply drift free of her skin.

The candles blew out, and then relit themselves.

"Holy crap," Beth said.

A shape formed above the center of the table. Next to the plate of cookies.

A little girl. About ten years old.

"I'm seeing someone, Kate," Sam said. "A young girl, long brown hair, light eyes, thin face and freckles."

"That's her," Kate exclaimed. "That's Mary."

Sam's heart beat hard against her chest. She'd successfully called a ghost who hadn't been in Entwine. Had she always been able to do that, or were her powers changing?

Sam expected the other ghosts to leave once Mary arrived, but their energy continued to lap against her skin in a warm wave. Beatrice and Robert disappeared. She assumed they were going to get Ray. She tamped down her worry though it continued to creep through her. If she lost Robert now . . .

Mary crouched, reaching for the cookies, but her fingers slid through them. A look of sadness rushed through her eyes, and then it was gone.

"Thank you for coming, Mary," Sam said.

"Why have you called me, Samantha Eveline Hamilton?" Mary's voice was hollow, distant.

"I heard that," Kate said. "How's that possible?"

"I can hear her too." Beth's eyes were wide.

Yasmin looked at their hands. "You're joined together in the flow of the Triumvirate. Imagine how strong you'll be when you finally meld your hearts together. You'll be unstoppable."

The last few words were said with such gravity, Sam's mind spun. Would they ever share their hearts with each other again? Was unstoppable a good thing?

She shook her head and looked up at Mary. "We've called you here so you can talk to your grandfather. He blames himself for what happened to you in the well."

A tremor distorted Mary's face. "I don't like to think about that day."

"I know, baby, but this will really help your grandpa," Kate said.

Mary looked at Kate, her lips trembling.

There was a sharp crack and a rush of heat dove down from the ceiling. A deep voice yelled from above. It wasn't Robert. Something heavy hit the ceiling with a loud thump. The walls shook and then steadied. If Ray touched Robert again, he might disappear forever. It took everything Sam had not to break the seance and rush to his aid. She gripped Kate's hand tighter.

A final bang sounded above, and Robert and Beatrice fell through the ceiling as if it were loose sand. Robert cradled her, catching them both to land lightly on the floor. They stood in the open space near the end of the table.

Someone followed them, almost on their heels. It had to be Ray. He landed on his feet as well. Or did he? His form kept shifting and moving. First standing, then sitting, then running, then crouching. Her eyes could barely follow.

Robert lifted a hand toward Sam. "May I introduce Raymond Parsons. The resident geist."

Mary squinted at Ray. "My grandpa never raised his voice. He never got mad at anyone. That's not him. This is a trick." The girl started to fade.

"Wait," Sam said. "Don't go." Already the connection grew weaker. She was losing Mary.

"Leave me alone," Mary said, just the bare outline of a girl left.

"Stop," Sam shouted at the same time as Beth and Kate.

Mary froze, materializing fully.

Sam's arms hummed with a different energy now, less chaotic, more even. Like they were finally on the same current for the first time, all three of them. Connected.

"She stopped." Sam gazed at her friends.

Beth's face was pale. A layer of sweat gleamed on Kate's skin. But they both looked calm.

Sam turned to Ray. "This is your one chance to talk to your granddaughter again. To tell her how you feel." The poltergeist's form kept swirling. He wasn't listening to her. "I'm not getting through to him."

Beth looked over at Yasmin. "Take the pipe from my right pocket. Now."

Yasmin waddled over quickly and retrieved the pipe. She held it up.

Beth tilted her head toward Sam. "Where is Ray standing?"

Sam knew immediately what Beth wanted to do. Sam pointed out the spot, and Yasmin placed the pipe at Ray's feet.

The maelstrom of movement stuttered. And then slowed. And then stopped. For the first time, Sam saw the man behind the poltergeist.

Ray bent down to pick up the pipe, but missed on his first try, his body struggling to settle into stillness. He took a deep breath and then grabbed the pipe. "I haven't seen this in years."

A surprised smile jerked his lips in something that resembled a smile.

"Grandpa?" Mary asked, her voice tentative and then her face warmed with color. "Grandpa!" she shouted at the top of her lungs. "Where have you been? Mama and I missed you."

Ray looked up at the sound of her voice. A look of wonder spread across his face. A sunrise blazing through the darkness. His body shifted again and then stopped. "Mary? Is that really you, angel girl?"

"It's me, Grandpa." Mary leapt off the table and ran into his arms. Ray hugged her, crying and sobbing so deeply Sam found tears in her own eyes.

He dropped to his knees, his arms still around her, though his body kept shimmering in and out of position. "I'm so sorry, I'm so sorry," he kept repeating, his voice hoarse. "I know you must blame me." He pulled back and touched her face with a trembling hand. "And your mother must hate me for letting you die—"

"Mama says that sometimes bad things just happen." Mary cupped his cheek with her small hand. "You tried to save me, Grandpa. I know you did."

"I did," Ray mumbled. "But I failed. I was too weak to hold onto you."

"And I shouldn't have been playing by the well." Mary smiled and took his hand. "None of that matters now. We can all be together again."

"Together?" Ray's voice was soft, filled with disbelief. His form shivered one last time and then finally settled. "We can be together?"

Darrin nodded "You can. We've been waiting a long time for you, Ray." Darrin grinned. "And your daughter, Phyllis, has been losing patience."

Ray smiled and this time the happiness shone through his eyes. "I bet she has. I'm ready." He nodded toward Sam. "I owe you, Necromancer."

"Keep safe, you two." Sam nodded at Ray and Mary. Seeing them so happy together brought more tears.

Darrin touched Ray's shoulder, and all three ghosts disappeared. Robert and Beatrice followed. All that remained in the dining room were the living.

"I'm so happy they'll both find some peace now." Kate took in a ragged breath. She was crying too.

"You two are such babies," Beth said, blinking back her own tears. "I can't believe we did it."

Yasmin handed them the tissue box. Tears were on her cheeks as well.

Sam laughed. It felt somehow right after the darkness. "We did this together. We actually saved a poltergeist. Who knows what else we can do?"

And now they had leverage to use against Caleb to find that tree branch. She hoped it would be the key to discovering the identity of the killer.

CHAPTER 22

ROBERT AND BEATRICE LED SAM DEEPER INTO THE FOREST around the manor. She gazed up at the branches of the beech trees overhead. The fickle sunlight played against their white bark.

Branches. Beech trees. A flash of Ellie's memory rushed through her. It was suddenly night. Paul was after her. Someone grabbed her arm. Sam jerked back, stumbling over some tree roots.

Robert caught her before she hit the ground, his strong arms scooping her up as if she weighed nothing. Sam buried her face into his shirt, breathing in his comforting scent. It was so natural to touch him now. Like they'd always known each other.

"Put her down right now," Beatrice said.

Robert did so, but kept a hand on the small of her back until Sam was able to take a few steps on her own. "Sorry," Sam said. "Flashbacks. Nasty side effect of seeing a ghost's memories."

Robert's eyes were worried. "It is quite all right, Samantha."

"No, it's not." Beatrice's hands were on her hips. "If you

two are determined to keep this up, then don't do it out in the open. Or are you hoping the Wardens drag you in, my lord?"

"Drag him in?" Sam took a few steps forward. "Where?" She didn't know much about the mysterious Wardens, but no one was dragging Robert anywhere against his will.

Beatrice frowned, her eyebrows dipping sharply. "Never mind about that right now. We've got an appointment to keep." She turned her back on them and headed into the forest.

"Do not fret over Beatrice's words."

Sam didn't reply, just followed Robert. She wouldn't allow him to be hurt because of what they'd done. "I'll protect you, Robert," she whispered. "I promise."

"Promises made in my woods are binding, girl." A voice came out of nowhere, yet seemed to come from everywhere. "Be careful with your words."

A vibration started at Sam's feet, like tiny ants dancing over her skin. It rose up through the soles of her boots, circling her calves, and then marched up her body with determination.

It didn't hurt, didn't scare her. Something about it reminded her of when she'd helped her first ghost. That rush of energy from what she always considered the Universe. This was nature at the purest level.

The leaves bristled. Whispered snatches of words sounded from above her, from the trees. One word jumped out among the many.

Necromancer.

The vibration against her skin grew deeper. Like the earth

underneath her feet was talking, or humming rather. She crouched and placed her hands on the ground, fingers sliding through the dirt, reaching the dampness underneath. The soil shifted against her skin, like it was alive.

"Do you feel it?" She couldn't keep the wonder out of her voice.

Beatrice gave her a quizzical look. "Obviously not like you're feeling it, lass. Looks like Caleb's showing off for you. King of the Forest and all that rigamarole."

"Well, you know how I like to make an entrance, Bea." That same voice which had spoken before echoed again through the trees.

With a great creaking noise, the large beech tree in front of them swayed, the trunk leaning.

The branches of the beech shifted back, and the center of the tree grew translucent. Sam saw a face within the trunk, then shoulders, then a body. An old man stepped out with a walking staff. It had to be Caleb.

Sam expected to feel an energy drain in the presence of such a powerful ghost. It was just the opposite. The forest continued to hum through her.

"Welcome to my woods. I'm Caleb." The ghost bowed low, and then straightened up with a look of pain on his narrow face. "I had heard of your power, Necromancer, but my birds didn't speak of your beauty."

Beatrice made a rude noise. "Let's not waste time with sweet talk. You know why we're here."

The old ghost smacked his lips together. "Were you always

this domineering when you were alive, Beatrice, or did death make you a shrew?" The words were dry, but his eyes flashed with a green light, almost the color of the forest leaves.

Beatrice didn't say anything, just shot him a withering look.

Caleb leaned both hands on his staff, bringing his impressive height down to mere mortal level. Sam saw carved symbols on the wood, just under his fingers. They looked a lot like the Celtic ones on Darrin's cuff.

"You did it, Samantha Eveline Hamilton. You got rid of the geist." Caleb tilted his head toward her. "Calling up Ray's granddaughter was a stroke of brilliance."

"I can't take full credit." Sam slid her hands in the pockets of her fleece coat. "It was actually my friends' idea. It took all three of us."

Caleb nodded. "Your Triumvirate is almost complete. The Wardens are quite intrigued."

Robert's jaw tightened. "Does Samantha need fear them?"

Caleb hunched his shoulders forward. "There are no plans to make a move on the Triumvirate. They wish to observe. For now."

Sam froze. What if they'd seen Robert picking her up? Well, if they had, it was done already. It didn't change the fact that they were here for a purpose. She cleared her throat. "Since the Triumvirate isn't in any pressing danger, I think we should stay on task."

"Quite right," Beatrice said with an approving smile. "We got rid of the geist, so you owe us the location of the journal."

"I'm surprised you didn't ask the Seeker to find it," Caleb said.

There was something about him she trusted. Trusted enough to be honest about Beth. Maybe it was the forest's call still vibrating through her body.

"I thought about it," Sam admitted. "Even though Beth's range has increased, it still hasn't hit the two century mark."

Caleb nodded. "Not yet anyway. You've all merely scratched at the top layer of bark. There will be much more you'll achieve in time."

"Are you an oracle now?" Beatrice said.

"While we all hope that Samantha's circle of friends continue to flourish in their abilities," Robert said smoothly, "we would be most pleased to receive the information you have promised."

Caleb chuckled. It had a dry quality like the crunching of dead leaves. "You have a pretty way with words, I'll give you that." He grew serious. "The last time I saw the journal, it was headed to an antique shop in town."

"Headed?" Beatrice cocked her head toward him. "Are you saying you don't know if it's still there?"

"I can't leave the forest." Caleb sniffed. "And my eyes in town are more limited. The crows are more comfortable here."

"We risked our existence to get rid of the geist for information that might not even be correct?" Beatrice's hands curled into fists. "If this is one of your games, Caleb, so help me . . ."

Robert put an arm around her shoulders. "If it is no longer

at the antique store, we will be able to track it with the help of Samantha's computation machine."

"Computer," Beatrice corrected.

"Don't worry, Beatrice," Sam said. "We'll find it. All we needed was a place to start." She tried to inject eagerness into her tone, but all she felt was worry. As soon as they found the journal, how long would Robert stay if they cleared his name?

Beatrice shrugged off Robert's grip and stalked closer to Caleb. "Tell us the name of the antique store. And don't think this is over. You owe me twice now. Once for the geist, and once for the lie. You promised us the actual location, not some scavenger hunt."

Caleb didn't back away. His face had gone still, like he was suddenly carved from one of his trees. "Our deal was clear. Information on the journal's location. I've delivered that." His voice dropped into a low dark place. "And since I've already been hiding Robert's talent of touch from the Wardens, I'd say we're even."

ROBERT STIFFENED. HE HAD NOT REALIZED HOW CLOSE they had been to discovery by the Wardens. Being in Caleb's debt was not a feeling he cherished.

Beatrice's face bled white. Robert helped her to sit on one of the tree stumps.

He glanced at Caleb. What they knew about the mysterious ghost was woefully limited. It would do no good to anger him further. "Thank you for diverting the Wardens' attention."

"And for keeping Robert's secret," Beatrice said numbly.

Robert inclined his head toward Caleb. "If you please, the name of the antique shop?"

Caleb's gaze flicked between Robert and Beatrice. Regret slid into the hard lines of his face, muting them. "The journal went to an antiquities dealer by the name of MacCallum & Sons."

"I know where they are," Samantha said, though she sounded as reluctant as Robert felt.

He looked at the fallen leaves on the ground. Would he simply fade away once they discovered Sarah Covington's true killer? How could they stop that from happening?

"Something has been bothering me since we discovered the journal missing," Robert said. "Do you know why my sister, Lillian, did not find it?"

Caleb sucked in his cheeks, looking like he had tasted something foul. "Well, I can tell you that for free. The Justiciar seized your house and arrested her. Said your sister knew you killed Sarah Covington and covered it up. Lillian died in jail."

Robert swayed on his feet, the movement causing Caleb's face to teeter back and forth like a solemn jack-o-lantern. "No. No. She was a widow with child. They would not have treated her thus."

Now Caleb sounded distressed. "All I know is Alastair pulled some strings. He had friends with influence."

Alastair, the Justiciar's lapdog. He had not realized Alastair's hatred extended beyond Robert. He turned quickly to Samantha and tried to steady his legs. "Is he lying?"

Samantha studied Caleb and shook her head slowly. The gaze which met his was full of sadness and understanding. He could bear neither.

"No, it cannot be," he said, unable to catch his breath. In his mind's eye, the forest disappeared, replaced by Lillian's face as he had last seen her. Carefree, excited to be a mother.

"My lord," Beatrice said. He felt her hand on his shoulder, but it was nothing to him. Merely the brushing of a leaf against his sleeve.

"Leave me be," he growled, hands twisting and grasping around what he wished was Alastair's neck. "Alastair destroyed my home, my name and all our lives." Robert's words burned their way through him. "If he were not already dead, I would seek him out and make him suffer for what he has wrought."

Energy coursed through him, much like when he threw the ledger across the table, but this was stronger. The tree stumps around them shook. Their wood whined in protest against the dirt. Clumps of sod and grass shuddered around their roots.

"Robert, please calm down." Samantha pulled on his arm, but he shrugged her off.

He shook his head. "Her death, her suffering . . . it is all my fault. She told me not to dally with Sarah . . . if I had given myself up right away rather than trying to flee . . . if I had demanded Lillian stay out of Scotland . . ." It had been absurd to think for a moment he deserved a chance with Samantha, a chance at happiness. He had caused too much pain.

Robert took a shuddering breath in, and the branches of the nearest tree rose almost straight up. He blew his breath out in a rush, and the branches cracked, leaves stripped from their limbs.

Caleb's face was ashen, but his voice was vibrant with a threat. "I understand your grief, but I won't allow you harm my trees any further."

Alastair was unreachable, but the urge to attack would not be denied. Robert flicked his hand toward one of the tree stumps, urging it to rip free of its bonds. With a great sucking sound, it rose up into the air and hurtled itself toward Caleb.

With just a nod of his head, Caleb sent the stump whirling past to land at the edge of the clearing. "You can't win here." His tone was proud, strong. "This is my land, my roots."

"Robert," Samantha shouted, her face suddenly inches from his. Her green eyes churned with flecks of brown and gold. "Stop this."

Lillian's face kept surfacing in his mind, covering Samantha's. Images of how his sister must have suffered swallowed his vision. "I cannot. I deserve this agony."

"Stop talking like that. Don't you think I blame myself for my parents' death?"

"It is not the same. You did not cause it."

"It still hurts." Her voice shook. "Their faces. My father pleading with me. I should have been able to do something. Anything." She pressed her forehead to his until all he saw was the storm in her eyes, flashes of lightning in the depths of her pupils. "We can't change the past."

"Let me go. I matter not. I am nothing." Already he felt the despair stripping away who he was. Soon there would be nothing left of Lord Robert Grenning.

"I refuse. You hear me?" Her voice roared in his ears though he knew she spoke in a whisper. "You are worthy. You are kind, gentle, caring. You are everything to me. And I'm not letting you go." The cool bite of her power dug into him, latching on tight, but it was what he heard in her voice which pulled him back from the spiral. Certainty.

She *was* in love with him. Even if she had not said the words. The fledgling shoot of hope grew inside him, bursting into bloom bathed in the glow of Samantha's love. He had faltered in his past, but he would not do so in the future. He would seize his second chance.

He concentrated on the pulsing force still within him. It fought, not wanting to disburse, but he pulled it apart until only pieces remained. He let it seep away, like water released from a tub, easing down the drain. He felt empty, alone. But he was not alone. Samantha held onto him.

Robert kissed her forehead, needing to feel her skin. Her touch centered him, reminded him of what he fought for. "I am sorry to have frightened you." He kissed her cheeks, and then her lips. And tasted salt. "You are crying."

Samantha looked up at him in wonder and touched his face. "No. *You* are." She held up her hand, tears on her fingertips. "Ghosts cry, I've seen it. But your tears are in my world, on my fingers. How?"

A stab of pain raked through him, clawing his insides. His hands clenched Samantha's shoulders.

"Are you okay?" Her gaze searched his face.

Should ghosts feel agony like this? What was happening to him? "I do not know, Samantha."

Caleb looked grim. "Of course, he's not okay. He moved my forest around like a geist, he can touch the living, and his tears are real beyond the realm of Entwine. Now he's suffering a price."

"I am willing to pay it," Robert said through gritted teeth. Then, just as quickly as it came, the pain eased, releasing. "To touch Samantha, it is worth any price."

SAM CUPPED ROBERT'S CHEEK, HAPPY TO SEE THE LINES IN his face ease. They'd need to figure this all out, but right now, she couldn't forget why they were here.

Sam faced Caleb. "I'm sure you already know I've made a Bargain with the recent murder victims."

"I sense the beginning of a deal." Caleb looked happy to be on more familiar ground. "Continue."

"As you also must know, one of them was murdered here in the woods."

"Ellie Croft," Caleb said. "But before you ask, I didn't see who killed her."

Beatrice made a *tsk*ing noise with her tongue. "I thought you saw everything that happened in your woods."

Frowning, Caleb's lips looked like two pale twigs. "This forest is too big for me to see everything at once, but the trees told me what happened."

"Ellie hit the killer with a tree limb," Sam said. "Would the trees know where that was? It has his blood on it."

"I'm sorry, girl." Caleb slowly shook his head. "There have been too many rains through this forest recently. I can't imagine anything like blood lasting on a branch."

"But it could, if it was sheltered." Sam held out her hands toward Caleb in a pleading gesture. „Could the trees tell you where the branch is now?" She'd asked Beth to find it, but she'd been blocked. Sam had her suspicions about why. Caleb most likely had protections against the forest itself being open to prying eyes.

Caleb sucked on his front teeth, the edge of his brown tongue sticking out slightly. "They could if I asked."

"I know you have a price," Sam said. "Tell me what it is, and we'll see if we can come to a mutually desired agreement."

"Consider this a gift." Caleb leaned easily on his staff, no tension in his body.

"What?" Beatrice said.

Sam stared at Caleb, stunned. There had to be a catch. She raised an eyebrow at Beatrice.

Robert took a step toward Caleb, any sign of his earlier troubles gone. "Do not trifle with this lass, or you will answer to me."

Caleb cackled, the noise almost screeching at the end. "Calm your nerves, young buck. I like this lass. And by helping her now, perhaps the Triumvirate will look upon me kindly should I need their assistance in the future."

Beatrice mimicked Caleb's voice. "Future favors? But you

said you always come out on the losing end."

Caleb frowned at her. "I didn't say the word 'favor' did I?" He shuffled back to his main tree, muttering under his breath. "I do something nice and all I get is the attitude. Ornery. That's what she is. See if I help *her* again."

Beatrice laughed. "You know I'm joking, you old coot."

Caleb harrumphed, but didn't say another word until he got to his tree to ask Sam's question. He whispered against the trunk. It sounded like the creaking timbers of a ship, yet with an undercurrent of softness like rustling grass in the wind.

Sam felt a mixture of excitement over finding the branch and worry it would all end in disappointment. She looked over at Robert and he gave her an encouraging smile.

Caleb turned back to them. "The branch you're looking for is about three hundred yards in that direction underneath an old oak."

Sam looked where he pointed. "Can you be more specific?"

"It's the only other tree in this part of the forest beside the beeches, so you can't miss it."

"Thank you, Caleb." Sam bowed low and held it for a moment, like she'd seen Robert do. "You might have just saved another life. Someone I deeply care about."

"I hope you find what you're looking for." Caleb fixed her with a strong stare. "As for any more touching, you two are safe from prying eyes in my woods." He stopped and let out a cackle. "Other than mine, that is. I'll continue to do what I can to protect you, but the sooner you can get Robert on his way, the better. The Wardens will eventually find out. They always do."

"If the Wardens come against us, they come against the Triumvirate of Pluthar." Sam didn't know what they could do against the Wardens, but it felt like something she had to say, needed to say.

The words sat upon the air like the vibration after a bell has rung.

"Pluthar?" Caleb's face grew as pale as the beeches around him. "I didn't think I'd survive long enough to see that happen again."

Sam took a step closer to the ghost. "There have been others before us?" It was the same question she'd asked of Yasmin. There was something neither of them were telling her.

"That information is not for sale." Caleb shooed them away with his hands. "Go find your branch."

"But I need to know."

Caleb struck his staff against the ground in a swift sure movement. The energy flowing around Sam hardened, holding her fast. She couldn't lift her feet. She might as well have been in concrete. "This is not a negotiation. Find your branch, save your friend." He lifted his staff and Sam stumbled back.

Sam stared at him. She'd find out what he knew. Somehow. "This isn't over."

"It rarely is." Caleb turned away and walked into the forest.

Sam flicked up the collar of her coat against the sudden chill creeping through the clearing. "Come on. Let's go get the evidence."

CHAPTER 23

THE LARGE OAK WAS EASY TO SPOT. ITS DARK BROWN TRUNK gleamed rich in comparison to the sea of pale beech trees surrounding it. The base could've easily fit three of Sam within its circumference. Long branches dipped down, some of them hitting the ground as if they couldn't support the burden of their knowledge.

Sam put on her gloves. She didn't want to leave her own DNA evidence behind. They already had a sample from Logan and Max. Beth had promised she'd have Graham's ready by the time Sam got back.

She dug through the dense foliage around the tree, searching for something pale, something resembling the branch she'd seen in Ellie's memory.

"Anything yet, lass?" Beatrice asked.

"No. But there's something shiny under here." Sam shoved her hand into an opening and something sliced along her finger. She hissed, pulling back. The glove was ripped and a shallow cut along her forefinger already welled with blood. Now she could see what the bright object was. "It's the top of a can. Dammit."

"I am without a handkerchief when I need it." Robert patted his trouser pockets looking frustrated.

Sam grabbed a tissue from her jacket. "It's okay. I'll just . . ." Her words trailed off, her attention drawn to the blood dripping from her finger and hitting the ground. "Am I seeing things?"

Robert and Beatrice drew close. Together they watched the next drop of blood slide off her fingers and fall toward the ground. Almost as soon as it hit the dirt, the earth sank around it and then smoothed out. No trace of the blood to be seen.

Beatrice swallowed loudly, looking ill. "It would appear Caleb's forest has a taste for blood."

"Or perhaps this is the price," Robert said. "With Caleb, something is always owed."

"You might be right." Sam let the blood continue to trickle. She raised her voice. "Okay trees, forest, whatever is listening, I think I just made a payment. Can you help me find the branch I'm looking for?"

A shiver ran through the oak tree's uppermost branches shaking the lush canopy of leaves. The branches danced against each other, sending several golden leaves drifting gently down to the ground in lazy circles. They landed on a pile of darker leaves she didn't remember seeing at the base.

The tip of something poked out from the cluster of brown. Something the same color of the beeches. It looked like a bone. Goose bumps formed on her arms, pulling the skin taut.

Robert's face was grim. "Though the sun is still bright, I feel the darkness of malice."

The ties on Beatrice's apron tangled in her hands. "This is definitely near where Ellie died."

All Sam had to do was bend down and take it, but her body didn't want to move. Sam knew Ellie's ghost wasn't tied to this spot, but a chill of death still crept up through the ground and seeped into her body.

"I would pick it up for you if I could." Robert touched her shoulder, helping to quiet the anxious fluttering in her stomach. "But I can only touch people, not objects."

"I know." Sam shoved the tissue against her cut. "I've seen some pretty horrible things. This feels different though. Darker."

Beatrice looked grave. "Ghosts feel it too, when death isn't natural. When it's murder." She calmed herself, growing still. "Like an infection in the skin in between Entwine and your world, joined at that terrible moment. An act of evil."

The death memories of Ellie, Monica and Wendy, crowded into Sam's brain. She wrapped her arms around herself, unable to stop the shiver shaking through her own body.

Robert drew Sam into a hug. "What has happened is in the past. The branch means we can save this fiend's future victims. You are one of the strongest women I have known. You will not fail."

Sam leaned back and met his gaze. It held acceptance and absolute belief in her. They'd only know each other a short time, but it felt like forever. Was there a way they could stay together?

Sam shook her head. Now was not the time. She moved out of his arms and then crouched. "Let's do this." She used her gloved left hand to move the leaves aside very carefully. There it was.

The branch was almost as wide as her forearm and just as long. Studying it, she saw the surface wasn't coated with the blood she'd hoped for. Just a fine layer of dirt and bits of leaf.

She wrapped her fingers carefully around the bottom base and lifted it up for a closer look, but the oak wasn't letting enough light through its limbs. She walked a bit further out into a patch of sunlight and twisted the branch, scanning for any sign of blood. The underside held deep furrows in the wood where it was just starting to split.

Wait. There was something in the largest furrow. Something gleaming. Sam peered closer, her nose almost touching the wood, and a large beetle skittered out. Her heart surged into her throat, gagging her. The branch fell from her grip. She fumbled to grab it back and failed.

Robert caught it before it hit the ground.

Sam's hand went to her mouth. What?

Beatrice's sharp intake of breath seemed as loud as a scream in the quiet forest.

Robert looked at the branch in his hand, then to Sam, then to Beatrice, then back to his hand. His eyes widened in a mixture of alarm and wonder. "How is it that I am really holding this? That my hand did not merely sweep through the wood?"

"I have no idea," Beatrice said. She patted her chest like she was trying to calm her heart. "But we're lucky we're still in Caleb's forest. *That* information would ensure several lifetimes in Entwine to certain ghosts."

Robert paled and handed the branch to Sam quickly. She took it from him and just held it, her mind trying to digest what had happened.

"Samantha?" Robert said. "You are as pale as the beech trees around us. Have I frightened you?"

She grabbed his hand and squeezed it. "No, nothing like that. Just mulling over the wonder of what you did."

Beatrice made a come-on, come-on gesture. "I'm sensing someone nearby. Let's get out of here before any more wonders assault the two of you."

Sam examined the branch again, before taking the clean rag from Kate's kitchen out of her purse and wrapping it up. There was definitely a dark red stain at the edge of one of the deep cuts. Her arm shook. It looked like blood. "Let's go."

IN THE KITCHEN, SAM AND BETH HELD THE BRANCH BETWEEN them. They both wore gloves so they didn't contaminate the potential evidence. Kate shone a flashlight into the crevices.

"It could be blood, right?" Sam said. She'd run almost the whole way back to the manor. They finally might have a chance of catching this psycho.

Kate nodded. "It definitely could be."

Sam took the branch from Beth and sat it on top of her

jacket again. It looked innocent on the kitchen island. Not the enormous clue she hoped it was.

The doorbell rang. Beth lifted her chin toward the front hall. "A neighbor?"

"I don't have any close neighbors." Kate squinted at Beth. "But I don't think the killer would ring the doorbell. So, no guns." Kate walked out of the kitchen.

Beth slid a knife out of her boot sheath. "She didn't say no *knives*."

Sam chuckled, but Kate's laugh from the hallway drowned hers out.

"Think it's hot Max?" Beth said.

Before Sam could make a guess, Kate rushed into the kitchen, pulling Michael behind her. Gone was his usual suit. Today he wore a t-shirt and jeans. But his expression was anything but relaxed.

Sam tossed a dishtowel over the tree branch. She rushed over to give him a hug. "You said you might swing by next week. Your parents are okay, aren't they?"

He gave her a hard squeeze and then released her. "My dad had a fall. Nothing serious, but my mom asked me to come early to help out around the estate. I also thought you could use another friend." He nudged her shoulder with his.

"It means a lot to me that you're here, but shouldn't you be with your dad?" And away from their murder investigation. And ghosts.

"My brother—Duncan—says he's recovering just fine." Michael grabbed Kate with one arm and Sam with the other for another hug. "Besides, I couldn't pass up the chance to see two of my favorite people together."

Beth cleared her throat. "Ladies, how about some introductions?" She popped a hand on her hip in her best I'm-a-TV-personality-pose.

Michael's arm tensed around Sam. Beth was in for a rude interruption of her regular programming.

"This is Dr. Michael Forbes," Sam said. "He's a very good friend of mine. A few years back, he saved Bronson's life."

The beam in Beth's smile didn't falter. Sam gave her points for that. "Bronson. How is the old man?"

"Good," Sam said. "We just chatted this morning. I caught him up on my trip."

She'd asked for his advice on what to do if they found the tree branch. He said he'd make some calls to labs who could process their findings discreetly. She didn't know how he had so many contacts, but they'd come in handy over the years.

"Very pleased to meet you, Michael. I'm Beth Marshall." The sparkle in Beth's eyes matched the sheen of her teeth.

"I know who you are," Michael said, dropping his arms back to his sides. Sam could have ice-skated on the look he gave Beth.

Beth crossed her arms. "Not a fan?"

"I don't watch a lot of TV," Michael said. "And when I do, I'm not much into fantasy." His words were pleasant.

Beth let out a pained sigh. "This again. Would you like me to prove I'm not a fraud?"

"Beth." Sam shot her a look that she hoped said, *drop it.*

"Michael doesn't believe in the paranormal."

Beth snorted. "Well then what does he think of—"

Kate poked her in the ribs with her elbow. "What does he think of your show? He's probably never watched it."

Michael pointed at the branch they'd left on the kitchen island, partially covered with the dishtowel. "What's that?"

"A tree branch." Sam smiled, knowing it probably looked fake. "Some tea?"

"What's going on?" Michael glanced between Kate and Sam.

"Nothing." Kate got down some mugs. "I've got some wood beetle problems. They helped me get a branch as a sample."

Sam had to applaud Kate's fib. Her delivery was smooth. But Michael didn't look convinced.

"Then why is Ms. Marshall armed?" His eyes skimmed over Beth. "Gun and two, no wait, three knives. I can't imagine the weaponry is necessary to repel ardent fans."

Beth took a step toward him. "I'm always armed. That's why I use a private jet for travel."

Michael ignored her. "Sam."

She heard the plea in his words. The plea for her to be honest. She'd come to Scotland to stand shoulder to shoulder with her past. If Michael truly cared for her, he'd stay her friend after he found out her secret. And if he didn't, best to find out now.

Sam put her hands on the marble island. The cold reminded her of the way iron felt. "We think it could help with the serial killer case in town. You've heard of it, right?"

"I have." Michael's posture stiffened. "Four women have been killed so far. If this is a clue, why do you have the branch and not the police?"

Beth laughed. "Because the police have no idea Ellie used the branch to attack her killer."

Michael's eyes locked with Sam's. "And how do *you* know that?"

Once she told him, there'd be no going back. Sam swallowed. "I see ghosts. I've talked with the victims."

Michael slid his hands into his jacket pockets, letting out a breath as if he'd been holding it since he arrived. "Thank you for trusting me. That's actually one of the reasons I came by. My brother had a vision about you."

Sam's breath caught in her throat. She stared at Michael, her mouth opening and closing. She'd been frightened by how he might react when he found out the truth, and now he was accepting it like it was nothing?

She staggered back a step. Kate took her arm, steadying her.

"Your brother has visions?" Kate's voice rose. "Does he black out? Can he drive?"

"He's learned to control those side effects." Michael took Sam's hand. "I'm sorry I kept this from you. It's become habit over the years to protect my family."

"You believe in the supernatural and your family has abilities?" Sam rubbed her face, feeling incredibly foolish. "And to think I worried for years about not telling you about my curse. I was so stupid."

Her stomach clenched. A wave of nausea rolled over her.

Had he been laughing at her lies all this time? Was this all a game to him?

"You weren't stupid," Michael said. "It's easier to act like I hate anything out of the ordinary. It throws the suspicion off the truth." There was a vulnerability in his face she'd never seen before. "I didn't tell you about my family because I was afraid." Michael looked past her, out the kitchen window. "Afraid you wouldn't believe me. Afraid you would. We've had to keep our gifts a secret from a lot of people. It's not safe."

"How long have you known about mine?" Sam's voice was rough.

Michael met her gaze. "The day you left for Scotland. That's when my brother had his vision." He touched her shoulder and the nausea faded. "I hated lying to you too, Sam. It hasn't been easy for either of us, has it?"

Some of Sam's anger and hurt softened under the pain in his voice. She was still upset, but she understood. Especially if he was protecting his family.

Beth opened a tupperware container of cookies and put them on the island. "So if you believe in the supernatural, why were you giving me shit about it?"

"I don't approve of your show or what you do with your gifts." Michael reached around her and grabbed a cookie. "For a smart charismatic woman, you're focusing on the wrong things." Beth looked like she couldn't figure out if there was a compliment in there.

Kate saved any potential retorts by grabbing a bottle of wine from the rack on the counter. "It's two o'clock. No one judge."

She got the opener out and several glasses.

Beth held out her hand. "No judgement here. I could use a glass. A tall one." She lifted her chin toward Michael. "So, what should I be focusing on, doctor?"

"Helping people." Michael finished his cookie. "Not exploiting their pain."

Sam thought about how he'd quieted her nausea with a simple touch. "That's why you became a doctor, isn't it?" Sam said. "Your powers are tied to healing."

Michael gave her an approving look like she was a star pupil in his class. "Partially."

"And emotions too." Sam's mind sifted through memories back to the day they'd met at Bronson's bedside. How she tended to feel calm around him, centered. "You can control someone's emotions."

"Influence them is probably more accurate." Michael looked around the kitchen. "But your abilities are much more interesting. I imagine this place is teeming with ghosts. My sisters come up with nicknames for the ones they help."

"You have sisters who see ghosts?" Sam took a glass of wine from Kate.

"Twins actually."

Beth took a long swallow of wine. "This is getting more and more looney toons even for me. Just how large is your family?"

"Large enough. I'm one of the youngest." The last was said with a hint of something Sam had seen before when Michael had talked about his family. Resentment.

"Your sisters who see ghosts," Sam said. "Are they necro-mancers?"

"No, they're mediums. From what I understand, there are only a certain number of necromancers in the world at any time."

Kate sat at the table. "I'm not surprised there's only a few necromancers. Sam helped hundreds of ghosts by the time she was thirteen. That's gotta be rare."

Beth nodded. "Yup. She kicked some major ass before she bottled up her secret sauce."

Michael looked at the branch again. "What's the plan?"

Sam took a cookie. "Bronson's checking on someone who'll run the DNA test."

"How long will they take?' Michael said.

"He wasn't sure. At least a few days."

"Too long." Michael took out his cell phone and texted someone. "I have an old buddy in Glasgow who can get the results to us in twenty-four hours."

Beth raised an eyebrow. "I hate to say it, but Mikey here is pretty useful."

He frowned at her. "I can leave tonight."

Sam finally felt they were moving forward. "Take the branch. We need answers now."

CHAPTER 24

"THIS IS TRULY THE PLACE?" ROBERT GAZED UP AT THE sign for the antique store, MacCallum & Sons, the establishment Caleb had sent them to in the search of the journal.

The sign looked like it had been beaten over the years, leaving behind just a pale tan of the original wood. The raised letters of the shop's name were still etched with bits of gold, reminding him of pieces of sunlight against the overcast skies.

Samantha smiled at him, holding her phone to her ear. "That's what Caleb said."

"Who are you speaking with?"

"You."

"Then why do you have that?" He pointed at her phone.

Samantha glanced at a couple who passed them by. "If I talked to the air, I would look crazy. Tetched, I believe you called it before."

Robert nodded. "Very wise."

"Are you nervous about finding the journal?"

There was no need to lie to her, and no point, since she could detect falsehoods. "I am not nervous, but I am worried what will happen if the journal is indeed inside."

Samantha shot him a quick look. "Because you might move on, and we'd never see each other again?"

"Yes. I find it is an outcome I am unable to bear." Robert wanted to touch her shoulder, stroke her cheek, anything to show her how he felt. But there were three ghosts on the street, and who knew how many more lurked inside the nearby buildings. Potential Warden spies.

Samantha studied him for a moment. "There are other ghosts nearby, aren't there?"

"What do you sense?"

"Three ghosts to your right, one inside the antique store and two more at the coffee place down the street." Samantha closed her eyes for a moment. "One more at the bakery and I think there might be one at the police station. That's further away." She opened up her eyes. "Am I right? I've never been able to sense this clearly before."

"You are right. It would appear you are becoming more powerful."

"Powerful enough to stop you from moving on? I've been doing research, but I can't find anything to help." Samantha turned her back on him and faced the street. "Even if you did stay in Entwine somehow, what kind of life would we have together? Long-term, it's a lose-lose proposition."

Robert walked around her until he could see her face again. "I might not have believed it initially, but I know now we were brought together for a reason. There *has* to be a way." Surely the Universe could not be so cruel as to bring them together only to tear them asunder. He wanted to tell her he loved her, but now was not the time. Not on the street.

"Us Hamiltons have never been quitters." She gave him a wisp of a smile.

"Neither were the Grennings. Shall we face the challenge together, my lady?"

Samantha put away her phone. "We shall," she whispered. "First things first." She headed toward the front door of the establishment, held it open, and let Robert slip inside.

The store was spacious. Built-in shelves along its edges cradled clocks and statuettes and ornate vases. Long counters filled the floor, their clear tops displaying wares inside. Though the heavily-shaded lamps kept the light low, the jewels and gold still sparkled.

Robert left Samantha at one of the front counters and wandered for a time. The store was very calming, sedate. Patrons spoke in whispers as if this were a church.

Samantha caught up with him by a knife display. "Do they have the journal?" he asked.

She nodded slightly. Without taking out her phone again, she could not talk freely with him.

"They won't find your journal," a voice said to Robert's right. He turned swiftly and found a ghost. A woman roughly Beatrice's age. By the quality of her dress, she had lived a very pampered life. Privileged.

Her severe black dress and jacket clung to her frail frame,

and gray hair flowed in waves against her skull. The only color present was the glow in her blue eyes.

"Excuse me, why would you say that?" Samantha kept her voice low.

One of the ghost's gray eyebrows raised. It had been plucked so thin, it was like a line of dust against her skin. "Excuse you? I doubt anyone would excuse your slovenly dressing habits if they had any modicum of class, but considering what is acceptable these days, I suppose I should be thankful your bosom is adequately hidden."

Samantha sputtered, her face already growing flushed, but before she could utter another word, Robert stepped in between them. He would like to have words with this ghost over her treatment of Samantha, but for now, they must be cordial.

"We have not been properly introduced. I am Lord Robert Grenning." He bowed low and held the position for several moments to denote the proper amount of respect.

"Well, Lord Robert, you certainly have manners." The ghost favored him a slight tilt of her head. "I am Imogene Clarissa MacCallum."

"You'll have to handle this." Samantha looked slightly pale. Imogene must be pulling energy from her. He realized she never looked this way around him.

He nodded, wanting to rush, but already sensing he would need to handle this delicately. "I would be more than happy to speak with Madame MacCallum."

"Imogene, if you please. A madame runs a house of ill repute." The bite in her words cut through the air like a whip.

Robert clasped his hands behind his back. "Imogene, please be so kind as to illuminate what your earlier statement alluded to. Why will your staff be unable to locate the journal we seek?"

Imogene crossed her arms. "Because it's wedged in between two file cabinets in the office. They couldn't find it when the other gentlemen asked for it last week, and they won't find it now."

Samantha gave him a pointed look. He knew what she wanted to ask.

"Thank you for this information. We will provide these details to the clerk." He attempted to act unconcerned for his next words. "I knew Sarah when I was alive, so the journal has a certain sentimental value for me. However, I am surprised someone else would be interested in the musings of a lovesick young woman. Perhaps a scholar or teacher looking for something of historical value?"

Robert felt Samantha fairly humming with impatience beside him.

Imogene cocked her head to the side like a bird about to pluck a juicy worm. "If you want to know what I know, there's a price. A Bargain with the Necromancer, and the truth about your interest in the journal."

A shrewd woman, indeed. Robert knew further hedging would be a waste of time. He glanced at Samantha. Ultimately, it would be her choice to accept a Bargain. She frowned but finally nodded. She mouthed, "If possible, yes."

"Very well." Robert's voice was brisk. "You will discuss your

Bargain with the Necromancer at a future date. I was wrongly convicted of Sarah Covington's murder in 1789. I believe the journal holds a clue to the killers' identity in my time, and it might shed some light on the fiend who has been preying on the young women here."

Samantha held her breath beside him, her attention solely on Imogene's reaction.

"Hmmpphhhh." The sound from Imogene was rich with satisfaction and approval. "The murders need to be stopped. That type of violence shakes the stability of Entwine."

The clerk from the back came around the counter and approached Samantha. "I am so sorry, Miss. The journal shows up in our inventory, but we couldn't locate it."

"Check between the file cabinets," Samantha said. At the man's surprised look, she smiled sweetly. "Well, at least that's where my missing things end up at home. Maybe we'll get lucky."

The clerk nodded slowly and walked away but not before Robert heard him say under his breath, "Crazy Americans."

Robert turned back to Imogene. "Now, it is your turn. Describe this gentleman."

Imogene nodded in a sharp quick motion. "I can do more than describe the gentleman who asked about the journal. I know his name."

"Who?" Samantha blurted out. Two women at a nearby case glared at her like she had interrupted their meditation.

"Logan Dunning, the Detective Chief Constable."

Robert shook his head slowly. This was not the news he

expected. Constable Dunning was a trusted friend, and if he was not mistaken, something more to Kate.

Samantha gasped softly. "Oh no."

Imogene looked delighted at the dour effect of her words, the edges of her mouth pulling back into a garish smile.

He turned to Samantha. "She is telling the truth?"

Samantha nodded.

"It might not mean what we think," Robert said. "There could be a vast number of reasons for his interest."

Samantha did not say anything, but Robert knew her thoughts. Kate would be bereft at this horrible news.

The clerk returned holding a leather-bound book. He walked over to them. "I found the journal, Miss. That'd be fifty pounds."

Robert recognized Sarah's journal, the unique stamping on the outside, but Samantha didn't even look at it. Her hand reached into her purse and emerged with crumpled bank notes. She let the paper drop to the counter and then tucked the journal into her bag. She made her way to the front door in a daze.

"Miss," the shopkeeper called out. "Don't you want your receipt?"

Samantha did not stop. He knew she feared telling Kate this news. He must comfort her. Robert brushed past Imogene.

"Wait a moment."

Her words stilled his passage. He turned and looked back at her.

Imogene removed a speck of something from the sleeve of

her jacket. Her nails were bleach white against the dark fabric. "About my Bargain—"

Robert leveled a stern look at her. "Catching this killer outweighs your petty needs. Your Bargain will have to wait. I thank you for your assistance in this matter. However, I do not appreciate the relish with which you delivered such distressing information."

Imogene reminded him greatly of Alastair. His body grew warm, flushed with anger. Just thinking of him brought back the agonizing memories. Of Lillian. Of what Alastair did.

He clenched his hands and felt something rush through his body, very similar to the sensation in the forest.

The sharp sound of glass clinking together broke the quiet air of the store. His gaze swept the shelves. The vases and statuettes chafed against each other in a dangerous dance. The patrons moved away from the glass, from the shelves, their eyes wide with confusion.

Robert took a long deep breath and blew it out slowly, releasing the energy as he had done earlier.

Silence descended again, the movement on the shelves ceasing. Imogene eyed him like he had suddenly grown two heads. He must leave before he caused anything which could be absolutely tied to him. Right now there was no proof. He needed to keep it that way.

He turned toward the entrance and found Samantha already gone. No one would be holding the door open for him this time. He must make his own way through.

The heavy wood loomed large in front of him, seeming more

massive than before. Robert sensed the thick metal contained within the wood. He must use speed as well as focus. He rushed toward the door and instead rammed into it.

Blood leaked out of his nose and down to his lips. Pain, bright and biting, spread from his face and crawled through his neck. He wiped his nose and gazed transfixed at the sight of his own blood on his fingertips. Blood which had not flowed in centuries.

What *was* happening to him?

Another stab of agony gripped his body. He doubled over, a vise around his stomach, his chest. Then just as suddenly as it came, it released. He leaned heavily against the door struggling for breath. If the Wardens found out about this, he knew they would not wait to detain him.

Robert suppressed the burning ache still flooding his body and looked around the store quickly. No other ghosts, save Imogene. She backed up a step, then another. He followed.

"Are you here alone?" His words were hard, though he felt as weak as a babe. He fought the wave of dizziness which threatened to capsize what little control he had left.

Imogene's earlier smugness had fled. Fear swam in her eyes. "I don't allow other ghosts in here, but you were with the Necromancer."

"If you speak a word of this to anyone, your promise of a future Bargain is off." His words were a growl.

"What are you?" she whispered. "I can tell you're not a geist. But you're not just a ghost."

Robert straightened, holding himself firm and strong by will alone. She must believe his next words. "Beatrice will know if you confide what you have seen with anyone. And if you do, losing the Necromancer's favor will be the least of your worries. You do not want me as your enemy."

Imogene's head bobbed up and down in agreement. "I'll keep quiet, I promise." She backed away in several stumbling steps.

Someone opened the front door to leave, and Robert slipped through behind him. He staggered toward Samantha. She stood waiting by a nearby bench.

"What happened?" Samantha's eyes searched his face, her voice dropping to a whisper. "Is that blood?"

"I collided with the door."

Samantha stared at him for a long moment. "Something's wrong. This shouldn't be possible. What if I'm killing your ghost self? Draining your essence away?" The color fled from her face.

"You are not killing my ghostly self." Robert had no idea if this was true, but he refused to believe the suggestion.

"It might be irreversible." She began to pace up and down. "There needs to be a balance. I know this. I've always known it just like the Rules."

"What balance?" Beatrice had not mentioned this to him before.

Sam stopped and almost grabbed his hands, but pulled back at the last moment. "Between ghosts and me. There's a balance usually. We've upset it somehow."

"Miss, are you all right?" a young lass said to Samantha.

Samantha shook her head and smiled. "Sorry. Just running through some lines. Theater." She walked off, toward the sidewalk. Robert followed. The girl gave Samantha a worried look but returned back to her friends.

Robert rushed to keep up. "What can I do to ease this burden from you?" He did not wish to see her in such turmoil. Not when they had larger obstacles to face than what was happening to him.

Samantha gave him a quick look and kept up the fast pace. "Nothing. Unless you know what's causing your sudden intrusion into the land of the living. And if it's a good thing or a bad thing."

Robert ran his tongue against his torn lip, tasting the salty tang of his blood. "All miracles come with a price. If my pain is the coin of passage into your realm, I will gladly pay it." He had said as much in Caleb's forest, and he still meant it.

Samantha stopped at the crosswalk, waiting for traffic. "This could be the Universe's payback against me. Making me care for someone only to kill him right in front of me."

"I am already dead."

Samantha crossed the street to her car. "You know what I mean. Look, after what just happened, I don't want to cause you any more pain. We might need to keep some distance until I figure this out."

Fear shone in the lines on her face. "Please," Robert said gently. "We can solve this puzzle together. Do not turn away from me."

She got into her car. "Don't follow me. I mean it." Samantha let out a ragged breath. "I couldn't live with myself if I destroyed you, and that's just what I might be doing." Her car's engine rumbled to life. "When I know more, I'll call for you, and we can go over the journal."

Robert watched her drive away. They had the journal, and his time might be measured by the few rays of light the sun still shed. If he was truly fading away, losing his ghostly essence, he wanted to say goodbye to Beatrice, and then be with Samantha for however long he had. He needed to tell her how he felt. In case this was the end.

He needed to tell her he loved her.

SAM GOT OUT OF HER CAR AND RAN AROUND THE SIDE OF the manor, toward the forest. She had some questions for Caleb. Questions about what was happening with Robert.

Her heavy purse, with the journal still tucked inside, swayed back and forth. Fear and worry fueled her stride, sending her into the forest faster and faster. Was she a destroyer? Would Robert cease to exist if they didn't stop? She couldn't touch him ever again. Wouldn't. Not until they knew what was happening.

The forest welcomed her, trees beckoning, their limbs stretched away and toward the sky, as if making room. Caleb knew more than he had revealed. The symbols on his staff matched the ones on Darrin's cuff. Darrin was employed by the Wardens. There was a connection somehow.

The bottom of her feet tingled through her shoes. Her run

slowed to a jog. Had she imagined it? If anything the jolt of energy got stronger. Her feet felt like a bad case of pins and needles.

Sam stopped. She was at the entrance of a small clearing circled by a tight copse of beech trees. Though sunshine filled the forest, her breath misted in the cool air coming from inside.

Necromancer.

All around her, the trees shivered her name. Her name? When had she come to think of herself as that?

"I'm Samantha Hamilton, not the Necromancer. You hear me, Caleb?" She looked around, but didn't see the ghost anywhere. The brush of electricity through her feet had disappeared, feeling returning to her toes.

Necromancer.

This time the word came from within the darkened clearing. But she couldn't turn back now. She needed answers.

Sam walked inside. Leaning her head back, she barely glimpsed the sky through the thick canopy of leaves above. Nothing moved in the clearing. Not the wind, not any insects, not even the crows who watched her from the beech trees. They could have been statues.

"Where's your boss?" Sam asked. "I've got a deal to make with him."

The crows flew toward her. Sam ducked, but they passed her by, disappearing through the opening to the main forest beyond.

The ground hummed underneath her, but it didn't numb her limbs like before. Whatever it was brimmed with life. Warm, inviting, revitalizing. The aches in her muscles, the tension in her shoulders, everything disappeared.

"Do I have to pay for that?" Sam asked. She turned around, knowing she'd find Caleb there.

He smiled, his lips looking like broken twigs. "Consider it a professional courtesy from one powerful being to another."

Sam slid her purse to the ground. "You've seen what's happening to Robert. It's gotten worse."

"Worse?"

"He bled."

Caleb jerked, clutching his wooden staff tighter. "That's impossible."

Sam shook her head. "I think I'm doing it."

Caleb had recovered somewhat. "The crows said you wanted to make a deal." His grey eyes assessed her carefully.

"Tell me what's happening. And if it's a bad thing, how to stop it." This was probably a mistake, but Sam was willing to do whatever it took to save Robert.

"And what are you prepared to do for me in return?"

Sam squared her shoulders. "What do you want?" There must be something he needed that only she could accomplish. Entwine was his home.

Caleb didn't say anything for several long heartbeats. Sam clamped her mouth shut and waited.

He walked toward her and stopped until she could see the deep greenish veins running under the pale skin of his neck. The power flowing around her intensified, like she'd suddenly come closer to the flame.

"I don't know what's causing this change in Robert, though I have my suspicions."

Truth. Her ghost lie-detector stayed green.

"Tell me your suspicions."

"No."

Sam grabbed at his hand, but her own wafted through his form. She shook her head in surprise. Robert had made her forget she couldn't touch all ghosts. "What do you mean, no? Just tell me if I'm killing him."

"Curious that you care so much." Caleb pulled a leaf from his hair and studied it. "You do a job, and then it's done. What happens after shouldn't matter to you."

"It does matter. I'm supposed to help ghosts, not hurt them." Even to her own ears, it sounded so odd after years of determined denial.

"Robert isn't just a ghost to you though, is he?"

Sam remained silent. She didn't trust him with information others would want. Others like the Wardens.

He looked disappointed. "Until you stop lying to yourself about who you are, what you want and why you want to save Robert, nothing I tell you is going to make a difference." Caleb shuffled past her, taking the energy of the land with him.

Lying to herself? She'd been more honest with herself, with her friends, these past few days then she'd been in years. And she knew what she wanted. To save Robert. "Caleb, wait—"

He grew transparent and disappeared without ever turning around.

"Dammit." The heat from her run and the argument with

Caleb was too much. She took off her jacket and flung it at the nearest tree. It caught on a thick low branch, just a few feet from the ground. "This is all your doing, isn't it, Universe? Caleb must work for you. Hell, you probably have the Wardens in your back pocket too."

She paced up and down the clearing, the sweat on her arms drying instantly in the cool air. "What's happening to Robert is my punishment, isn't it? For turning my back on you." Hot tears crept into her eyes. "My first ghost after years of peace, and I let my guard down, finally caring for someone again. Stupid. I was so stupid."

There was nothing in the clearing to hit or pull or yank without harming the plants and trees. So, she settled for the one thing she could do. She screamed.

It came from her very core, pulling with it her rage and resentment first. Then came misery, turning her voice hoarse. Finally, despair folded her onto her knees, her fingers gripping the soil and grass underneath her.

"If you take Robert from me, I . . . I . . ." she faltered, unable to continue.

"Hush, lass. I am here."

Sam squinted up at him, the sunlight making its way into the clearing, the branches overhead seemingly farther apart.

She didn't speak, didn't think, just reacted. Sam surged to her feet and kissed him, feeling the press of teeth under his lips until they opened to her.

The kiss became urgent, almost rough and bruising. He lifted her up onto the wide branch her jacket had landed on. He pulled off her jeans, while she got rid of her top. A breeze blew against her bared skin, raising goosebumps. By the time her bra and panties joined the rest of the clothes, Robert was naked.

Sam's gaze danced over his form, caressing it just like she couldn't wait to do with her hands. When she met his eyes, something feral looked out from behind the brown. Her heart stumbled and then it ran, pounding against her ribs.

He pushed her back along the low tree limb, until her shoulders hit the main trunk. His hands started at her calves, then her thighs, over her ribs, up to her breasts.

Sam arched into his touch. A moan escaped her lips. She ran her hand down his chest, lower, and gripped him, wrapping her fingers around his width. He pinched her nipples, just hard enough to make her whimper. Then his tongue flicked over their tight buds. Sam moved her grip back and forth along the length of him, in time with the pull of his lips on her breasts.

Robert moaned, shoulders tensing. He grabbed her hands and put them on his chest. Urging her legs wider, he pushed himself not inside her, but over her wetness, back and forth while he kissed and bit along her collarbone, her neck.

Sam rocked against him, the orgasm rising up through her body until it spilled out. She didn't make a sound, just clawed at his shoulders, her nails drawing blood as another wave of pleasure crashed over her.

Before she emerged from the haze, he slid into her. Filling her completely. She sighed. Finally.

Their movements were frantic at first until they found the right steps to the dance. The leaves shook on the branches with each thrust. The tree trunk cut into her back, but she begged him deeper, wrapping her legs around him.

Her chest slid against his, sweat slicking over their skin. The forest fell away. All she saw was him, all she felt was him, and all she wanted was him.

Pleasure raced through her, like fire licking through dry leaves and kindling. Her head whipped back, hair catching on the bark, cries exploding from her lips.

Light filled her eyes. She looked at her arms, her hands, everything was burning with light. Including Robert. Wherever they touched, skin on skin, he blazed.

Like it had when they first kissed, Sam felt his essence, who he was, meld with hers. Joined.

Robert bucked against her, the rhythm escalating into a frenzy. She clenched her legs around him, hands gripping his hips. His body froze, then trembled with his cry. An answering release rose through her. Their hands found one another, twining together as they had from the beginning.

They held each other, and after a while, the sounds of the forest returned, and the faint traces of twilight dimmed the copse.

Sam felt like she'd run a marathon, but in the best way possible. "I don't think I can move."

Robert staggered back, releasing her. "My legs feel as though the bones were removed." He made it to the nearby tree stump and sat.

Sam fell the few feet out of the tree limb, catching herself against the trunk. "I've never done it in a tree before." She giggled and then clamped her hands over her mouth. "I sound like a teenager."

"I seem to bring that out in you if you recall the library assignation." Robert patted the stump. "Come sit."

Sam looked at his face, memorizing every line, every crease, the scar by his lips and the dusting of freckles across the bridge of his nose. *I don't want to lose him.* Tears returned, but they didn't burn this time. They healed.

She'd broken her own vow never to touch him again, but she hadn't been able to stop. He'd crept into her heart before she'd known it. Perhaps from the first moment he had come through the darkness and into her life.

"Do not cry, lass." Robert pulled her onto his lap. "Are you worried about the journal?"

Her eyes strayed to her purse on the ground still holding Sarah's diary. "Yes, but the tears aren't for that."

Robert's gazed at her. "Surely you do not regret—"

"No." She smiled. "That was beyond description. And I'm a writer."

He laughed softly. "What then?"

She recalled Caleb's words from earlier. Maybe she hadn't been entirely honest. And she was sure the Universe had its own lie detector. If anyone's power had a hope of bringing Robert fully into the living realm, it was hers.

Sam cupped his face in her hands. She'd been naked this whole time, but now she was about to become truly vulnerable.

"I am the Necromancer. And I want you, Robert Grenning." The forest grew quiet, the wind dying away. Like she knew it would. The Universe was listening. "I will find a way for us to be together because I love you."

Robert's eyes widened, moisture making them glisten in the emerging moonlight. "I love you too." He stroked her cheek with shaking fingers. "Fate will not separate us."

She leaned her forehead against his, never breaking his gaze. "You are mine."

The words came from deep inside her, breaking through the remnants of her doubt, her worry, her walls. They felt right. Like she'd been waiting to say them for a long time.

Robert didn't break their gaze. "As you are mine."

A popping noise sounded in the distance, like their words had been siphoned away. There was no going back now. Whatever the outcome, their feet were firmly on this path.

CHAPTER 25

BETH RAISED AN EYEBROW AT SAM. "SO WHEN YOU SAID YOU are the Necromancer, it made that same popping sound like when we did the ritual?"

Sam glanced around the semi-deserted library. They were at a table along one of the walls, but Beth's voice carried if the looks they were getting from the front desk were any indication. "Yes, but it's not the same thing. I'm the Necromancer for *now*. It doesn't mean forever. And keep it down." Why had she even told Beth about it? Old habits definitely died hard.

Beth pushed back from the table, Sarah's open journal in front of her. She spoke quietly. "I think you might *want* to be the Necromancer again. No take-backs this time."

"Oh really. What makes you think that?"

Beth unwound her scarf and let it pool on the table in a crimson puddle. "Even though it's been years, you've embraced what you can do again pretty easily. Robert, Beatrice, the seance, speaking with some forest ghost." She gazed at Sam. "The Rules. I know those came back to you in a heartbeat. You're more alive now than when I saw you at Kate's wedding."

"I don't enjoy what I can do." That wasn't entirely true, but she wasn't going to agree with Beth.

Beth sighed. "Okay fine, maybe you don't enjoy every part. But you want to help Ellie and the others, right?"

Sam nodded. "I'm a decent human being. Of course, I want to help."

"But you risked your life for them with the memory journey."

"To save Kate."

Beth grabbed her wrist. "Stop making excuses and start listening to your heart."

"Why do you even care?" Sam realized she really wanted to know the answer.

Beth released her wrist. "Because you're important, Sammy. You won't admit it right now, but there's a part of you that knows being the Necromancer is the right thing. You've got a purpose. Not many can say that." Sincerity shone from Beth's eyes.

Sam clicked one of her laptop keys to bring the screen back to life. "I can't talk about this right now, okay? We've got enough shit on our plate with finding the killer's identity. Anything in the journal yet?"

The light in Beth's eyes dimmed back to its usual coldness and she pointed at the journal in front of her. "Sarah had quite a lot of gentleman callers." Beth held up her hand and ticked off each with her finger. "She had a lord, a Freemason, an American, a railroad magnate, and a married man. It reads like a romance novel. No offense."

"Okay, let's try searching for the railroad compass symbol." She typed it into her laptop, but nothing came back that looked remotely promising. "Do you know the names of anyone yet?"

Beth flipped through the pages. "I'm only halfway through, but let me see what I can find."

Sam typed in *Freemasons compass symbol*. She scanned the images on the screen and froze. There it was, but fully rendered, not faded like the killer's tattoo. A compass was on top, with the sharp points facing downward over two rulers joined together at a right angle. The description called the rulers a square.

She couldn't move. Back into Ellie's memories. Hands on her throat. A wrist with the symbol next to her face. Breath stalling. Dying—

Beth shook her shoulder and broke the spell. "You went totally white," she said. "What is it?"

Sam gestured toward her screen. "Our killer has the Freemasons' universal symbol on his arm. The square here at the bottom was faded, but I just got a ghost flashback. We're on the right track."

"Good. I found a list tucked in between some of the pages. Gerald Ramsey, Shamus O'Toole, Robert Grenning, Oscar Dunning, and Francis Mitchell."

Sam touched her arm. "Shamus O'Toole. Remember how Max went on about his famous pancake recipe in Kate's kitchen?"

Beth nodded. "And isn't Logan's last name Dunning?"

"It is. There's a creepy portrait of Oscar in the police station." She didn't want to tell Beth the rest before she told Kate, but she needed to share with someone. "Logan was looking for Sarah's journal too."

Beth took in a quick hiss of breath. "Well, shit. Not looking good for the Constable. Any others ring a bell to you?"

"No, but I knew there had to be information in Sarah's journal tied to what's happening now. The killer then and the killer now are connected."

"So, you think the killer in Robert's time has a descendant now who's murdering these women?" Beth didn't look convinced. "I admit it's interesting that three of our suspects have relatives Sarah fooled around with, but that's hardly enough to go on."

"It's more than interesting," Sam said. "It's connected."

"Explain away, Professor." Beth crossed her arms.

Sam swallowed, but it was difficult past her dry throat. "We've been fighting against the idea of Fate ever since we were kids, but I don't think we can ignore it any longer."

Beth looked like she was going to protest, but then remained silent.

"Kate calls me out of the blue to help with a ghost issue. I wouldn't be able to help, but then suddenly Robert emerges from the Rinth, and I see my first ghost in seventeen years." Sam tapped on the table. "Then I confirmed Kate's B&B is his old manor home. And his former housekeeper turns out to be Kate's ancestor."

"Still could be several coincidences," Beth said. "In a row. Similar like."

"True, but then you're compelled to find a smoking pipe no one asks you to find, which brings you to the B&B right when we need you."

"That had nothing to do with the murders. It ended up being related to the poltergeist."

"But since Kate didn't tell you about the murders, finding the pipe was the only thing that was going to bring you here, especially when *I* would be visiting." Sam leaned her elbows on the table. "You admitted you knew you'd have to face me if you found the pipe, but you couldn't deny the physical consequences if you didn't see it through, so you had to come."

"True. Seeing you again was not on my bucket list."

"All right, so something needed to push you here not only to protect Kate, but because of the Triumvirate we're all part of. Caleb made it sound like we were preordained or something."

Beth's lips tightened. "I don't like the sound of that."

"I don't either, but I can't help feeling this was orchestrated." Sam shook her head slowly.

"Okay, so say I buy your 'destiny' explanation for why we're here. It doesn't explain the killer connection."

Sam leaned back in her chair. "What are the odds that my first ghost out of retirement was wrongly convicted of a murder that was really tied to a string of murders like the ones we're facing now? And that they happened in the same town? And that the killer's true target is Beatrice's relative, a family she's been watching over for centuries like she watched over Robert? Again connecting Robert to me, to Kate, to the journal, to the murders . . ."

"Fine. I'm too tired to debate any longer." Beth pinched the bridge of her nose.

"I only hope that there's enough blood on that branch to get some answers."

"There'll be enough."

"What makes you so sure?"

Beth snorted. "If you're right, and Fate is directing this ghost-and-serial-killer show we're stuck in, it won't leave us hanging." She gave Sam a long look. "Still think you can do take-backs on your Necromancer statement?"

Her phone buzzed. A text from Kate. She'd spent the day with Yasmin and her husband, David.

Michael's back. The lab is calling him tonight with the results.

She showed it to Beth. Beth gave her a smug smile. "I told you. Get used to being the *Necromancer*."

Sam closed her laptop, the metal underneath her fingers chilling her. She'd figure out a way to get rid of her curse. She'd promised it wouldn't ruin her life again, and she intended to keep that vow.

SAM PACED UP AND DOWN OUTSIDE THE MANOR'S MAIN entrance. She just needed some air. Michael was back, but they were still waiting for the results.

Clouds skidded against each other in the turbulent sky above. Sam's dark green wool coat did little to stop the cold creeping up her arms.

Sam suspected the results would point to Logan. He'd been after the journal, and out of all of Kate's suitors, he seemed the most . . . enamored.

Sam smelled Beth's citrus perfume and turned around.

"You really should come inside," Beth said. "It's looking nasty."

Beth stood there in a chic puffer coat, zipped up against the wind. The burnt orange color of her coat looked like fire against her dark hair. Gone were her usual high heeled boots. If the scraped and wounded leather on the work boots was any indication, Beth was ready for things to get messy.

"Can't come inside," Sam said. "I need to think, and moving helps." She started pacing again.

Beth matched her steps. "Are you worried about the DNA results?"

"More about how we're going to prove everything. Knowing the DNA piece is a start, but we can't use that in court. Or the testimony of a ghost. We have to have other evidence to convict him."

"Once we know who the murderer is, if we can't find the evidence we need, I'll take care of it." Beth slid her hand inside her open jacket and pulled out her gun. The metal looked oily in the shadowy night, like the surface moved with its own storm clouds. She slipped it back into its holster.

"We're not killing anyone." Sam faced Beth and placed her hands on her hips. "There has to be another way."

Beth mimicked her stance. Her usually immaculate bob swirled against her cheeks in the wind. "The longer he's free, the more women he could kill. Even if we protect Kate, who'll protect his future victims?"

"Have you ever killed anyone?" Sam kept her voice bland. No judgment. Just clinical. She didn't want Beth to close up on her again.

Beth glanced over Sam's shoulder, her mind clearly somewhere else. "No. Unfortunately, he survived."

Sam was surprised. Not that Beth had tried to kill someone. But that he wasn't dead.

Beth's gaze shifted back to Sam. "My soul's already black. What's a little more sin if it helps to save a friend?"

Beth's soul might be smudged, but Sam didn't believe it was truly black. Not yet, anyway.

Sam gripped Beth's shoulder and met her gaze. "Let's agree to try it my way first. We'll do some detective work, hire an investigator if we have to. There has to be some evidence to tie the killer to the crimes."

"I'll agree, if you promise not to stand in my way if Plan B is needed."

"We won't need a Plan B. We won't have to stoop to his level."

Beth looked like she was going to argue further, but Kate interrupted them.

"Michael's got the results." She stood in the doorway. "He won't tell me. He wants us all there."

Sam's stomach dropped, leaving an emptiness behind. She knew what this meant. Michael wanted Kate's friends around her. It was bad news.

"We're coming," Sam said. She heard Beth fall into step behind her and they went into the manor.

They joined Michael in the kitchen. He smiled when he saw them, but it held no warmth. "My guy was fast. I definitely owe his dad a free check-up." His feeble attempt at humor confirmed Sam's suspicions. It was Logan.

Sam put her arm around Kate's waist. "Thanks for doing this for us, Michael. What did the results say?"

Michael gazed at Kate. "The DNA is from a Dunning. Either Logan or Graham."

Kate froze under Sam's arm, her entire body rigid. "No." It was just a whisper, but Sam heard the raw pain inside as if it were a scream.

Sam tried to hug her. "No one wanted it to be Logan—"

Kate pushed her back with such force, she stumbled. "Logan would never murder an innocent person. Ever." Her eyes flashed like they held a flame.

"Why don't we know which one it is?" Beth said.

Michael ignored her and concentrated on Kate. "It could be either brother. They share many of the same markers."

"There is some additional evidence that points to Logan." Sam didn't want to tell Kate, but what if she ran to Logan, trying to get him to prove his innocence? She needed to know the danger.

"You already told me about the men listed in Sarah's journal." Kate's eyes narrowed. "They have the same ancestor. It doesn't prove a thing."

Beth sighed. "There's more. Tell her Sammy."

"He was after Sarah's journal. Only the killer might have known there was a connection."

"I told Logan about the journal. I didn't say it was related to a ghost situation," Kate said. "Just that we thought it could give us a clue to the killer now. He was trying to help."

"You told Logan?" Beth's voice rose. "What were you thinking? He's always been on our list of suspects."

"He's never been on *my* list." Kate's hands balled into fists.

"We don't know anything for sure," Michael said. "Come on, let's have some tea and discuss it." Kate didn't budge when he pulled on her arm. "Any cookies left over?"

Kate and Beth glared at each other for another long moment and then Kate turned away. She slammed a plastic container down on the kitchen island. "You ate all the snickerdoodles. These are the only ones left."

Sam opened the lid. Peanut butter cookies. Right now she couldn't eat a thing, but they needed some normalcy. She took a cookie and offered one to Beth. "You're right, Kate. You know both brothers better than we do. And if you told Logan about the journal, it could easily be a misunderstanding."

Michael set mugs on the counter. "But until we know otherwise, both of them are on the list. We need to be smart about this. All of us."

Beth nibbled on the edge of her cookie. "Help us keep you safe, Kate. Please."

Kate gave them each a quick glance. "I know. I just can't understand how my gut is so wrong." She took out some soda bread and put it on a plate. Next followed some cheese chunks.

Sam knew she was trying to process everything by doing something mindless.

Michael looked at Sam. "So, what's your plan to get the evidence we need to prove the killer's identity?"

"Who says I have one?"

Beth grabbed a slice of soda bread and some cheese from the plate. "You plan everything. We all know it. And you were fretting about it before."

Sam didn't even try to argue. They were right. Having a plan made her feel calm. In control. "Well, I don't have anything concrete yet, but let's go through the evidence we have so far."

"Tree branch," Michael said.

"Can't use it." Kate got down several boxes of tea. "We've contaminated it now with our test."

"She's right." Beth rocked back and forth from foot to foot. "Ghost testimony, out. We don't have any other physical evidence."

"We need to find some then," Michael said. "A search of their homes might turn something up."

"Do you think the killer kept trophies?" Beth said.

"You mean like mementos from his kills?" Sam didn't remember Killer Paul taking anything when she'd been in the ghosts' memories, but it could have been after they'd died.

"Logan mentioned each woman had something missing." Kate's voice was low like she hoped they wouldn't hear her.

"That detail wasn't in the paper, was it?" Sam looked at Beth who shook her head.

Michael pushed mugs toward Sam and Beth and then filled

them with hot water. "Do they both live in town?"

"I know where Graham lives." Beth leaned forward, dunking a chai teabag into her cup.

Kate put her half-eaten cookie down. "That's right, from the B&E you performed to get his hairbrush."

"Everyone's a critic," Beth mused.

A shadow of a smile graced Kate's lips before she seemed to realize this wasn't anything happy they were discussing. The expression quivered, and then died.

"Did you see anything else when you were there?" Sam chose Earl Grey tea.

Michael lifted his chin toward Beth. "You broke into Graham's house? Kate was serious about the B&E?"

Beth shrugged. "Apartment actually, not house. And he left the slider unlocked, so technically I wasn't breaking in." She turned to Sam. "I didn't have time to search, but I can go back."

Sam blew out her breath through her nose. "Well, anything we do find in their places, we can't use legally."

"We don't remove it." Michael poured creamer into Kate's cup. "We call the police with an anonymous tip, and they can find the evidence without knowing we were involved."

Sam nodded, warming to his idea. It might work. "We'd have to make sure Logan wasn't the one who went out on the call. Even if he's not the killer, he might cover up evidence proving it was Graham. They are brothers after all."

Michael broke off a piece of the soda bread. "Let's worry about that when we find the evidence. I'm sure we can figure out something for Logan. A distraction."

"You'll never get into Logan's place." Kate's hands fluttered to the locket around her throat like a touchstone. "But Sheila has an extra key."

"Sheila at the police station?" Sam said.

Kate nodded. "His secretary. She feeds his cat when he's on holiday."

Beth took a sip of tea. "Are you close with her? Can you get the key so we can make a copy?"

"No. She's very protective of Logan." Strands of Kate's red hair caught on her cheeks when she shook her head. "She doesn't like me much."

Michael squeezed Kate's shoulder. "Don't worry. I'll get the key. I can be very persuasive when I want to be."

Beth raised an eyebrow. "No one disagrees that on the *surface*, you're a fine specimen of a man, but if Sheila's loyal to her boss, she's not going to give up the key willingly."

Michael frowned. "I'll get the key."

"You're going to use your abilities on her, aren't you?" Sam said. "Manipulate her emotions."

"It'll get us what we need."

Beth snorted. "And you look down upon what I do. Who's harming the innocents now, doctor?"

Michael smiled brightly, but his eyes held something darker. "This small deviation is nothing compared to your public display of greed."

Kate gazed down at the counter. "Maybe we should figure out another way?"

"Beth's going with you." Sam's pronouncement was met with stunned silence.

Michael's face reddened. "You can't be—"

"I won't be saddled with—"

Sam held up her hands. "You're my friend, Michael." She paused and took a deep breath. "But up until yesterday, I didn't know you'd been lying to me about what you could do."

Michael stiffened. "You lied to me too, remember?"

Sam nodded. "True, but you know what I can do. I can't harm the living." She touched his arm. He tensed, but didn't pull away. "I don't understand your abilities, not really. I can't let you use them without having someone I trust to be there, just in case."

Beth's mouth dropped open for a moment and then she closed it. "Did you just say you trusted me?"

Reluctant understanding filled Michael's eyes. "I guess we both need to get to know the real Sam and Michael, don't we?"

Sam grabbed his hand quick and squeezed it. "We do. The ones we hid from each other." She looked at each of them. "Logan's place needs to be searched as soon as possible before there's another murder. I don't want to see another victim again. No more."

Kate lifted her mug. "Noon tomorrow. Most of the constables will be at lunch."

"Looks like we've got a lunch date," Michael said to Beth.

Beth's shoulders slumped. "Shoot me now."

CHAPTER 26

BETH WATCHED THE GROUP OF CONSTABLES LEAVE THE police station and head toward the bakery on the corner. The clock in the center of town sent out the last thundering bell marking the noon hour.

"So what's your plan?" Beth asked Michael. She flexed her fingers. Her hands were still cold inside her cashmere-lined gloves.

"I'm going to talk to Sheila."

Beth gave him what she hoped was a sufficiently withering look. "We not only need his keys, but Logan's alarm code too. I've got leverage on Sheila from my contacts. This could be over and done with quickly."

"Why am I not surprised you dug up dirt on someone?"

Beth waved her hand at him. "If it's prudent, who cares? Sheila's got a gambling problem. Let me talk to her."

The blue eyes Michael turned to her were colder than the wind rifling through Beth's hair. "I'll get what we need without your *methods*." The last word sounded like it dirtied his lips.

"You mean your persuasion voodoo or whatever the hell you do." She didn't bother to hide her doubt. He probably just relied on his good looks to get what he wanted.

Michael frowned, but it barely brought out a line in his smooth skin. "Persuasion voodoo? Is that a dumbed-down TV explanation you're used to regurgitating?" His voice lowered. "With how you've been flaunting your skills, I'm surprised the government hasn't scooped you up, put a leash on you, and sent you sniffing for national secrets. Good thing most intelligent people think you're a fraud."

She tensed and then let it release. "So, I should be worried about black SUVs pulling up and yanking me off the street?"

Michael's gaze grew serious. "No. If the government wants you, you'll never see them coming."

Beth's snark died on her lips. She might not know Michael well, but her gut told her he wasn't lying. Her shoulder blades itched, and she restrained from turning around, suddenly feeling eyes on her everywhere.

"This isn't about me," Beth said. "You plus Sheila better equal pay dirt." She leaned in. "Otherwise, it's my turn."

"Well, come on then. We've got about forty-five minutes before they trickle back in from lunch." He headed up the steps into the station.

As they had hoped, it was pretty deserted, with only a few constables in the back. Sheila sat at the front desk, sipping on a green smoothie.

Logan's assistant turned out to be exactly what Beth had expected. Heavy make-up, teased short brown hair, enough perfume to bathe in. For days. Beth guessed she was in her early fifties, but trying to cling to her forties by the tips of her acrylic nails.

She scanned the waiting room, which was empty except for them. No surveillance cameras. She didn't know what Michael really planned, but she'd give him his chance. Sitting down in a waiting room chair, she grabbed one of the magazines. It was from last year. She wasn't planning on reading anyway.

Michael approached the front desk. "Excuse me," he said smoothly. "I was wondering if you could help direct me to the local hospital?"

"Are you sick?" Sheila's question was one part helpful, the other part wary. Beth heard the distinct sound of anti-bacterial lotion being pumped.

Michael laughed, and it slid against Beth's skin like a gentle caress. She shivered. Jeez. Maybe he did have some abilities after all.

"No, I'm not sick," he said. "I'm a surgeon from the States, and I would love to check in with the local hospital and talk with some of the doctors there. My sister is here with me in the waiting area. Could you perhaps give us directions?"

His voice was warm and inviting. Maybe he was going to try for the romantic angle with Logan's assistant? Beth glanced over at him and realized he looked the part. Dashing yet approachable in his blue wool coat. Blond hair windblown. In a pose worthy of a supermodel, he leaned toward Sheila, hand casually placed on her desk near a photo frame. If he wasn't such an ass, she'd find him attractive. But he was. An ass.

Sheila flushed, and a hand crept to fluff her hair. "Of course, Dr. . . ."

"Forbes," Michael said with a welcoming grin. "And you are?"

"Sheila." Her smile revealed magenta lipstick on her teeth. "The hospital is just a few blocks over. Really not far at all."

Michael nodded, and then appeared to suddenly discover the photo frame. "Is this a picture of a Maine Coone? What a handsome devil." His words dripped with envy.

"It's a she." Sheila's voice was warm. "Felicity. She's the Detective Chief Constable's kitty, but I love her just like she were my own."

Michael sat on the edge of Sheila's desk. Beth was surprised she didn't keel over from a heart attack. From the rate of Sheila's breathing, Michael was giving her serious palpitations.

"I've got a girl kitty too." His voice lowered like he was confiding a secret. "Short-haired domestic, though Cleo is anything but domestic. Gorgeous black fur, grass-green eyes, and a regal demeanor." Again came that soft chuckle, warming Beth's skin. "I swear, she thinks she owns my place."

Sheila laughed, though it was really more of a throaty giggle. "Oh, they all do, don't they?"

Beth controlled her urge to barf from all the saccharine in the air. Sheila ate it up, if her possessive grip on Michael's arm was any indication.

Michael pulled out his phone, and when they started to goo and gaaa over cat pictures, Beth turned away and stared up at the portrait on the wall. She squinted at the name plaque.

Oscar Dunning. Logan and Graham's creepy old relative. Not surprising one of them was a killer.

They'd found nothing in Graham's apartment earlier. Just some old take-out containers. He hadn't been there in a few days, but no trophies, no stash of murderous mementos. Which left Logan to investigate.

Michael's voice reached her, and she caught the last part of what he was saying. "Tough on your chief. I know what it's like to have crazy hours as a doctor. And with these murders I've seen in the papers, he can't have much time to spend at home. His poor kitty."

"I know," Sheila said. "But that's why I help take care of the little girl. He gave me a key to his place for just that reason." Her words brimmed with pride.

"If only I had someone I could trust like you." Michael injected a note of sadness into his tone, like this subject had troubled him for quite some time.

"Your wife can't take care of Cleo?"

"No wife, or girlfriend, either." Michael sighed. "But even with your attention, I'm sure Felicity gets bored being alone so often."

Beth looked up at the clock. Twenty minutes had passed. They needed to be gone soon if they wanted to miss any early lunch stragglers coming back. *Come on Michael. Get this done.*

Sheila patted Michael's hand. "You would think Felicity would be bored being alone so often, but Logan, Detective Chief Constable Dunning, had a scratching post window seat designed just for his baby. It stretches across the whole side wall. Felicity watches the birds all day long."

Michael whistled. "That must be amazing. Maybe something like that would help my cat? Keep her occupied. I would love to see how it was constructed. But not from a photo," he added. "Seeing it in person would help me know how to build it."

Sheila's reply was swift. "Oh, Logan is out on a call right now. Maybe you can check with him tomorrow? I'm sure he wouldn't mind letting you see his handiwork." She ripped off a page from her small notepad. "Here, let me write down your information for him." Her voice dropped slightly. "If you leave your cell phone number, I can make sure he calls you."

Beth glanced at her watch. Michael had a few more minutes. Otherwise, Beth would have a nice private chat with Sheila about the money she owed. She shifted in her seat and glanced at them. Michael had taken Sheila's hand in his.

"Unfortunately, I'm flying back home tonight, so I won't be able to see your chief tomorrow," he said. "Maybe *you* could show me?"

"I don't think so, oh, my, your hand is so warm. So relaxing." Sheila's words were slurred on the edges like she'd been drinking.

"Or if it's easier, I could just borrow his key for a few hours and no one needs to know you've helped out a fellow cat-lover." Michael's words were soft with a sing-song quality. "And I'll need the alarm codes too. Don't want to frighten Felicity."

"Alarm codes," Sheila repeated. "Just helping."

Beth nodded along with Sheila.

"Logan will be very grateful you took care of this for him." Michael squeezed Sheila's hand.

"Grateful," Beth whispered. Michael was so right. One less thing for Logan to worry about. She swayed toward Michael like he was the Pied Piper. A part of her brain screamed loud enough she heard it through the warm haze of thoughts, though it sounded like a whimper.

Snap out of it.

She slid her fingers down to her boot sheath. The touch of the cool steel of her knife instantly cleared her mind. Holy crap. She was at a distance and felt it this bad. Sheila must be on a Michael-high.

"Our secret," Sheila murmured.

"Yes. It'll be our little secret," Michael whispered.

The look on Sheila's face was one of pure happiness. Like all her dreams had been granted in an instant. She looked younger, more vulnerable, and for a brief moment, Beth felt bad about what they were doing. But then she remembered this was to protect Kate from a killer.

Sheila took out her purse from her desk drawer, rooted around for a few seconds, and then announced, "Here they are." She placed a set of keys in Michael's open palm. "Front door, deadbolt, and shed out back."

"And the codes?"

Sheila got a notebook out from another drawer, opened it to a specific page and gave it to Michael. He scanned it, and then handed it back.

"Thank you," Michael said, and it sounded genuine. He

leaned down and kissed her on the cheek. Then, he whispered something in her ear, but Beth couldn't make it out.

He got up and joined Beth. His voice all business. "Come on. She won't remember a thing." He buttoned up his coat. "Kate will come by later and drop the keys someplace where Sheila will find them. She'll think she misplaced them."

"The codes? Don't we need to write them down?"

Michael tapped his temple. "Photographic memory. They're here."

"You're kind of freaking me out right now," Beth said. "I felt what you did from the waiting room."

Michael held open the door and let Beth walk through in front of him. "Sorry. I'm usually more careful, but it took longer than I expected to find a common thread to get inside Sheila's emotions. And a plausible reason for her agreement. I need both for a real connection."

Beth paused at the threshold and turned around to look at him. "Are you telling me if you're not careful, you can accidentally sway a group of people?"

A chill started in the middle of her back and crawled up to her neck. Maybe she'd written Michael off too early as a harmless doctor with a superiority complex.

Michael gave her a long stare. "You're afraid of me." He studied her like she was an interesting zoo animal.

"Fear can be healthy. I trust my instincts."

"And what do your instincts tell you about me?"

Beth slid her hands into her pockets. "You're dangerous."

Michael laughed, but it held a shadow of something dark.

"Some members of my family would agree."

"I can't figure you out." Beth shook her head. She didn't trust him, but was thankful he was on their side.

"And you don't like that. I can tell." Michael still looked amused. Beth wanted to smack the smile off those well-shaped lips.

"Enough small talk." Beth headed toward the car. "Let's grab the others and hope we find something at Logan's. Otherwise, we're screwed."

LOGAN'S HOUSE CREAKED IN THE WIND, AND THE floorboards shifted under Sam's feet. She knew it was only her imagination, but it felt like the house was anxious to get rid of them, get rid of the evidence they'd found, like it wanted to cut free a cancerous tumor.

The wooden box was just big enough to hold a ream of paper, but Sam knew it didn't have something that mundane inside. The longer she looked at it, the more it seemed to gather the shadows around it. Like it breathed in the darkness.

Clouds had smothered most of the sky. The pale illumination through the windows didn't touch the wooden box with anything but a glancing blow.

"It'd be nice if we could turn on the lights," Kate whispered to her left. "It's two in the afternoon, but it feels like midnight."

"We can't risk it." Michael held up a flashlight. "Did you two want to look through the box before the ghosts get here?"

Sam shook her head. "From what you've told us, it sounds like we found the trophies. If only there was a way to tie the trophies to them without Ellie and the others having to relive what happened."

"There wasn't a connection I could see," Michael said. "I didn't want to dig further without them being here. We need to put everything back the way we found it."

Though Logan's nearest neighbor was a good distance away, Sam agreed with his caution. If this box held what they feared it did, when they called in the tip to the police, they needed to make sure no one knew they'd been here.

Kate paced to the window and back. Then to the front door and back. In the gloom and the small space, she couldn't really go far. Michael and Sam exchanged a long look. Sam nodded, getting Michael's message.

"Maybe you want to go wait with Beth?" She touched Kate's shoulder lightly. "We can handle everything."

Kate shrugged her off. "No." She gave Michael a stern look. "And don't think you'll convince me to leave either. I need to know the truth."

"Wouldn't dream of it. I know that don't-fuck-with-me tone." Michael checked his phone. "Yasmin texted. Logan's still at the station. Nothing from Beth on anyone approaching. We're still good, but we should be quick."

A gray Maine Coon rubbed around Sam's ankles and meowed up at her. She crouched to pet the purring cat. "Sorry to intrude on you, Felicity. We'll be gone before you know it."

The cat's purr cut off like a plug had been pulled. A growl rumbled up through Felicity's body, vibrating through Sam's hand. She stood, knowing what this meant. She'd yet to find a cat who didn't have this reaction to ghosts.

"They're coming," she told the others.

The skin on her arms grew taut, the brush of energy grazing her shoulders, lifting the hairs on the back of her neck. The air thickened.

"Finally," Kate said, though the fearful expression on her face suggested she'd have been happy if they'd never arrived.

Felicity stopped growling and shot Sam a suffering look. Without another sound, she stalked back into the hallway.

Robert materialized first. A fine sheen of sweat coated his face as if he'd run the entire way from the manor. "I have told them of what you need. They are fast upon my heels."

They both took a step toward each other, and then stopped. Her gaze roamed over his face, his body. They hadn't seen each other since the forest. "I've missed you."

Robert took another step closer. "I have missed you as well." His hands opened and closed. She knew he was struggling not to touch her, but they couldn't risk anything. Not with the other ghosts showing up at any moment.

A larger rush of energy slid against her skin and then dissipated. Suddenly, the four victims stood before her.

"Everyone's here," Sam said. She nodded toward the women and received worried and wary looks back.

"Good," Michael said. "Let's get this done."

Kate grabbed Sam's left wrist. "I need to hear this for myself."

Michael's eyes widened slightly. "Kate can hear ghosts too now?"

"If Kate or Beth touch me, they can," Sam explained. "We think it could be a Triumvirate thing."

Michael just nodded like she'd told him the time, and then clicked on his flashlight, shining the beam onto the hardwood floors. "Let's get this done."

Sam glanced at the ghosts. Wendy and Amber had settled by the windows. Wendy's yellow sundress was the only warmth in the gloomy light. Amber still looked shell-shocked, but she'd only been a ghost less than forty-eight hours. Sam couldn't imagine what she was going through.

Monica tugged on her jacket, straightening the ever-straight hem. Her gaze looked resigned.

Ellie had her hands on her hips and had positioned herself in front of the box, staring at it as if it were evil incarnate. "So you think he took things from us, stole from our dead bodies?" Ellie's words dripped with contempt.

"That's what we're afraid of, yes." Sam knew it was better to be direct with Ellie. Anything else wouldn't be fair to her.

Monica joined them. "You've looked inside already." It wasn't a question.

Kate nodded. "We have, but we don't know if what's inside belongs to you and the others." Tears threatened in her eyes, her entire body rigid. "Frankly, I'm hoping you don't recognize a single thing."

"I don't believe it was the DCC either." Monica gave Kate a sad smile. "I've always thought he was a good man."

Ellie shook her head. "We don't know anything until we see what's inside." She looked over at Sam. "Open it."

"We're ready, Michael," Sam said. Kate's grip on her wrist trembled, but she held fast.

Michael lifted the lid carefully with his gloved hands. The hinges didn't make a sound. They were well oiled. Well used.

Sam didn't know what she expected, but it wasn't the disparate cluster of things huddling inside. The glow from Michael's flashlight caught the charm bracelet on top. Dolphins and angels reached out from the worn silver, trying to escape their chains.

One of the ghosts gasped. Sam couldn't tell who. All of them except for Ellie looked like they were going to be sick. Ellie just looked like she was going to kill someone.

Michael lifted the bracelet up, but it snagged on the gray woolen cap underneath. He carefully worked the errant angel's wings out of the fibers. Several strands of red hair gleamed in the light. Sam's stomach somersaulted. Would they find something more gruesome?

He placed the bracelet and hat carefully inside the lid. The blue fabric Sam had glimpsed underneath the hat was a pair of navy socks. They matched the blue of Monica's jacket perfectly.

The last item was in a small plastic bag. Flat. Blood red.

Sam's gaze latched onto Michael's. He had a look she recognized when he'd come from the hospital after someone had died. This was bad. She didn't want to know what was in the bag. Or why the killer had kept it pristine.

"Okay, everyone gather around," Sam said. "Let's see what you can identify." Robert ushered Wendy and Amber closer.

Wendy's face was devoid of expression, but her eyes looked wounded. "The bracelet is mine. My Da gave it to me when I was thirteen."

"And this?" Sam gestured to the hat.

Amber tried to take it, but her hand slid right through the wool. "Dammit. I keep forgetting I'm dead. That this is all real." Wendy slid an arm around her waist. Robert stood behind both of them, a hand on each shoulder.

"I know this is difficult, lass," he said. "But at least you are not alone. Samantha will find the fiend who did this and ensure he is punished."

Amber nodded, tears spilling down her cheeks. Wendy led her back to the windows.

"The socks are mine," Monica said. She turned a concerned gaze toward Ellie.

"Are the things theirs?" Michael asked.

"So far," Sam said.

Kate's hand fluttered to her chest, fingers finally gripping the locket around her neck. "This can't be happening."

Sam's heart skipped a beat. She didn't want to do this, to make Ellie's pain even worse, but they had to know. "Take it out, Michael."

The plastic crinkled against his gloves. He popped open the plastic bag and took the lacy piece of fabric out. Looking like he wanted to be anywhere but here, Michael slowly unfolded it. Red lace panties.

"That sick son-of-a-bitch." Ellie's words jabbed into Sam's skull. Her eyes glowed red, swirled with patches of black. The paintings in the living room banged against the wall like there was an earthquake. Glasses and plates in the kitchen cabinets rattled.

Anguish burrowed into Sam's skin, pushing runners of pain through her veins. Rage devoured the anguish.

He had to die, but he needed to suffer. Suffer like they had.

"Sam, control your ghosts," Michael said, his voice commanding. "If anything breaks, we've lost." He rushed into the kitchen.

Ellie's thoughts, her feelings stampeded over Sam's, taking over. He'd die a slow death. She'd see to it. She rushed over to her purse and pulled out an iron dagger.

Kate grabbed a painting before it hit the ground. "Something's wrong with Sam," she called out.

Michael ran out of the kitchen toward Sam. She slashed at him. The dagger ripped through his shirt, but didn't reach his skin. He tried to grab for her wrist, but she was too fast.

"Sam, break out of it," Michael said. "You can block a ghost's emotions. Do it."

Get to the front door. She had to get to the station and find the DCC. Finish this.

"Samantha, stop."

Robert stood in front of her. Not touching her, but blocking her way. *Slash him quick and he'll move.* The realization of what that could mean sliced through her as cold as the iron in her hand. She'd lose him. The iron was death to ghosts. Robert would die.

Sam scrabbled her way to the surface, breaking through Ellie's emotions.

The anger rode her hard, but she fought it. She flung the dagger and it hit the floor with a dull thud.

Michael grabbed her from behind. She instinctively head-butted him and felt teeth, bone.

"Shit," he exclaimed and the coppery scent of blood filled her nose.

She tried to wriggle free, but he hooked one of her legs with his own, tangling her, holding her.

"We need to calm down, otherwise we'll never put the killer away." Everywhere Michael touched, her back, her shoulder, even his breath on her temple weakened Ellie's hold on her.

Sam met Robert's gaze. He was inches from her. "I will help." Robert lifted his hand toward her and she felt the buffering of Ellie's anguish until it became a bare whisper in her mind. The barrier clicked into place inside her.

"That's right," Michael said in a soothing melodic voice. He loosened his grip on Sam, cradling her now. "We all need to relax."

Out of the corner of her eye, Sam saw Ellie rocking back and forth just like she was being rocked in Michael's arms. The red glow in her eyes faded.

The other ghosts watched Michael as if they couldn't bear to look away for even one second.

"Everyone okay?" Kate asked. She looked like she was going to throw up.

Sam nodded and pushed Michael gently away. "I'm okay." Not quite. She felt like she might join Kate over a trashcan. Her breakfast protested in her stomach. "Did you know your powers extend to Entwine?"

"Holy shit," Kate muttered.

Michael looked surprised, but pleased. "I guess I do now. We need to put everything back, wipe any prints, get out of here and call this in."

"I'm so sorry," Ellie said, glancing at each of them. She looked shaken and drained. "I didn't mean to do that to you. I just couldn't stop thinking of him taking those off my body after I was dead. I just—"

"It's okay," Sam said. "It's my fault for not being prepared." She gazed at all the women. "Thank you for being brave. For helping us find the truth. Michael's right though. We have to leave. All of us."

Robert nodded. "We shall head back to the manor and await your return. Come, lasses." He gathered them close and put his arms around them. They disappeared.

Michael returned to the living room after putting the box back where he had found it. "I'll make the call."

"Sheila might recognize your voice," Kate said. She was pale, sweaty. Sam knew she was going to come undone soon.

"I'll call it in," Sam said. "But we'll need that distraction for Logan. If he gets here first, the box will be gone."

"Beth's handling that." Michael looked up from finishing

a text. He hustled them out of the house and reset the alarm.

Sam looked back as they walked through the woods to their cars. Logan's cat stared at them from her window perch. Even with his top-notch security system, why would a smart cop like Logan leave damning evidence where it could be easily found?

Arrogance, maybe? Even the smartest person can screw up, and who would ever suspect the Detective Chief Constable of murder? But the ghosts had confirmed it. Logan was the killer.

CHAPTER 27

"PLEASE, JUST A FEW MINUTES," KATE SAID TO CONSTABLE Reid. They stood in the narrow police station hallway leading back into the holding area. "He's been asking for me." Kate needed to see Logan. To decide for herself if she could believe he'd killed all those women.

Constable Reid gave her a stern look. "We know he's been asking for you, but if the evidence is right, you might have been his next victim. I can't let you see him."

Kate pulled out her cell phone and called Beth, who was waiting outside. "Just give me a minute," Beth said. Kate wasn't above using Beth's celebrity if it meant she got to talk to Logan.

A few moments later, Beth sauntered back accompanied by another constable. His baby-face filled with awe.

Beth had her television smile plastered on, the charm oozing from every pore. "Of course, I'll sign your log book," she said. "Always happy to please a fan."

"It's Beth Marshall," the constable said to Reid. "*The* Beth

Marshall. She said she might consider doing a show here. In our town."

"That'll do, Campbell," Constable Reid said. "I'll take it from here."

Once Campbell disappeared around the corner, Reid's face lit with a huge smile. "I'd heard you were in town. We love your show at the station, Ms. Marshall. We watch it every Thursday night. The way you found those dog tags for that military widow." He shook his head slowly. "You gave her closure. You help so many people."

Beth's fake smile turned into a real grin. "Thank you so much Constable—"

"Call me Ted."

"Ted. It's nice to have my work appreciated. That's one of the reasons why I started my show. I knew I could do what others couldn't. I could give people peace."

Kate had heard the spiel before, but Beth really sounded like she meant it. "So, can we see Logan? Just for a few minutes?"

Ted shook his head. "We've still got him in a holding cell waiting to be booked. He's not supposed to have any visitors."

"Did you grill him yet?" Beth said. "About the murders?"

"A bit, but we've been instructed to wait for the big brass. They want to question him personally." Ted looked pained. "I still can't believe it."

Beth put a hand on his shoulder. "That's exactly what Kate's going through. Can you help me give her closure too, Ted?"

Ted gazed at both of them for a long moment. Finally, he

nodded. "All right. Wait here." He gestured toward the wooden bench against one of the walls. "I'll get it cleared and then bring you back." He walked down the hall and disappeared around a corner.

"Stop fidgeting, Red. This was your idea after all."

Kate sat on the bench. "Thanks for pulling some celebrity muscle. I wasn't going to get in."

"I know." Beth unzipped her leather jacket and took the seat next to Kate. "I didn't realize I had such a following over here. I might end up doing a remote show after all."

Kate's glance grazed the plaques on the wall. Most of them were for Logan's achievements. She let out a shaky breath." Do you think he did it?"

"It doesn't matter what I think. And I hardly know the guy. Why do you think he's innocent?"

"Gut instinct." Kate leaned back, her shoulders touching the wall. Images rushed through her mind. Prisoners, handcuffs, crying. She pulled back, feeling ill.

"You okay?" Beth looked at her. "We can go if you've changed your mind."

Kate shook her head. "Nope. It's fine." Was she suddenly not going to be able to handle any object without getting a glimpse of the people it had touched in the past? She needed help with her abilities. Help from those who might know what she's going through. "You think Michael was telling the truth about his family? He said he had a brother who gets visions."

Beth didn't look pleased. "What I saw here at the station

proved he's got skills. But there's more he's holding back. I don't trust him."

"Because he didn't gush all over you like the constables?"

Beth's reply was cut off by Ted's return. He led them down the hallway to a door in the back. He opened it with a key card and ushered them into a small room with three cells. Each had a single cot, toilet, not much else. All were empty save one. The one with Logan.

Logan rushed to the front of his cell, hands gripping the metal bars. "Thanks for coming, Kate." He nodded toward Beth. Logan was still in his own clothes, though the white shirt he wore looked slept in. The lines on his face were deep. Dark circles bruised the skin underneath his eyes.

Kate blinked back tears. "Are you okay?" As soon as the words left her mouth she realized how idiotic they sounded. "Stupid question. Of course you're not okay."

"Five minutes." Ted glanced at his watch.

Logan shook his head, a glimmer of the usual sparkle in his eye. "It's all right, Kate. They'll figure out soon enough they have the wrong man."

Ted stiffened, but didn't say anything.

Beth tilted her head. "So, you're saying it's Graham?"

Surprise flooded Logan's face. "Why would you think it's my brother? Did he say something?"

Kate wanted to smack Beth. No one knew about the DNA test. They couldn't explain how they found the branch, and it wouldn't be allowed in court.

"Ignore her," Kate said. "She thinks everyone who's even

sent a glance my way is a potential killer."

"I didn't do what they're saying." Logan stepped back from the bars, looking taller. For a moment, he wasn't a prisoner, he was the Detective Chief Constable. "Once they go through the evidence, they'll figure out the truth."

"But your fingerprints were on the box." Ted looked like he hadn't meant to let that slip, but it was obvious he was just as upset over Logan's arrest as Kate was.

"They found your fingerprints?" Kate suddenly felt dizzy.

"Someone's framing me. That's the only explanation."

Beth pointed toward his arm. His sleeves were rolled up. "Look."

Kate's mouth was dry. Seeing the tattoo Sam had described made her skin crawl. "The killer had this tattoo."

"This thing?" Logan looked down at his arm. "A lot of men in town have this. We're all part of the Freemasons. Joined when we were lads."

"Kate, why would you say the killer had this tattoo?" Ted's voice shifted out of friendly and into cop.

Beth hit Kate on the shoulder. "We were talking about it last night. Sam's worked with some cops on her books and we suspect the killer is local due to the radius of his kills. Since many of the men here have the tattoo, it stands to reason the killer might too."

Ted nodded. "Two minutes and then I have to take him back."

"Did Sam find something?" Logan said. He cast a quick glance at Ted. "With her research."

Kate nodded. "I didn't want to believe it. Fought not to believe it."

Realization dawned in Logan's eyes. "I would never hurt you, Kate."

The DNA test said it could be Logan, they'd found the evidence at his house, his fingerprints were on the box, he obviously liked her, and he had the tattoo. Though she didn't want to believe it, everything pointed to him being the murderer. And she'd almost let him into her heart.

"I don't know what to believe anymore. I'm sorry." Kate turned away from Logan's anguished face. "Let's go, Beth."

Beth looked surprised. "But you still have another minute left."

Kate didn't say anything more, just headed for the door. The last thing she heard before starting down the hallway was Logan's yell.

"I'm innocent, Kate. *Innocent.*"

SAM HELPED KATE CLEAN THE LUNCH PLATES IN THE kitchen. Or more accurately, she cleaned while Kate just stared at nothing. Sam knew her mind was someplace else. *With* someone else. Logan.

Beth had told her what had happened at the station, but Kate wouldn't talk about it. That had been a few days ago, and Kate still moved through the manor like she was sleepwalking.

For what felt like the hundredth time, Sam thanked Stu and

Aggie silently for keeping the girls a little longer. Kate was in no shape to take care of anyone. Not even herself.

"Beth and Michael will be back in a little while." Sam dried her hands on a dishtowel. "Yasmin promised her tonic would help you finally sleep." She tried to inject some energy into her tone, but it sounded brittle in the heavy quiet of the house.

The manor felt empty with just the two of them. The manor ghosts hadn't been around since Logan got arrested. Robert had also left, only temporarily. He'd said he didn't want to intrude, and Kate needed her more right now than he did. Though she knew he was just trying to be noble, she could use the company, the support. It wasn't like Beth and Michael were on the positivity squad.

Now that their killer had been caught, she'd expected to have Ellie and the others to show up. That's what used to happen when she'd done this before. But she hadn't seen any of them since that day at Logan's house. Perhaps they needed to see his conviction for their murders in order to move on.

Glancing at the sky through the kitchen window, Sam frowned. It seemed much darker than a few moments ago. "Looks like we're in for another storm. Why don't you go sit in the study, and I'll make us some tea."

Kate didn't argue. She turned away and shuffled out of the kitchen and into the hallway.

The doorbell rang, and Sam's heart pounded into her ribs, almost making her drop the kettle. She put it down carefully on the stove.

It was just a doorbell. Logan hadn't qualified for bail, so

it wasn't like he was going to show up on their doorstep. But since they'd found the trophies at his house, Sam had felt skittish, perpetually in flight mode. Her head told her it didn't make sense. Her body refused to listen.

She fought not to sprint into the hallway. Slow steps. Everything was normal.

"Who could that be?" Kate said. "Stu and Beth have keys." She'd stopped only a few steps toward the study. The chandelier above cast a yellow glow on her face carving out deep shadows under her eyes. She stared at Sam. "You don't think it's the police? That they somehow found out we were in Logan's place?"

"No. I worried about that too, but they would have found something by now." Sam walked over to Kate and took her hand. She hoped Kate wouldn't feel the tremble working its way through Sam. Maybe she'd take some of Yasmin's tonic too. "Come on, it's probably some girl scouts."

"Scotland doesn't have girl scouts." A little of the old Kate poked through in the tone, and Sam smiled.

"Humor me." Sam peeped through the spy hole in the door. "It's Graham. Were you expecting him?"

Kate blew out a long breath. "No, but I'm not surprised. I've been avoiding his calls. I just couldn't." She reached around Sam to grasp the door handle. "Guess it's time to stop being a coward."

She opened the door. "Graham." Kate's voice sounded shaky. Tears threatened in her bloodshot eyes. "I'm sorry. About Logan."

Graham's khaki jacket was wet. The harsh beat of rain on

the pavement swelled into a deluge. He looked as if he'd been sleeping just as poorly as Kate. "Oh, Katie. There's no need to apologize."

Kate opened the door wider. "Come in, come in, so I can blubber in the privacy of my own home."

Graham stepped through the doorway quickly. His hair was drenched from the downpour outside and slicked close to his head.

"I'm so sorry for what's happened with your brother," Sam said.

"Thank you." Graham smiled, though the edges of his mouth barely lifted, as if his face had forgotten the full movement and only recalled a shadow.

Kate took his jacket and hung it on a hook in the hallway. "Sam was going to make some tea. Would you like some?"

"Tea would be wonderful," Graham said, and then sneezed.

Kate gave him a sharp look. "We need to get you dried off. At least your hair so you don't catch a cold. Go on into the study, and I'll get a towel for you." Suddenly animated, she hurried toward the bathroom next to the kitchen.

"Poor lass." Graham shook his head slowly. "I think she was in love with my brother."

"He seemed like such nice guy, but I guess that's what they always say." Sam couldn't help the regret in her voice. "You had no inkling of what he was doing?"

"We don't really get along. We haven't been close since we were kids." Graham's voice was even, but Sam heard the hurt underneath. "But I never would have suspected him of something this heinous."

Kate bustled out of the hall bathroom. It was like she had stepped from a black and white movie into color. "Why aren't you in the study getting warm?" She pushed Graham down the hall and toweled off his head while she did it.

Maybe Kate just needed someone to fuss over to help keep her mind off things? If that was the case, Graham could stay as long as he wanted. Or maybe it was time for the girls to come back?

When Sam joined them in the study with a steaming pot of tea and muffins, they had settled into the cozy armchairs by the fireplace. Graham held Kate's hand, and she cried into a tissue.

Kate glanced up at Sam. "Poor Graham has had to put up with my break-down."

"Nonsense." Graham stood up and helped Sam place the tray on the coffee table between them. "We're both a mess."

"Kate believed Logan was innocent at first. I'm sure you did too." Even if they were estranged, Sam imagined it would be difficult to suspect your sibling of being a serial killer.

"I did in the beginning. But the trophies confirmed it." He cast a sidelong look at Kate, who stared away from them and into the fireplace. His voice became quiet. "Along with the women he chose."

Sam couldn't disagree. She handed Kate a plate with a pumpkin muffin on it and a fork. "You haven't eaten all day."

"I'm not hungry."

"Do you want me to force-feed you in front of Graham?"

Sam stared at her until Kate finally picked up the fork and took a bite of muffin. Sam doctored some tea for Kate and handed it to her.

Kate put her plate down on the table. "I know the trophies look bad, but Logan claims he was framed." She studied Graham. "Maybe I should listen to my gut and not my head?"

Sam didn't know what Kate was playing at. Because if Logan wasn't the killer, Graham was. Was she trying to bait him into making a confession?

She wished her iron daggers weren't in her purse near the front door.

"I'm not surprised he's denying it." Graham poured himself some tea, his eyes brighter than before. More alert. "I guess we're just lucky he didn't collect body parts from the victims. There was one killer several years back that took pinkie toes."

Kate gasped, but her tears had dried up. "That's awful."

"I think that's enough talk about the trophies." Sam shot Graham a hard look. "So, how's the cab business, Graham?"

"I want to talk about Logan and the trophies," Kate said. "That's the only evidence they have to convict him. Easily planted."

"True," Graham said, his tone placating. "But they had his fingerprints on the box and Logan has a state-of-the-art security system."

Kate tilted her head. "So, it was someone he knew, someone he trusted."

Sam's mind went over Kate's words. But if it was Graham, why not frame someone else in town? He wouldn't have known about the DNA test. It wasn't like Logan trusted him, so he wouldn't have the codes to his house. No. It had to be Logan.

Graham put down his teacup. "I'd like this to all be a nightmare too, I truly would. But he's guilty."

Kate's shoulders slumped. She tortured the pumpkin muffin with her fork. "I guess you're right."

"I've been wondering why he would have kept such dangerous evidence." Graham's words were a bit rushed. A flush crept its way through his skin. "I've heard it said that some killers use trophies to relive the murders."

A flash of Ellie's memory crowded into Sam's brain. Running for her life. She nearly dropped her own cup, but clenched it tight before it slipped from her grip. Where had that come from? She hadn't had any flashbacks since they'd caught Logan.

"I've heard that too," Kate said softly.

"Most of the things he took were pretty mundane." Graham's words were slower than before. "Except for Ellie's. I feel terrible for the Crofts. To think he kept their daughter's panties. It's horrible."

Sam froze in the process of putting more sugar in her tea. They hadn't released any information on what the specific trophies were, let alone which one was taken from which victim. And Graham had just told her he wasn't close to his brother, so why would Logan be tempted to share his crimes? Released from the starting gate, her heart broke into a gallop.

Before she could even act surprised at his trophy comment, Graham said, "I mean, I didn't know Ellie personally, but that just seems so much worse than taking Wendy's charm bracelet."

Again information he shouldn't have. She didn't know how he had done it, but Graham had framed Logan. He was the killer.

Rather than the nauseous rush she'd become used to this past week, adrenaline eased through her system, like a weapon. Her legs and arms felt strong, ready. Her eyesight sharpened. An acrid smell reached her nose. Graham was sweating.

She had to get Kate out of here and find a weapon without spooking Graham.

The easiest option was the back door in the kitchen. And the kitchen had knives. Not the daggers she was used to, but she could handle most blades.

Sam would need the element of surprise to take down Graham. He was her height, but had more bulk. She had to be careful.

Kate clanked her cup down on the saucer. "Wait a second, how do you know—"

Sam crossed her legs, hitting the tray with her foot and knocking Kate's cup onto the heavy rug. It didn't break, but tea spilled everywhere.

"Sorry, about that." Sam fake-mopped up the mess with a napkin and tilted her own cup just enough to make a bigger spill. "Damn it. Let me get some towels from the kitchen. Kate, can you show me where they are?"

Kate stood and gave Sam a quizzical stare. "Sorry, Graham. We're obviously rusty in the hostess department." She squeezed his shoulder and smiled. "We'll be right back."

Graham gave them a bland smile, but the planes in his face sharpened.

Sam walked slowly and casually out of the study.

He was suspicious, but she hoped he wouldn't try anything just yet. The short walk to the kitchen seemed like miles.

"Is Beth staying on for a few more days?" Sam tried to keep her voice even. Sound traveled in the manor, so she couldn't warn Kate outright. But she could text Beth.

Kate gave her a pointed look. "I don't know what Beth's plans are. But I don't think she's booked a flight back yet."

Sam slipped her phone out of her pocket and sent a quick message to Beth.

Graham is killer. At manor. Hurry.

When they reached the kitchen, Kate went over to one of the drawers and took out some towels and cleaner for the rug. "I realize I've got to be wrong about Logan. You don't have to make up an excuse to talk to me about it."

Sam leaned in close, grabbing Kate's shoulders. "Graham is the killer," she whispered in her ear. "Run out the back door. Call the police. I'll stall him." She shoved her phone into Kate's hand.

Kate stiffened under her grip, her gaze shifting past Sam's shoulder. "Watch out," she screamed.

Sam whirled around.

Graham's fist smashed into her cheek. Her teeth sliced open the inside of her mouth, blood spurting down her throat. Her body spun toward the marble island. She couldn't twist out of the way in time. She hit the marble hard, cracking her head, pain pounding through her temple.

"Graham, stop!" Kate yelled.

Sam slid to the floor. Light fading. Cold against her cheek.

Graham's voice rasped against her senses. "Oh, Katie. Please call me Paul."

CHAPTER 28

ROBERT PACED UP AND DOWN OUTSIDE MACCALLUM & Sons. Beatrice sat on a bench watching him.

"Do you think it has been long enough for her to comfort Kate?" Robert said.

Beatrice sighed. "I don't know why I thought I could persuade you to leave her alone. You're obviously drowning and like it that way."

"You do not understand—"

"Excuse me." Darrin suddenly materialized in front of Beatrice. He had a jacket over his usual black tunic and trousers, but the cuff on his wrist still gleamed. The expression on his face could only be likened to sorrow. "Robert, the Wardens would like to see you."

Tightness gripped Robert's chest and squeezed.

Beatrice stood. "What do they know?"

"I was only told to bring him." Darrin had true regret in his eyes. "As much as I'd like to disobey for you, Beatrice, they would merely send someone else who isn't as cordial."

"I will come willingly." The idea of facing the Wardens robbed his legs of strength, but there was no escape. He grasped Beatrice's arm. "If I do not come back, will you tell Samantha my last thoughts were of her?"

"No one's having any last thoughts," Beatrice hissed. "Keep your wits about you and be careful. They might not know everything. Don't volunteer any information."

Robert hugged her hard and then released her. "Sage advice, dear Beatrice. I am so blessed to have found you once again."

Beatrice fixed Darrin with a stern stare. "The Wardens will hear from me if my boy doesn't come back. Understood?"

Darrin nodded, looking worried. Robert wondered again at what power Beatrice truly held in Entwine. "They want to talk to him. That's all." He took Robert's wrist, and his Runner's cuff glowed. The symbols flared bright, leaving an afterimage in the air, almost like they had leapt off the metal. Suddenly they were no longer outside the antique shop. They were someplace else.

Robert was not certain what he thought the lair of the Wardens should look like, but he would not have expected the extreme bustle of a train station like the ones he had seen on Samantha's spirit box.

Darrin had taken him to a platform which overlooked the activity below. Ghosts rushed about like they were late for something vital. Here and there were gates, elaborate archways really. Some were made of metal. Others gleamed with polished wood. There were even some in the distance which appeared to be made solely out of flowers and trees.

Each gate was manned by ghosts who looked like professors or librarians, checking names off a list. Ghosts stood in line next to Runners. Many looked happy, but a few gave Robert the impression they were going to bolt any moment.

Burly ghosts walked along the lines. Though they did not have any weapons, cuffs like Darrin's gleamed on their wrists.

"Is that where Ray went?" Robert pointed at the gate where the most unhappy ghosts appeared to be waiting. That one was made of black metal corroded with rust and something else. Something that looked like blood.

"No. He went there." Darrin lifted his chin toward a gate made of stones like the ones you would find near a river or lake. Smooth, calming, all in colors of blue and gray.

Robert swallowed, feeling very small in the scheme of things. Would he eventually have to go through one of these gates if Samantha did not succeed in their quest? "Are these gateways to Heaven and Hell?"

Darrin took his arm and led him back away from the gates, down a long hallway. "Everyone has a different idea of Heaven, Hell, Valhalla, the Underworld. It depends on the person they were in life."

The further they moved down the corridor, the more it changed. The cold utilitarian lines shimmered, transforming. Wallpaper grew up upon the walls, filling in like grass in a field. Light bulbs disappeared, replaced by sconces filled with flickering candles. Even the concrete underneath their feet changed into a wooden floor with a series of rugs along the length.

"What just happened?" Robert said.

"The Wardens like to make their visitors feel welcome." Darrin stopped in front of an ordinary looking door. "They get them so rarely." He knocked on the door and gave Robert a warm smile. "I'm glad to see you made the leap from the Rinth. I always knew you could do it."

Robert drew himself up to his full height, preparing to meet the rulers of this Realm. "Much like that leap, my heart questions my chances again. Any suggestions?"

Darrin considered his words. "Be honest, be clear with what you want, and be respectful." He leaned in close. "They can destroy your essence if they so choose."

The Runner turned and headed back down the hall. "I don't want to have a distraught Beatrice on my hands. Play nice," he called back over his shoulder.

"Come."

The voice from behind the door was gentle, but Robert did not mistake the command underneath.

He took a deep breath and remembered Beatrice's advice. He would not reveal more than he was asked. Robert turned the handle and opened the door.

THE SOUND OF SOBBING SEEPED INTO SAM'S EARS, MOVING deep inside her, chilling where it touched.

Sam struggled to push the haze away from her mind, but

it swirled tightly like a freezing fog. There was something important she had to do, but she couldn't seem to remember. Every time she got close, it moved away, blurring, disappearing.

The darkness around her grew lighter, like moonrise behind wispy clouds. There was a shape in the distance. A hallucination?

Dressed in jeans and a long sweater, her mom looked just like she had most days. Her long blonde hair curled back over her shoulders, and her light green eyes warmed when they lit upon Sam. She knelt by her.

Knelt? Sam realized she was lying on the ground.

The way her mom's head tilted, the feel of her hand on Sam's cheek. She knew deep in her heart. No question. This was really her.

"Mom?"

"My poor girl." She gathered Sam in her arms, and the smell of ginger washed over Sam, taking her back to when she was a child. "I've missed you so much."

"This can't be happening." Sam tried to hug her back, but she couldn't move. She realized she wasn't dreaming, but she wasn't quite awake either. Somewhere in between. "Where's Dad?"

"He's fine." She pushed the hair back from Sam's face, and Sam closed her eyes, basking in her touch again. It was her mom. Her *mom*.

"Why did you wait so long to come back?" Sam didn't care that she sounded like a child. At this moment, she felt like one.

Her mom's eyes grew sad. "It's the price of being the

Necromancer. You give up seeing your loved ones for the power."

"But I never wanted this power. I tried to get rid of it."

"I know, baby. But it's part of you. And it's changing. If you continue to grow with the Triumvirate, who knows what other rules you'll be able to break? Maybe we'll be able to see you again. You've always been stronger when the three of you are together."

The Triumvirate. Fate had definite designs on their lives. She wasn't sure she liked it, but if it allowed her to see her parents again, she might be able to live with it.

Her hand stilled on Sam's temple, and she leaned in close, whispering in her ear. "You have leverage, you know. You can make your own Bargain with the Universe."

Make her own Bargain? What leverage? "I don't understand?"

Her mom pulled away. "There's no time. You're in the woods, and Graham has drugged you. Kate's okay for now, but he'll kill you both unless you stop him."

Kate. At the mention of her friend's name, the details of what had happened at the manor collided together in her mind. Graham was the killer. He'd knocked Sam out.

Sam willed herself awake. Nothing.

"It's not working, Mom." Sam struggled to move again. The invisible bonds still held her tight.

"Take a deep breath." Her mom breathed with her. "Call to the Triumvirate."

"But that didn't work before."

Her mom smiled, and it was so familiar, tears rushed into Sam's eyes.

"I'll try, Mom."

Kate, Beth. Hear me, help me to wake up.

Only silence.

She screamed louder in her mind. *Dammit Kate, I'm trying to save your ass. And Beth, we still have crap to do. I need you both right now.*

An echo filled the darkness around her. Not an echo. Voices. Shouting her name.

Sam, Sammy, Ms. Perfect, Princess. Kate and Beth. She grasped onto their voices, holding them close.

"Go, honey," her mom said. "Wake up. Save yourself."

Sam's eyes flashed open. The mist in the air made the moonlight hazy in the gloom. She heard the wind rustling the leaves. This wasn't a dream. She was awake. The trees of Kate's forest loomed all around her. A shiver hammered her body.

From her position on the ground, she felt eyes on her and saw Kate tied to the oak tree. Her arms were bound in front of her. Chartreuse nylon rope wrapped around Kate's waist, binding her to the tree.

"You okay?" Kate mouthed.

Sam tried to clear the fogginess from her mind. She moved her arms just slightly. No restraints. No sound of Graham anywhere. Could he have left them alone?

Hope sparked through her, giving her strength. She looked around more closely. A dark, lumpy shape next to her looked familiar. Her purse. What was her purse doing here? More importantly, were her daggers still at the bottom?

Kate had seen her daggers in the forest during her vision. They were important. She hoped Graham had missed them.

She pushed herself up slowly and reached for her purse.

"I see you're finally awake," Graham said.

Sam's head spun. Graham sat to her left. There were two of him, no one. She leaned over and threw up. Acid burned up her throat. She struggled for breath, her stomach clenching several times until she was done.

Graham handed her a wad of tissues. When she didn't take them, he pressed them gently into her palm. "You'll want to get yourself cleaned up. You have a wedding to attend."

"What?" Sam managed to croak. He sounded like this was all normal and natural. She wiped her mouth with the tissues. Throwing up had helped clear some of the wooziness, but her head pounded with each pump of her heart. She'd hit the marble island hard. Probably had a concussion.

"Katie and I are getting married." A pleased smile spread across Graham's face.

"You sick psycho," Kate growled. "No one's getting married to your crazy ass."

Graham's gaze held pain. "I'm not crazy, darling. I know it might seem that way." He walked the few steps over to Kate and crouched so that they were on eye level. "But there are reasons for all my actions." He looked at his hands, flexing them. "Even the unpleasant ones."

"I don't care what reasons you had." Kate glared at him. "Killing those innocent women was unforgivable."

Graham cupped Kate's cheek. She flinched her head away, but he grabbed her by the chin and yanked her back to face him. "Don't you understand? They were inferior. Just copies of you. They were nothing."

Sam needed to get him off this path and stop Kate from goading him. Stalling was one thing, but they needed to keep him calm.

"Where did you get your disguises, Graham?" Sam said. Her stomach rolled dangerously, but there was nothing more to come up. "They fooled everyone. I had no idea it could have been you. Very ingenious."

Graham nodded, looking like his suspicions had been confirmed. "Their ghosts told you everything."

"They did. Though everyone had a different description. It was truly clever." Sam meant what she said. Sick, but clever.

The tension eased from Graham's body and he released Kate's chin. "I bought them online with stolen credit cards. I didn't want to take the chance of any witnesses figuring out it was me." He gave Sam a long look. "I didn't factor a Necromancer into the equation, but it worked out the same."

Sam nodded slowly. "I'm surprised you didn't leave the disguises at Logan's place. More evidence to point to your brother."

Graham stood from his crouch. "Wigs, prosthetics, they all pick up trace DNA. Too much to leave behind. I never planned on what happened with Logan." He gazed off into the distance toward the manor. "No matter our troubles. I just needed a place to keep their things. A safe place. He wasn't supposed to be involved."

Kate cleared her throat. "Then how did his fingerprints get on the box?"

"It used to be his." Graham gave her a wink. "I know what you're doing, Katie. Trying to stall. Having cold feet before a wedding is quite natural. You're probably worried about what you'll be wearing." He walked behind the oak tree and came back with a garment bag. He unzipped it, the sound harsh against Sam's ears. Crystals gleamed and winked on the cream wedding dress inside as he showed it off.

"It's beautiful." Kate smiled at him but shot Sam a frightened look when Graham zipped the bag back up.

He sighed. "I'm sorry I don't have anything for you to wear, Sam. You were unexpected really, but Katie pleaded for me not to kill you at the manor, so I had to bring you along." His face brightened. "But you can give the bride something. How does that go? Something borrowed, something blue."

Sam fumbled with her bracelet. "How about this, Graham?" A cool breeze wafted the hair back from her sweaty face and she felt more clear-headed. She lifted the silver rope bracelet toward him, making her hand shake so he'd think her still weak.

"That's perfect," Graham said. He went to her and plucked the bracelet from her hands. "And so thoughtful." He leaned in to give her a hug and whispered in her ear. "No hard feelings, but after the wedding, I'm going to have to kill you. My father always taught us: no loose ends."

CHAPTER 29

THE HOUSE WAS TOO QUIET AND EMPTY. NOT EVEN THE wind seemed to want to disturb the silence. Aside from the signs of struggle in the kitchen, there were no clues.

Beth holstered her gun and leaned back against the bottom railing of the staircase. She rubbed her chest. It felt bruised. No matter how she tried to control her breathing, her heart continued to pummel her ribcage with ferocity.

Being worried over someone else's safety wasn't something she was used to. She hated it. That's what letting people in did to you. Made you almost suffer a coronary.

But Kate and Sammy needed her. Neither was going to die on her watch. Not happening.

The cops and Michael were on their way, but Graham had a head start and a car, which meant he could be miles from here.

Her best bet now was her gift. Anything that could give her and the police a location. Who knows how long Graham would keep them alive? Especially Sammy. Beth had just gotten her back. She couldn't lose her again. Not like this.

Beth stomped back into the kitchen, her worn work boots clomping against the hardwood floors. She surveyed the scene again. Chills rushed up her arms even under her lined motorcycle jacket. A broken dish, a salt shaker collapsed on the counter, and blood smeared on the marble countertop. She'd left everything the way she'd found it.

Okay, we need an object. Clothing, jewelry, glasses. What do we have?

Beth thought about Sam first. She had no idea what she'd been wearing after they'd left for town this morning. No specific jewelry. Beth hadn't seen her purse in the house, but Graham might have dumped it anywhere. She couldn't afford to waste time on dead ends or maybes.

Her thoughts shifted to Kate. She never went anywhere without her locket. The one with the picture of her kids and Paul. Wherever the locket was, Kate would be.

No one was here to ask her to find it. An essential thing to activate her gift. But she'd found the pipe without anyone.

She lowered herself onto the kitchen floor and sat cross-legged, emptying her thoughts of everything but Kate's locket.

The oval shape of the locket formed in her mind. The filigree work on the outside leading to the engraving on the back. *With my love. Always.*

"Okay Fate or Universe or whatever you are, I need you to work that mojo on me again. Help me find Kate's locket."

The ticking of the clock in the corner sounded deafening. Beth shook out her hands and tried to relax. Closed her eyes. Waited.

The only reply she got was the creaking whoosh of the refrigerator powering down.

She sighed. It wasn't working.

She scrambled to her feet and grabbed her cell phone. Maybe it would work if someone told her to find something over the phone. She'd never tried it. Had never needed to.

Michael didn't answer. She dialed Yasmin's shop. Voicemail. She finally reached Lacey, her personal assistant on the show.

The line clicked, and Beth didn't bother to say hello. "Lacey, it's Beth. I need you to do something for me."

Lacey's sleep-tinged voice sounded faint. "Beth, what's going on? Are you in trouble again? We're supposed to start filming soon."

"I need you to ask me to look for something. It's important."

Lacey sighed. "What do you need me to say?"

"You can't just say it, you really need me to find it. It has to be important to you."

"Beth, I don't really understand how your gift works, but how am I supposed to care about you finding anything at two in the morning here. I'm half asleep."

"Dammit, Lacey." Beth punched the back door. "If I don't find them, they're dead."

"Crap," Lacey said, sounding alert. "Okay. I'm with you. Sorry. What do you need me to do?"

Beth took a deep long breath and nursed her knuckles. "Tell me to find Kate Banberry's locket."

"Beth, you better fucking find Kate Banberry's locket and save her."

The conviction in Lacey's voice was true. But all Beth felt was the blood throbbing in her hand.

"Shit." It wasn't working either. "Got to go." She hung up on Lacey's protests.

Beth paced up and down the kitchen running through her options again. No neighbors nearby. She could drive into town but that could eat up time. The only people left in the manor right now besides her were the dead.

The *dead.*

Her steps stilled. Stopped. The dead who used to be people.

Could a ghost ask her to find something? She saw Sam with Entwine's eyes, all glowy and shit, like the ghosts saw her, and Yasmin mentioned she was tied to the ghostly realms. Maybe she was already connected enough to Entwine to make this work?

"Beatrice, Robert, Anyone? I need your help. Kate and Sam's lives depend on it," she shouted. Glancing around the kitchen, she said softly to herself. "Okay genius, how are you supposed to know anyone heard?"

The toppled salt shaker slid down the length of the kitchen island and smashed into the sink. Salt sprayed everywhere in a white mist.

Beth realized she'd stopped breathing. This might just work.

"Okay, folks, ghosts, whoever is here, I need you to ask me to find something. And you have to really want me to find it, so put some oomph into it otherwise it's not happening." She paused for a moment. "Find Kate Banberry's locket. Repeat that phrase over and over again."

Please, Universe. Please.

Her thumb burned, where she'd cut it years ago with their blood sister ritual. She looked at it and drops of blood welled up from the scar.

"What the fuck?"

She grabbed a napkin, pressing it to the wound, and the faint brush of voices reached her ears. The ghosts. How was she hearing them? Her thumb pulsed, matching the cadence of the sounds.

It wasn't just one voice. A chorus with a woman's strong yell rising above the rest. Beth had never heard Beatrice, but she believed it was her leading the battle cry.

The tingling began at her scalp. It always reminded her of being caught out in the rain. Drops hitting her hair, then sliding down her skin, skimming over her body, finally soaking in.

Her body warmed, matching the heat in her thumb. The earlier chill extinguished under the energy filling her.

It was working.

"Keep going!"

Every part of her vibrated as if tuned in not only to the ghosts' voices, but to something more. She reached out her hands toward the shimmering air in front of her and a blast of cold shot through her.

The familiar sparkles solidified into something that always reminded Beth of looking into the surface of a frozen lake about the size of a large dresser mirror. The center clear, but toward the edges, frosted, ready to crack at any moment.

The reflection of her black eyes stared back at her. She tapped the icy mirror in the center. The ghosts' shouts still rang in her ears. The center darkened, the only light coming from the glow of Kate's locket. She saw its oval outline blazing.

A thick silver cord of light rose up in front of Beth, sliding back and forth like a snake looking for the right time to strike. Before she could exhale, the cord shot forward, latching onto to the flicker of gold inside the mirror.

The cord pulled taught, yanking Beth forward. Her body remained in the kitchen, but her spirit form followed the cord's path.

Images shifted in front of her eyes. Kate bound to an oak tree. She knew where this was, recognized it from when Sam had shown her where the branch had been found. The view moved to the back of Graham's head. A body lying on the ground, still, unmoving. Graham blocked the face, but Beth knew it had to be Sam.

Sweat pushed through her pores. Tears gathered in her eyes. This couldn't be happening. It wasn't fair. Kate was still in danger, and Sam might be dead already.

The view frayed around the edges. Beth slammed back into her body, stumbling until she ran into the kitchen island.

Leaning on her side, she clung to the cold marble. The ghosts went silent, or whatever connection she'd had was gone.

Her arms and legs felt like they had weights strapped to them. All she wanted to do was curl up in a ball on the floor.

But there was no time to recover.

Her hands shook when she dialed the police station, and then sent another text to Michael. She opened the back door and clung to the frame, legs wobbly.

"Kate's in Caleb's forest by the old oak," she said to any ghost listening. "Please help her. Buy me some time. And pray Sam's still alive."

She checked her gun, her knife, and her resolve. She'd need all of them to do what it took. Whatever was necessary to save her friends.

Without a glance behind her, Beth slipped out into the night.

THE DOOR SWUNG OPEN, AND ROBERT GAZED INTO WHAT reminded him of a gentleman's club. One where whiskey, negotiations, and privacy were the order of the day. Rather than potential torture.

Robert stepped into the room slowly, looking for the owner of the voice he had heard. Heavily stuffed leather chairs were arranged two by two in a room about half the size of his manor's study.

In the far corner by the fireplace, the murmur of conversation reached his ears, though he could not tell who the occupants were. The high backs of the chairs effectively hid their identities.

Someone got up from one of the chairs near a window.

A window which displayed beautiful blue sky and sunshine. Where were they?

"Lord Robert Grenning, so nice to meet you at last."

The speaker was just a girl. Well, if he had to admit, she was most likely in her fourteenth or fifteenth year, but much younger than he had anticipated. Perhaps she was the Wardens' apprentice?

Her hair was short, cut tight to her head. Large eyes regarded him with interest. Along her right ear, bits of metal crept all the way around to circle back to the lobe. A tattoo began under her chin, swept around her neck and clavicle to disappear at her left shoulder. The same types of symbols on Darrin's cuff and Caleb's staff.

Robert bowed low. "I would say the pleasure is all mine, but I confess being summoned by the Wardens has left me confused." He gazed at the chairs by the fireplace. "Are we waiting for the Warden to finish up his meeting?"

The girl smiled, and it was indulgent. "We're not waiting on anyone. I'm Sloane. I summoned you." She walked over to a small table by the window. "Would you care for a drink?"

Robert swallowed his surprise. How could a realm such as Entwine be run by children? Were all the Wardens this young? "As we both know, a drink is a meaningless offer to a ghost."

Sloane gave him a wink. "Come on now. We both know you're more than just a ghost." She sat down in one of the chairs and gestured to the other. "In fact, we've never seen one who can do what you do."

He sat on the edge of the chair, back straight. They knew.

Fear spiked through him, sending a wave of adrenaline from his chest to his stomach. Sweat collected on his forehead. "I can assure you, it is not by choice or design."

She sighed. "We're not going to destroy you, if that's what you're worried about. Though we've done much worse for fewer transgressions." The casual way in which she said this chilled Robert more than a blade against his throat.

His spine remained straight, taut. "Then why am I here?"

"We need your help."

"No." Beatrice's fears were playing out. He stood. "I will not be your assassin against the living."

Sloane's fingers drummed out a single beat on the chair's armrest. "Sit. No one is going to make you a gun for hire. Really, where do you ghosts dream up this sh—stuff?"

Robert sat. "What are you?" Beatrice had said Wardens straddled both realms, but what did that mean?

Sloane gave him a long look and suddenly appeared much older than her years. "That's something I'm willing to share with the Necromancer. But for now, we need her help, and you're the best person to convince her."

"You do not seek to harm either of us?"

"Of course not."

The tension slid from Robert's shoulders so greatly, he actually slumped back in the chair.

Sloane took a drink from her glass. The bitter scent of whiskey made Robert's mouth water. "Though she's got to fix this thing between you first."

"This thing?"

"This." Sloane punched him in the mouth, her movement so quick, her hand blurred in his sight. The blow tore open the wound he had suffered at the antique store, and pain seared through him in a hot line from his cut lip to his fists. "You've got to get the balance righted between you and the Necromancer, otherwise you'll both end up dead and of no use to us."

He swallowed his blood and his anger. To strike out against these creatures without more knowledge would be foolish. His fingers unclenched. Slowly.

"Good. You know your place." Sloane handed him a napkin. "You're special, Robert. There's no denying it. But *we* run Entwine."

He wiped the blood dripping down his chin. Samantha had mentioned the balance as well. "And how do you propose we right this balance you speak of?"

Sloane smiled, and it reminded him eerily of Caleb's grin when he knew something he did not wish to reveal. "Samantha knows. Or she will soon enough."

The door burst open, and Darrin rushed in. "The Necromancer is in danger."

Robert stood almost at the same time Sloane did. The only one who presented a danger was the killer, and Logan was in prison. Which meant they had the wrong man. "Take me back now. I can defend her."

Sloane pinned Darrin with a stare. "This was supposed to have been handled."

Darrin blanched. "There were complications."

"Go with Darrin," Sloane said. "Save the Necromancer. Do what needs to be done."

Robert nodded. "I would die for her, but you know that well enough already. I will not fail."

Sloane gestured to Darrin. He grabbed Robert's arm, pulling him back through the door. They took off at a run toward the platform they had arrived on.

"Hold onto me tightly." Darrin stopped when they reached the platform. "We're doing this the hard way." Without warning, the gates and the ghosts below them disappeared.

Trees exploded around him, like Darrin had ripped open the fabric of the forest. Robert stumbled forward, using the oak tree for support. Darrin had been right about this not being the easy way.

The images before him jumbled in his mind before settling. He was at the tree where they had found the branch. Darrin was gone. Samantha sat on the ground, eyes wide. Kate was bound to the tree.

His eyes narrowed. The killer was Graham.

CHAPTER 30

HER PURSE WAS TOO FAR AWAY NOW, AND GRAHAM WOULD easily see her reaching for her daggers if they were still there. The mist had cleared, leaving an easy path for the bright moonlight.

Sam scrambled for anything to say to stall longer. She'd texted Beth. Someone should be looking for them. "If you want to do this right, we should really go into town and wake up a priest."

"We don't need a priest to declare our love." His face was aglow with happiness, like a child on his first trip to Disneyland. His eyes kept darting back and forth between them and the surrounding forest. They looked glassy, reminding her of the crows.

"But it won't be legal," Kate said. "If you're going to be the step-father to my girls, it should be legal."

With Graham's attention focused on Kate, Sam took her chance. "Caleb," she whispered into the grass. "We need your help." Crows observed them from the branches of the oak tree.

Caleb's eyes in the forest. She didn't know the extent of his powers, but right now he might be their only shot.

Graham laughed and it was warm and rich, like they were all sharing a good joke rather than shivering in the cold with a mad man. "I don't need an official title to be a father to your children, Katie. I knew the sacrifices, and I was willing to make them."

"Why take on Paul's name?" Kate said softly. "I really want to know."

Sam inched closer to her purse.

"I knew you missed Paul desperately." Graham crouched again and took Kate's bound hands in his. "That you'd never let another man into your heart. So I became him. I learned to cook." He smiled with a wistful glow in his eyes. "You'd be amazed at my chicken marsala. I can dance too, just like he could."

Kate gripped his hands with her fingers. "But why me, Graham? We were friends, sure, but you went through an awful lot of trouble to be the man I needed. Why?"

Sam was almost to her purse. She unzipped the top carefully.

Graham reached into his back pocket and pulled out his wallet. He opened it up and pointed at something behind the front plastic slot. "Our mother died when I was only ten. Logan was seven." His voice shook. "Our Da beat her. Until one day she didn't come home from the hospital." Tears were in his eyes. "You're a good mother Kate. You remind me so much of her."

Kate's eyes widened. "I'm so sorry, Graham. Let's go back to the manor and talk. I'll make us some tea."

Sam had searched her entire purse. Nothing. Graham must have the daggers.

"No, I can't take that chance," Graham said. He stood. "Your other friends will be back by now. They wouldn't understand."

Sam got to her knees. She felt more steady. She might be able to rush him if Kate kept him talking.

"Then how are we going to be married in the forest?" Kate said.

Graham opened his arms wide, like he embraced the trees, the sky. "These woods have always been special to our family. Generations of Dunnings have been married here symbolically. No priest required."

To Sam's right, the air ripped apart in a loud snap, and Robert was instantly there.

Robert held onto the oak tree like he was ill. Then he straightened and glanced at Sam with just the barest flick of his dark eyes, and then his gaze returned to Graham. He didn't bother to speak. He just barreled into Graham, and both men went down in a tangle of limbs, rolling over the exposed tree roots.

She didn't know how he was here, but hope spiked inside Sam. She got to her feet and ran toward Kate.

THEY TUMBLED ONTO THE GROUND. HARD ROCKS DROVE into Robert's back, his arms, his thigh, but he did not loosen his hold on the villain.

"What the hell?" Graham exclaimed. They came to rest with

Graham on his back. He shoved Robert from him, but Robert regained his footing easily. He had brawled many a time in his day.

Graham shifted left to right, slashing at the air with Samantha's iron daggers. "I didn't realize Sam could call ghosts to her aid. But I do know these daggers can kill you."

Graham smiled, and the movement pulled away his mask of humanity. Evil gleamed in the light of his eyes, clung to the wicked curve of his lips.

Samantha had made it to Kate. He must give her time to free her friend.

Regardless of their hopeful escape, if he did not stop Graham, he would keep pursuing Kate. Beatrice would lose her kin. His hope of being with Samantha would perish. And Graham would continue to kill. Robert had caused Lillian's death and the death of her child. No more would die because of his inaction.

No more.

The anger burst from his heart, saturating his body in burning heat. The power he had felt before was back tenfold. He clenched his teeth and raised his hands toward the fallen branches in the clearing. Pain squeezed his bones in a harsh grip, but he ignored it, pushing forth with his hands. With a heavy shifting of dirt, the branches rose in the air. There were three large branches and a smaller one bristling with sharp barbs, the size of the finest of blades.

He thrust his hands toward Graham, and the branches flew. Graham fell flat to the ground, dodging the larger ones, but the smaller branch sliced along his neck and shoulders. Graham didn't cry out. Instead, he scrambled to his feet and charged in Robert's direction.

Robert managed to twist out of the way, but one of the daggers slashed along his left arm. The skin lost all feeling, the limb dead, like the iron had stolen what little life he possessed where it touched.

"Hurry, Sam." Kate's whisper carried from the oak tree.

Graham turned toward the sound. Sam had grabbed one of the sharp rocks from the ground and scraped it against Kate's bonds.

He saw Graham's intention in the fevered glaze over his eyes. Robert tried to grab him around the waist, but his left arm was useless. Graham slipped through, daggers raised and raced toward the women.

Graham was almost to the oak tree. Samantha had risen to her feet, shielding Kate. No weapon save the small rock.

Graham would cut her down. Cut both of them down. Robert had not lied to Sloane. He would destroy himself if it meant Samantha lived.

Robert blinked out and then re-materialized in between her and Graham at the last moment.

Both daggers sliced into him. One to his hip, the other to his gut.

"Robert!" Samantha screamed.

He reached down with his right hand and grasped the blade in his stomach, his skin instantly blistering. He pulled it free and flung it at Sam's feet.

What felt like acid devoured his skin, eating into his hip bones, burrowing deep. He did not have the strength to pull the remaining dagger free. He slid to the ground, unable to stand.

Samantha fell next to him and cradled him in her arms, rocking him back and forth. "No, no, no," she whispered over and over again. Hot tears hit his cheeks, his lips, tasting of salt.

Graham stood immobile, just staring at Samantha. But Robert knew his hesitation wouldn't last.

Robert grasped Sam's hand with his wounded one. Her fingers trembled. "Take this." He put her hand over the dagger still embedded in his hip and tightened his grip, despite the pain as his skin burned away in tatters. "And kill him."

"Robert—"

His hand slipped from the iron. He could no longer feel the dagger in his side or Samantha's touch. "I am forever blessed to have known you, Samantha Eveline Hamilton. To have loved you."

Her eyes flashed, holding that distant storm he had glimpsed before. He had given her a chance. He prayed it would be enough.

Samantha's hand hovered for a moment over him, and then pulled the dagger free. She picked up the other one from the ground. Determination hardened her face. "I'll save all of us, Robert. Somehow."

She stood and faced Graham. A wind whipped through the forest, lifting the leaves from the ground to swirl about her feet. Robert had never seen her more exquisite, more primal.

She twirled the iron daggers in her hands like they were a part of her, and then tilted her head toward Graham. "Come on, you bastard."

CHAPTER 31

Rage rose through Sam, her focus narrowed until all she saw was Graham.

He feinted toward her, but she'd already seen the way his eyes had shifted and anticipated his move. Both daggers sliced through his shirt, drawing blood.

He drew back and pulled out a knife from a sheath on his belt. "You'll have to kill me to stop me. I don't think you have it in you."

Graham moved slowly to her right. Sam kept herself between him, Kate and Robert. Kate had picked up the stone Sam had been using and was working on her restraints.

"I'll do what needs to be done." Sam looked for an opening, but Graham was prepared now. This wasn't going to be easy.

He shook his head and circled back to her left. "I don't think so. Now, your friend Beth, her I'd be worried about. She's no innocent. But you, you're too soft."

Before the last word was out of his mouth, he lunged at her. She twisted out of his reach, but had forgotten how close Kate was. She tumbled back over her legs. Graham charged her.

"Sam, roll left," Kate yelled.

She obeyed instinctively and Graham's blow mostly missed her, just skimming her hair.

How the hell did Kate know what would happen?

She got to her feet and risked a quick glance toward Kate. Her eyes were white. Like during a vision. She was seeing the future.

"Drop now," Kate commanded, her voice almost a growl.

Sam fell to her knees and Graham sailed over her, his momentum carrying him several feet past her. She sprang up and stabbed him in the side. He spun around and she lost her grip on the dagger.

Sam slashed at his face, cutting open his cheek. He grabbed her wrist and squeezed it until she dropped the other dagger. She pulled him toward her and head-butted him hard.

Graham stumbled to his feet. "You bitch." He rammed into her. She fell back. He smashed her head into the frigid ground. Once. Twice.

Pain brought sparks to Sam's vision. She tasted blood in her mouth. She shoved a knee into his groin, but he just grunted and straddled her.

"Stop it!" Kate screamed. "I'll marry you, I'll do anything. Just stop."

His hands circled Sam's throat, the fingers pressing into her skin. She gasped, air already choked off. Flailing, she only managed to lose more air. Graham wasn't moving.

He looked back at Kate. "You were trying to escape." His

voice was calm. "Father always said there must be consequences. Otherwise, you don't learn."

Kate continued to plead with him, but Sam couldn't follow the words. A burning ache began in Sam's lungs and flooded her chest. She couldn't hold on much longer.

Play dead.

Every part of her wanted to fight, to struggle, but she let herself go limp.

The vise around her neck released by just a fraction, then a bit more. It wasn't enough, but it was the best she was going to get. She took a quick inhale, and then smashed her bent knees into Graham's back, pushing him toward her. So she could reach his face.

Her hands clawed his cheeks, then higher, stabbing into his eye. Hot bits of flesh slid under her fingernails, coating her fingers. Graham pulled back, screaming high and long.

She expected his grip to fall away, but it was like concrete had replaced his fingers, and he squeezed harder.

His breath on her cheeks smelled like Kate's oatmeal cookies. Her stomach roiled.

"Hold on, Sam." Kate's words were soft, but reached her ears. "Hold on. Help's coming."

Sam bucked and twisted, a fish on a hook. With the bloody mess of his left eye sliding down his face, he continued to crush her windpipe.

"No one's coming to save you, Samantha Hamilton." Graham's tone was filled with triumph, but also held a shadow of sadness. "No ghosts. No one."

The moon above grew dark. She couldn't feel her hands, her feet. Kate had told her to hold on, but how could she when she was weightless? The pain was gone. Everything was quiet.

A woman with long red hair shoved her face into Sam's. "This isn't good," the woman said. She backed up and pulled on the edges of her blue blazer. "We need to hurry."

CHAPTER 32

SAM STUMBLED AWAY FROM THE STRANGE WOMAN. SHE stood in a small forest clearing in front of a gaping, dark hole. Sounds wafted up from the darkness. Gurgling, crying, screaming.

"Who are you?" Sam said.

The woman frowned. "She's becoming his latest victim."

"I think there's been some mistake." Sam didn't know what was going on, and she wasn't going to wait around to find out. She took a step back, and then another.

And ran right into someone else. She turned around and found a young woman in a bright yellow sundress. Also with long red hair.

"It's okay, don't be afraid." The woman in the sundress reached for her, but Sam jerked away. Other voices surged up around her. There were more people in the clearing. And they all had Scottish accents.

A young girl clung to an older man's hand. "I'm frightened, Grandpa."

The man shook his head slowly. "She just needs help re-membering, Mary. Necromancer, you saved me. Saved me from being a geist. I'm with my family now."

Necromancer? Definitely crazy time. And what the heck was a geist? "I need to go home now." Sam wasn't sure where home was, but it definitely wasn't here.

An older woman,who looked like a housekeeper, sighed. "You're going to have to do your thing, Caleb." She looked over at a tall man who reminded her of a bunch of stick-like limbs all barely held together. His staff glowed.

Okay, maybe this was all a dream. Who has a staff, and a glowing one at that? She just needed to wake up.

Another redhead joined the housekeeper. She looked like she was dressed to go clubbing. "This is just like what hap-pened to me when I died. You can fix her, right?"

"Died?" Sam edged away from them, but it brought her closer to the pit. Pain radiated up from its depths, clutching at her skin. She had to get away from these nut jobs, but that wasn't the way to escape.

"Entwine needs you desperately, lass, but not as a resident," Caleb said. He walked forward, and Sam couldn't move. She didn't know if it was from fear or something else.

He stopped, so close that she saw faint shoots of green running through his skin, like he was about to bloom. "This should help you remember." He placed his hands on either side of her temples.

She tried to break free, but tendrils from his fingers pushed against her. It felt like needles diving into her skin. Sam cried out, but almost immediately the ache was gone replaced by an insistent voice.

Come on Sammy, be alive. Whoever is listening, save her.

Beth. It was Beth. Images shot through her. Beth at ten, trying not to cry while Sam bandaged her wounds. At Sam's treehouse reciting their blood sister oath. At the manor, when the old Beth smiled back at her.

Oh God, don't let her die. This is all my fault.

Kate. Again images flashed in her mind. An eight-year-old Kate being bullied at school until Sam saved her. In her wedding dress, beaming with love. In the kitchen, holding out her hands for the pipe, fear and strength in her eyes.

The next voice was the loudest though it was ragged at the edges with pain. *I am forever blessed to have known you, Samantha Eveline Hamilton. To have loved you.* Her entire body froze. Robert. The man she loved. How could she have forgotten?

Everything clicked into place. They were in the forest with Graham. Robert had been stabbed, Kate was bound, and Graham had been trying to kill her.

Sam looked over at the pit, knowing now it led back to Graham. Tears blurred her vision. She couldn't save Kate. She'd failed the victims. Who would bring Graham to justice? She'd never be with Robert, never see him again. The iron would destroy him in Entwine.

"I'm dead."

She felt numb. All the struggle, all the hope, all the love—all that she'd gone through this past week meant nothing. Nothing.

She turned her back on the ghosts. On the disappointment in their eyes.

"You're not quite dead yet, lass," Caleb said drily.

Sam turned around. Her heart woke up, beating hard in her chest. "There's a chance still?"

"We've got a plan."

Beatrice gave her a quick nod, and then shot off orders like a drill sergeant. "Ellie, Amber, over there. Darrin hold Mary's hand. Ray between Monica and Wendy. Caleb, you're with me. Let's give her everything we've got."

A glow began in their feet, moving up through their bodies. The higher it traveled, the brighter it blazed. Sam had to squint to look at them.

Beatrice broke formation and stood in front of Sam. She cupped her cheek, and the touch sent a buzzing through Sam's skin, like she was too close to an electric socket. "Take what we give freely to you." The words sounded formal. Then her voice lowered to a growl like Kate's. "And kick his ass."

The ghostly energy slammed into Sam, and she tumbled back toward the pit. Toward the pain. Toward life.

Sam fell, weightless once again. The darkness gave way to the light of the moon above. She plummeted back into her body. Graham's fingers still gripped around her neck. Her chest didn't burn, she didn't feel the need to struggle for breath. The ghosts' energy was her air.

"Back away now." Beth's words snapped in the distance. The sharp crack of a gunshot echoed in the air.

Graham jumped off Sam. He put his hands into his pockets.

Sam smelled the iron. He still had one of the daggers.

"Beth, go right," Kate shouted and then quickly stood.

Graham flung the dagger, barely missing Beth. Sam reared up and tackled him around the legs, her chin smashing into the backs of his knees.

Graham fell to the ground, but twisted, grabbing onto Sam. "Why won't you just die?"

"Get away from my friend, you mother-fucker." Beth pointed her gun at Graham, about ten feet away. "I promised her I wouldn't kill you, but that doesn't mean I won't shoot out both your kneecaps."

Graham tightened his hold on Sam. She struggled, but he wouldn't let go.

"Allow me," Caleb's voice reached Sam's ears. "This is my forest, and I made no promise to spare anyone."

Kate didn't move, shock filling her face. But Beth nodded at Caleb and lowered her gun like this was expected somehow. How could they both see him?

He lifted his staff. A piece of the blackened sky split away from the clouds and descended upon Graham. Caleb's crows.

Graham screamed, his arms flailing, letting go of his grip on Sam. Fear overriding the madness in his eyes. The maelstrom of black grew so thick, Sam only saw Graham in brief flashes. The metallic scent of blood misted in the air.

"Stop." Sam got to her feet. "We need him alive."

"Are you sure?" Caleb asked. His eyes gleamed like the dying glow of the sun. He suddenly looked more ancient than Sam had ever suspected.

"I'm sure," Sam said. Graham needed to pay for his crimes and to provide proof that would free Logan.

Caleb lifted his carved staff again toward the murder of crows, and they spun away from Graham in a dark funnel, disappearing into the forest. Graham's bloody chest rose and fell. He wouldn't be attacking anyone else tonight.

"Sam?" Michael's shouts pierced through the air. "Kate, Beth?"

He skidded to a halt by the oak tree, his eyes scanning the scene. His gaze stopped on Caleb. "Do I want to know what happened here?"

"We're all good." Beth rolled Graham over and secured his hands with zip ties behind his back. Tatters of clothing and flesh littered the ground.

"The cops are moments behind me," Michael said.

Kate let out a shuddering breath. "Good. They can take Graham and get Logan out."

Fear clutched at Sam's stomach. Where was Robert? He couldn't be gone. She scanned the area around the oak tree. Was she too late?

She rushed over to Caleb. "Robert, is he . . ."

"I am sorry, lass." Caleb's face looked like weathered wood.

"He's gone?" Her legs felt like they might buckle.

"Not quite, but soon." Caleb pointed toward one of the beech trees across the clearing. "He's there."

In the distance, she heard sirens. Michael's hand on her arm startled her. "Go find Robert. All of you. I'll keep the cops off your back for as long as I can."

Sam gave him a quick hug and then raced toward the tree Caleb had indicated. Robert was on the other side of the massive trunk.

He was still there. And yet . . .

Her steps faltered and then stopped. Her mouth grew dry. Caleb was right.

They'd need a miracle.

CHAPTER 33

ROBERT LEANED AGAINST ONE OF THE EXPOSED TREE ROOTS. Blood coated his white lawn shirt, and his breath hitched with each inhalation. His upper half was visible, but he'd almost disappeared below the waist. Just the faint outline of his form remained, like a chalk drawing washing away under a sudden rain.

Beatrice sat beside him, her arm around his shoulders. "We have to hurry." Panic fluttered at the edges of her words.

Sam dropped to her knees. Her heart stilled, feeling like it stopped. She couldn't lose him, but how was she going to save him?

"Robert, I'm here." She glanced back at Kate and Beth. "He's fading."

His eyes opened. "You are alive." He smiled, tears in his eyes. "You are alive." His voice shook. He reached a hand toward her, and she grabbed it, pulling it to her lips, her cheek.

The power from the ghosts still hummed underneath her skin. She wondered if he felt it. "I'm so sorry. My daggers did this." They'd done what they'd been meant to do. She swallowed a rising sob.

Kate's hand gently gripped her left shoulder. Beth touched Kate's. They would hear the ghosts now.

"It is not your fault." Robert's tone was gentle. "I knew the risk, and it was worth it." He looked over at Beatrice. "I am glad to have found you again, dear Beatrice."

She tutted at him. "That sounds suspiciously like a goodbye. No more of that. Samantha will figure out a way to stop this."

"We'll fix this," Beth said. The conviction in her words bolstered Sam, helping to push the fear back.

Kate squeezed Sam's shoulder. "I won't let you down, Beatrice. We're a Triumvirate."

Robert smiled at Beth and Kate. "I am happy to see you surrounded by your friends again." His face contorted with pain. "Did I weaken you for battle? Taking your energy? The Warden said we have upset the balance."

The Warden? Sam shook her head. "Whatever has been happening, it's not hurting me. And I beat Graham with everyone's help. Yours included."

The lines around his mouth eased slightly. "One less sin for the devils to wrench from my soul."

"Hush now, my lord. You are not going to Hell." Beatrice frowned at him.

"Whatever we're going to do, we better do it quick," Kate said. "I'm not sure how much longer Michael's going to be able to keep the cops from coming this way."

Beth glanced back over her shoulder. "He's probably using

his 'feel-good' abilities. But we need to get this moving."

Sam leaned over and kissed Robert lightly. He was cold. "Beth's right. We're going to fix this. You hear me?" she said against his lips.

His arms wound about her, pulling her closer. The warmth of his blood seeped through her clothes, and she felt the skipping beat of his heart against hers.

His heart? Sam couldn't speak for a moment. She pulled back, but placed her trembling hand on his chest. "You have a heartbeat?"

Beatrice's hand rushed to her mouth, and then she lightly touched Robert's chest, placing her hand next to Sam's.

Robert smiled, but it was weighted down by sadness, barely lifting his lips. "It started thundering in my chest right after I was stabbed. Bittersweet, is it not? What I longed for happened at the moment I knew I had not cheated death after all."

The bottom of Robert's shirt faded away under Sam's gaze. Nothing was left from his hips downward. The iron would take him away piece by piece unless she figured something out. Quickly.

Robert had thought he'd been stealing energy from her through their connection. Could she give it to him willingly with purpose? As if hearing her need, the gift from the ghosts thrummed faster through her veins.

"I'm going to try something." Sam looked back at Kate and Beth. "I'm going to give him the energy the ghosts gave me earlier, when they helped save me. It might counteract the iron."

Beth gave her a short nod. "You can do it, Sammy."

Sam took a deep breath, reached for the area where his hip had disappeared, and willed her energy into his body. Fatigue filled her, but she kept pressing. Where her fingers touched, his clothing, his skin shimmered back into being. Dizziness swallowed her vision, and she pulled back, bracing herself against the damp ground. His lower body stuttered for a second, and then his hips came back, but nothing more.

"Did it work?" Kate said. Her hand on Sam's back helped keep her upright.

Lethargy pulled at Sam's limbs. "A little." She tilted her head toward Beatrice. "Can I get more energy from the ghosts? For Robert?"

Caleb stepped out of the beech tree. "No. I managed to protect the others so they didn't lose too much, but they're pretty tapped out."

"Could we help?" Kate looked at Caleb. Fear mingled with strength in her eyes. "We are the Triumvirate of Plantar."

"Pluthar, Red." Beth nodded at Caleb. "Can we help or not?"

Caleb shook his head. "Ghostly essence is needed to repair him."

Sam got to her feet. If only the ghosts she'd helped in the past were here. She'd demand they give her some of their essence. It would be the least they could do after all she had done for them.

Her gaze flicked to Caleb. "I should have gotten something out of the Bargains."

His face smoothed out as if she'd finally said something intelligent. "You should have."

"Yet, I never did."

Caleb hesitated for a moment and then nodded. "True."

"How do I get whatever is owed to me?" Sam kept her voice respectful, though she just wanted to throttle the answer out of him. They didn't have much time.

"Every Necromancer must discover this on their own." Caleb rocked back on his heels, looking calm, like Robert's life wasn't in jeopardy.

Sam shoved her face into Caleb's space, until the other ghost backed up a step. "Don't play games with me."

Beatrice rose to her feet. "I don't understand you, Caleb. One minute you're sacrificing everything to save these two, and now you're stonewalling them. *Help* her."

Caleb shook his head slowly, though this time there was an emotion in his gaze. Resignation. "The Rules must be obeyed. By us all."

Robert's voice was weak, but it reached her ears. "Perhaps you simply need to ask for your payment."

"At least one of you has some sense." Caleb's mutter was like rough rocks scraping against each other.

"Asking for payment," Sam said softly. "That's it."

"What are you talking about, Sam?" Kate looked worried. "Who are you asking for payment?"

"The Universe." Leaning back her head, Sam gazed up at the dark sky above. The moon had hidden behind the clouds, which made the stars glimmer even brighter. She felt the watchful eye of whatever it was up there, the one who had given her this ability. There had always been that bond with something unseeable, untouchable, but she hoped not unfeeling.

She'd never addressed it directly before. The cops were going to hear this, but it couldn't be helped.

"I, Samantha Eveline Hamilton," she shouted, "demand payment for all the Bargains I have struck in your service."

Sam heard Michael's voice in the distance explaining to the cops that they couldn't disturb her. Except for that, the night was silent.

"Samantha." Beatrice's voice jarred her. "Hurry." Robert's eyes were closed again. Everything below his waist was gone once more.

She would not fail. She would not lose him.

"Kate, Beth. Come here." They rushed to her side. "Hold my hands." The humming energy they all had when they touched sparked and danced underneath Sam's grip. She let it fill her. Maybe this would get the Universe's attention.

Facing the sky again, she didn't yell this time, didn't shout. "I am the Necromancer. You will deliver my payment *now.*"

The stars seemed brighter than before. One by one, they blazed. And fell, arcing toward her.

CHAPTER 34

SAM LOOKED AT THE LIGHTS OFF TOWARDS THE HORIZON. "Looks like someone heard me." Though part of her was relieved something was happening, another part worried at what she'd awoken.

Caleb took up position on her right, placing his staff in front of him. The runes upon its surface pulsed, their power chattering against Sam's senses.

The glowing streaks of starlight descended, hitting the treetops. Someone moved through the trees ahead. More than one person, ethereal and glowing. Ghosts.

She recognized them. She recognized them all.

Ellie was the closest. She led the other victims to stop near Sam and Caleb. Sam craned her neck, but still couldn't see an end to the stream of ghosts. They filled the forest.

"They're all here," she whispered to Kate and Beth. "More than I remembered."

She saw Mrs. McCarthy who she'd met when she was eleven. She'd helped her say goodbye to her husband. Next to her was

Thomas Henricks, who'd drowned, but they couldn't find the body until Sam accepted his Bargain.

The children who'd never made it home from school when their bus had collided with a semi. They were playing a game of ring around the rosy, looking like normal healthy kids again. Near them stood the patients at the hospital who'd perished in a fire. Their burns gone. All their wounds healed.

Clustered around one of the trees were the union workers from the factory disaster. They weren't bloody any longer, and they had all their limbs. They were whole. She'd forgotten she'd done that when she'd given them peace.

She'd been so wrapped up in her pain, her grief, she had minimized the good she'd done over the years. At the bookstore signing, Cynthia had been right. Sam had forgotten.

Wind whipped through the trees, ruffling Sam's hair, cutting through her clothes, but leaving the ghosts untouched.

"Who are they?" Beatrice's voice wavered between wonder and suspicion.

Sam said the only words which felt right. "They're my ghosts."

"Well, you were certainly busy," Caleb commented. "And all before you turned fourteen." He studied her. "There is definitely more to you than anyone knows, isn't there?"

Sam didn't answer, didn't know how to answer him. She'd never met anyone else who could do what she did. It was more than just talking to ghosts.

She dropped Kate and Beth's hands. The spirits shifted, parting down the middle to make way for someone. A young boy.

Sam lifted her hand to her mouth, but didn't stifle the sudden sob. Her throat burned. Tears flooded her eyes.

Zachary Lerner, Cynthia's son. He'd fallen through the screen of his third-floor bedroom window when he was five years old. Cynthia had descended into such a deep depression, Zach had been scared she'd hurt herself. Sam's gift had allowed Zach to give his mother the forgiveness she needed so she could forgive herself.

He'd been her first ghost. Her first Bargain.

She'd only been five years old herself.

Somehow she'd known the words, had known the Rules, and instinctively known who she was.

What she was.

"You got bigger," Zach said, still sounding like that same little boy she'd met all those years ago.

Sam crouched, so she was on eye level with him. "I did." She didn't try to stop the tears now. They streamed down her cheeks, hot, cleansing. "I checked in on your mom before I flew to Scotland. She's doing really good."

"I know. I watch over her," Zach said. "Me and grandma."

Sam longed to smooth back the thick bangs that fell over his eyes, but she wouldn't be able to touch him. He'd died before his life had really even begun. "I'm glad you're not alone."

Zach's right hand went to his chest, his fingers grasping at his t-shirt. She thought he was in pain, but when he pulled his hand back, she saw a glow flickering over his palm like a tiny lightning storm.

"Glad you finally asked for this. I've been holding it forever."

Zach reached his hand toward her, stopping a hairsbreadth from her cheek.

A liquid rush of warmth flowed over her skin, sinking through her in the way she imagined sunlight felt to the plants and trees. Life-giving.

"Thank you," she told him, but he was already backing away for the next ghost to take his place. One by one they stood before her, lifting their hands, giving her their payment, though that word paled with what they gave. Her vision glimmered on the edges. Her heart pounded hard against her ribcage like it couldn't contain all they had shared.

Graham's victims were the last. Pinpricks of heat rushed from her heart down to her arms, her fingers. Sam had almost forgotten this part, when the Bargain was fulfilled. She lifted her hands toward the women, and the embers which had sealed the Bargain emerged through her skin. The specks of light glowed brightly through the air.

The sparks surrounded Amber, Monica, Wendy, and Ellie. Then they sank into their ghostly forms, blazing them bright before they returned to normal. The dark bruising around their necks was gone. They looked beautiful and at peace.

Sam felt an emptiness now that the connection was gone. But it faded when she looked at the happiness in their faces. They would never get their lives back, but they'd gotten justice. And now they could move on if they wished.

Ellie walked over to her. "The others are spent from what they gave to save you. But I've got a little left." She leaned in close, sending her energy over Sam like a brush of a feather against her skin. "I hope this saves your man." Then all four women disappeared.

Payment is made. The words felt more like a presence sliding through Sam's mind rather than a voice.

The breeze kicked up into a full wind. Pieces of leaves and dirt clouded the air, churning.

Sam sensed the forces behind the storm. Bright flashes of energy rode on the wind. Greens and yellows swirled up from the ground to cluster at Caleb's feet. Around Beth and Kate the colors were darker, but stronger too. The strands of power flowed from them to Sam, like vines.

Sam knew she could stop the storm with just a flicker of her finger. Or ride on the edges of the lightning brewing behind the clouds. The ghostly essence inside her boiled, aching to be used.

"Quickly now," Beatrice yelled.

Her words snapped Sam's focus back. Robert. She rushed over to him. Only the top of his shoulders, his neck, and his head remained. A slice of nothingness cut through his neck, reaching toward his chin.

His eyes were closed and he barely breathed. She dropped to her knees and grabbed his shoulders.

Her thoughts filled with images of their future together. Him meeting Bronson, Beth, Kate, and the girls. Their wedding. Having children of their own. Growing old.

I love you with everything I am, everything I will be. She willed the energy coursing through her body to flow into Robert.

The ghostly energy inside her pooled around her heart. It

burst through her pores and into him. Sam reared up, going blind for a moment, every part of her body rigid.

Robert sucked in a breath and screamed, but Sam didn't let go. Not even when it felt like her skin would shrivel, like her heart would explode, like her bones would disintegrate.

Her breath came in fast pants. Her skin slicked with sweat. Finally the last of the energy slid out of her. She felt completely empty.

Sam looked down at him, expecting to see him back as he was. He was no longer bloody, and had his form again, but just barely. Under her gaze, his feet flickered and disappeared. "No. This isn't fair. Not after all that."

"What's wrong?" Beth and Kate had joined her by Robert.

Kate looked at the ground. "Is he gone?"

"No, but it didn't bring him back fully. He's fading again." Sam rose, the hot breath of frustration lifting her. "It wasn't enough." She slammed the palm of her hand against the beech tree, wanting to punch it until her fists were bloody. "All of that and it still wasn't enough."

"You're asking to break the way of things. The Rules," Caleb said. "Iron kills ghosts. Rule #18."

"I know the damned Rules," Sam growled at him. *You have leverage. You can make your own Bargain with the Universe.* Her mom's words drifted up through her mind like they'd been waiting for this exact moment to nudge her memory. "I know the Rules. And I can break them."

Beatrice nodded, giving Caleb a defiant lift of her chin. "Do what you have to, Samantha. Save our boy."

Sam was going to need help. "Beth, Kate, you've got to hold whatever energy is still in Robert together."

Kate looked uncertain. "How? We can't see him."

Sam looked down at her thumb, a bloody scab on the surface. "Unless we bind the Triumvirate. Officially. Can I have your knife, Beth?"

Beth slid it from her boot sheath, but held onto it, giving Sam a knowing look. "You want us to recite the blood sister oath. It might be our last chance."

"Maybe our only chance." Sam looked at both of them. "Will you do it?"

Beth didn't reply. Instead she cut her thumb on the same scar they all had.

"I love you, Samantha Eveline Hamilton and Katherine Amanda Peterson." Beth met their gazes. "When you need me, I will be your heart, your courage and your strength. We are sisters in blood." She handed the knife to Sam, who did the same.

"I love you, Tiffany Elizabeth Marshall and Katherine Amanda Peterson," Sam said. "When you need me, I will be your heart, your courage and your strength. We are sisters in blood."

Kate held out her hand for the knife. "I had a vision. If we do this, everything is going to change."

"I'm not afraid of change." Beth smiled, a glimmer of tears in her eyes as she looked at both of them. "I'll do everything I can to save Robert."

In that moment, Sam didn't think she could love Beth any more than she already did.

"There's darkness ahead." Kate cut her thumb, watching the blood well up.

Sam put her hand on Kate's shoulder. "There will always be darkness. We need to be the light for each other."

Kate nodded, several tears spilling down her cheeks. "I love you, Samantha Eveline Hamilton and Tiffany Elizabeth Marshall. When you need me, I will be your heart, your courage and your strength." Her words slowed. "We are sisters in blood."

Sam held out her thumb toward the other two. Beth put hers on Sam's mixing the blood. Kate did the same. They stared at each other. Wind whipping through their clothes, dirt clogging the air, clouds tumbling in the sky.

Somehow over the storm, Sam heard the same popping noise she'd heard all those years ago. Beth and Kate looked at her. Beth resigned, Kate worried. They were bound for certain this time. There would be no turning back.

"He's there." Sam pointed to where Robert lay. His legs below his knees were gone. She grabbed her friends' hands, and this time when she felt the chains shift inside her, connecting them, they were strong, solid. "My sisters, I need you." The words came from somewhere deep inside, but they felt right. "Hold him. Be my strength."

Kate shook her head. "What do we do?"

"I know what to do." Beth's eyes were completely black. "We'll hold him, Sammy. Finish it." Beth grabbed Kate's hands, lifting them up over Robert's body like she truly saw him. Blue light danced along their hands, their arms. Kate's mouth hung open in surprise, but Beth looked focused. Glowing drops of energy fell from their arms onto Robert, filling in the missing pieces.

Sam turned her back on both of them. The rest was up to her. It was time to do what frightened her the most. What she'd been running from since she'd been thirteen. What she'd planned to bury.

She'd never known how to summon the voice which had always frightened Beth and thrilled Kate.

The voice she used for the Bargain.

But something shifted within her. The last puzzle piece slid into its rightful place, revealing the picture which had only been hinted at before. She'd always had the ability at her disposal.

Heat rushed up from her core, burning up her throat, past her tongue. Her voice dropped into deeper octaves. It thundered through the forest in a shout which drowned out the maelstrom of wind and debris pulsing through the air.

"I am ready."

The shadowy night shivered, and something gathered around Sam. Something immense.

What is your need?

The voice was calm, and familiar somehow, though Sam couldn't place it. Like something from a dream.

Her skin flushed. Would this really work? She looked back at Robert.

The Bargain wording must be carefully done. She'd been able to wiggle out of helping a ghost when the intent didn't match the words. She wouldn't put it past the Universe for taking liberties with interpretation.

"My need is that Robert Grenning shall be made whole in body, at the age he was when he died, remembering everything that has happened in his life and beyond, and he shall become part of this living world. Read what is in my heart and know the truth of what I desire."

I have always known you and what is in your heart. What do you offer?

She exhaled her breath. It was quickly lost in the wind. "I will serve you willingly from this day forward, never to shirk my duty again." She knew this was what it wanted, had always wanted. Would it be enough?

The Bargain has been struck.

Everything slowed, and then froze. Beatrice's mouth open in a wide "o" of shock, leaves hung in the air, caught in a perfect dancing swirl with chunks of dirt, and Caleb staring right at whatever it was she couldn't see.

The glowing embers, like what she'd given back to Ellie and the others, drifted down from above to seal the Bargain. They dissolved against her skin like always, but they burrowed deep within her this time. Seeking, searching. Bands of warmth wrapped around her temples, her heart. They constricted painfully.

Pressure built inside her. Then, without warning, a shock wave burst from her, stealing all sound. For a single moment, she felt every ghost throughout Entwine, knew their names, their loss. She cradled all the living within her, echoing their heartbeats, their dreams.

She was everywhere. She was life and death and something

in between. The living and the ghosts, entwined together through her, connected, bound.

Then, it was over.

She was just Sam. Careening forward.

Someone caught her.

"You did it, Samantha." Robert's voice.

"Robert?" She gazed up at him. He was whole. She patted his shoulders, cupped his cheeks, squeezed his arms. He was really there.

She buried her face in his chest, breathing in the scent of him, hearing his heartbeat against her ear. Her body sagged against his. Tears spilled over her lashes, soaking her cheeks and his shirt.

He lifted her chin back until she met his gaze. It was filled with wonder. And love.

"You kept your promise, Necromancer." Robert tucked a strand of hair behind her ear. "You are mine."

Sam put her hand behind his neck and pulled him closer. "As you are mine." She kissed him, pouring her joy and her relief into the press of her lips, until she forgot everything but him.

"Get a room." Beth's voice held relief. They broke apart. Sam frowned at Beth, but it didn't dim her smile. "Nice to meet you, hunky hunky Robert."

Robert bowed toward Beth and Kate, a flush coloring his cheeks. "I am most honored to make your acquaintances finally."

Kate's eyes gleamed. She looked exhausted but more relaxed.

"Wow, hunky is right. Now I know why you fought so hard for him." She punched Sam in the arm. "I'm still freaked out about what we just did, but we are so definitely the Triumvirate of Awesomeness."

Sam laughed, and it mixed with the tears. She was bound forever to these two, with or without the oath. She squeezed her sisters to her and one word came to mind.

One she hadn't thought possible to find again. One she'd never thought to be worthy of. One which had fled the day her parents died.

Home.

CHAPTER 35

SAM LEANED BACK IN THE KITCHEN CHAIR, ENJOYING THE sunlight blazing through the back door. It had been a week since Graham had been captured. Logan had been released. Sam finally felt able to relax.

The kitchen was full. Emily and Patty colored at a small side table with Kate. And Beth tried for the hundredth time to explain how the coffee maker worked to Robert.

"No, you measure coffee into the filter, then you can press the button." Beth's voice was surprisingly patient.

"Gosh, Mr. Robert, don't you have a coffee maker?" Emily looked up from her drawing.

Robert glanced back over his shoulder at Emily and smiled. It was the heart-warming one that had charmed the socks off the required referee when he got his Citizen's card. His forged identity papers from one of Michael's contacts had come in handy.

"No, I do not, Miss Emily. However, I have found I quite covet the taste of this dark brew and must endeavor to get a machine of my own."

Emily gave him a quick nod. "You sure do talk funny, but I like you."

"Me too," Patty piped up.

"I shall do all I can to retain your good favor, my lasses." In his jeans and polo shirt, Robert still managed to look courtly when he bowed toward the girls. They giggled, the sound high and sweet.

Kate got up from the table with the girls and pointed to Robert. "You'll have your hands full with the charm oozing out of that one. The new maid already asked me if he was single. Bronson set her straight."

Since Ray was gone, Kate had already begun preparations to open the B&B back up for business. Bronson had flown over to assist. Sam was happy to have him by her side again.

"If she tries anything, I can handle her." Sam cracked her knuckles loudly.

Beth bumped Robert's shoulder, and he turned back to the coffee machine, though he kept stealing glances at Sam as if unsure whether she really meant to harm the maid in question.

"Okay, Casanova, how many scoops do we use for a pot?" Beth said.

"I assume the use of that name is a jest of some kind, so I will ignore it in the hopes that coffee will soon be brewing. Five scoops?"

"You got it." Beth tried to fist bump him, but Robert just stared at her hand until Beth sighed and dropped it.

Patty touched Sam's elbow. Like Kate, there was color in

her face now. The heavy burden of carrying her secret was gone. Kate had a long conversation with both girls about abilities and what they meant. Even if Emily never developed any special gifts, Patty would still need the support of her sister.

"Yes, sweetie," Sam said. "Did you want me to look at your picture?"

Patty shook her head, sending wisps of light brown hair around her shoulders. "No. I wanted to thank you. You kept your promise." She threw herself into Sam's arms and a scented plume of strawberry lip balm rose into the air. "You saved Mommy."

Sam kissed her head and rocked her gently. "We all saved her, monkey. You, me, Beth, Michael—"

"And Mr. Robert." Patty shifted in her arms and watched Robert finally hitting the button for the coffee maker. "He's different, isn't he?"

They had specifically not told the girls Robert used to be a ghost, but the girls weren't stupid. Emily knew something was off, and Sam suspected Patty could sense what he was. "Is different bad?"

"Oh no, Auntie Sam. I meant, he's like me, like you. Different. Special."

Sam squeezed her. "You've got a much better outlook on things at your age than I did. My parents tried to help me through it, but it wasn't the same. I felt a bit lonely."

Patty looked over at her. "You'll never be alone now. We're family." Her voice lowered into a whisper, though it was still almost as loud as her talking voice. "And you've got all your ghost friends too."

Michael walked into the kitchen in time to hear Patty's theatrical whisper. "Ghost friends? I only brought pastries for the living. Hope that's okay."

Beth grabbed the box from his hands, her fingers almost crushing the thin cardboard. "Please say there is chocolate in here."

"There is."

"Bless you." Beth looked like she was about to hug him, but turned away and dove into the box.

"But I was going to make pancakes," Kate said. Her eyes narrowed on Michael. "Did you buy these because you don't like my cooking?"

"I love your cooking, as you well know. "Michael poked her arm. "Are you fishing for a compliment? A little boost of self-esteem?"

Kate gave him a poke back. "Oh yes, Mr. Look-at-me-in-my-perfect-everything. Like you don't angle for compliments all the time."

Patty slid off Sam's lap and ran over to join in. "My Mommy's the best cook there is."

Sam ignored the rest of the hubbub and watched Robert walk toward her. Her heart still fluttered like they'd just had their first kiss.

He held out his hand. "Would you accompany me on a walk, my lady?"

She grasped his hand, and marveled again he was alive. They

strolled out of the kitchen and into the hallway. They'd almost lost each other, and now they were walking together, just as normal as could be.

"Thank you again for clearing my family's name," Robert said. His voice held a hint of tears. "I cannot say just how much this means to me."

Sam kissed his cheek. "I'm just happy I could help, though it'll be some time before it's done." Sam had contacted an old reporter friend. They were going to work together to dig up more evidence against Oscar Dunning. She squeezed Robert's hand. "But it's a start."

She stopped in the entryway. Everything looked warmer, more friendly, like the house had been brought back to life as well. The wallpaper glowed under the gleam from the chandelier. Even the desk at the front looked proud and beautiful. No longer discarded, no longer forgotten.

"What are you thinking?" he asked. He'd cut his hair a bit shorter, but it still lay thick and unruly against his cheeks.

"I never thought I could be this happy again."

"Beatrice says self-acceptance is the key to true happiness." He delivered this with the severity of a doctor prescribing medicine. "I am blessed to still be able to see her, though I do not know how that is possible."

Sam laughed. She was still worried about the Bargain she'd made, and what being brought to life meant for Robert. But everyone had made it through the ordeal in one piece. "So, do you agree with Beatrice? Is self-acceptance the key to true happiness?"

He took her hand and kissed her knuckles. "Only after I died did I realize what it meant to be truly alive. Truly happy. I love you, Samantha Eveline Hamilton."

"I love you, Lord Robert Grenning." Nestling her head against his neck, she put her hand over his beating heart. The thrumming rhythm echoed the pounding in her chest. Being the Necromancer had brought Robert to her and had saved them both. But she couldn't have done it without Kate and Beth.

She thought of the lines in the synopsis she'd just sent to her agent. It was a new book she was going to write. One she needed to write.

Glimpsing the future, seeking objects, and communing with the dead. Gifts? Maybe. Maybe not, but they'd brought three girls together. They were sisters in every way but blood. Until they performed the ritual.

And now they would never be alone.

ACKNOWLEDGEMENTS

I HAVE TO THANK EVERYONE WHO HAS BEEN WITH ME ON THIS incredible journey, from the first moments I decided to finally pursue my dreams, through the ups and downs of being a writer, and into the final stretch—holding my book in my hands. Holding my dream in my hands. Your support and belief in me has meant the world.

Of course, I would have crashed and burned without the guidance of my critique group. Anne, Troy, Jess, and Dion, you said yes when I asked you to form a group with me and it was the start of something amazing. I remember how nervous we were in the beginning, how fragile we were during critique, but we learned and grew together. I can't wait to see the magic each of you creates on your own journey.

And without Jessica Petersen, *Entwine* wouldn't be the book it is today. As my editor, she helped me polish this story until it gleamed. She also designed an exquisite cover—I'm so in love with it! I'm always amazed at how much we can each accomplish when we don't stand in our own way.

Special thanks to Pam Binder and the University of Washington. She taught the first writing class I had ever taken during their evening writers' program. I had never shared my work before with someone who didn't already love me. I was so scared my writing wasn't good enough. But the course, and my newly-established critique group whom I met there, gave me the confidence and the validation that this was what I was meant to do.

Pam also led me to the Pacific Northwest Writers Association. The PNWA Writers Conference was the first place I truly tasted the flavor of writerly energy. Through attending, learning, and volunteering, I grew incredibly as a writer and as a businesswoman.

I come from a very creative family, and from the beginning they had my back. No one ever questioned my desire and drive to be a writer. They know what it's like to have a dream others might not understand. Kim, Mary-Kate, Charlie, Charles, John, and Carol—thank you.

My parents knew of my dreams, but sadly aren't here to see their fruition. They instilled in me the magic of storytelling and the joy of reading. They taught me I could be anything I wanted to be and for that, I'll be forever grateful. I know they continue to watch over me on this amazing journey.

From the halls of junior high, until now, so many years later, Karen Weir has been there throughout. We're best friends for a reason. Thank you for your unwavering belief in me.

Losing my mom, getting cancer, and being laid off—all within a four month period—dropped me into a dark place.

But like Sam's glow in this book, I saw the light shining brightly through the shadows. This was my chance to stop wasting time and go after what I wanted. What had always burned deep in my soul.

To be a storyteller. To touch lives. To bring the light so others can find their way.

Thank you, Universe.

ABOUT THE AUTHOR

A NEW YORK TRANSPLANT, TRACEY SHEARER NOW CALLS the Pacific Northwest her home—a land teeming with ghosts, writers, and coffee shops.

The loss of both her parents and her own battles with cancer continue to fuel her love of stories that explore how important our connections are to each other. And through her work as a mentor and coach, Tracey enjoys helping other writers realize their dreams.

Under the close supervision of her two rescue kitties, Cleo and Feta, Tracey is working on the next books in this trilogy.

You can find her on Twitter at @TraceyLShearer and also at traceyshearer.com.